COPY
FIGHTS

COPY
FIGHTS

THE FUTURE OF INTELLECTUAL PROPERTY
IN THE INFORMATION AGE

Edited by
ADAM THIERER and WAYNE CREWS

Foreword by DECLAN McCULLAGH,
Washington Bureau Chief, *Wired News*

CATO
INSTITUTE
Washington, D.C.

Library of Congress Cataloging-in-Publication Data

Copy fights: the future of intellectual property in the information
age / edited by Adam Thierer and Wayne Crews.
  p. cm.
 Includes index.
 ISBN 1-930865-24-4 (paper : alk. paper) — ISBN 1-930865-25-2
  (cloth : alk. paper)
  1. Intellectual property—United States. 2. Copyright and
electronic data processing—United States. I. Thierer, Adam D. II.
Crews, Wayne.

KF2979.C665 2002
346.7304'8—dc21

                                                    2002071635

Printed in the United States of America.

CATO INSTITUTE
1000 Massachusetts Ave., N.W.
Washington, D.C. 20001
www.cato.org

Contents

Acknowledgments

Much of *Copy Fights* springs from the 2001 5th Annual Cato Institute/*Forbes ASAP* Technology and Society conference, "The Future of Intellectual Property in the Information Age." The first such event that we, the editors, were involved in as newcomers to Cato would have been impossible without the help of Cato's expert conference staff, who kept us sane prior to and during the event. They are Christie Raniszewski, Julie Johnson, Laura Major, and Megan Brumleve. Jerry Brito, manager of media relations, did a magnificent job of getting attention for the event.

The contributions of our research assistant Lucas Mast were indispensable in corresponding with our many contributors, helping us organize our conference, and helping us organize the book.

Gene Healy suffered nobly, having been charged with reviewing all of these chapters in 2002, on top of Cato's regular torrent of policy studies.

And to David Lampo for keeping the fire lit under us to get this book out on time, thanks! Finally, Mary McLaughlin did a terrific and fast copyediting job, and Patricia Bullock made all the editing changes with lightning speed.

Foreword

The Cato Institute has performed a terrific service for anyone interested in the future of technology. It has assembled a provocative, beguiling, and thoroughly engaging collection of essays on the law and policy of intellectual property.

Over the past few years, intellectual property has morphed from an arcane topic of interest mostly to academicians and patent attorneys to the stuff of newsmagazine cover stories. Courtrooms' klieg lights have illuminated how copyright law has been stretched in ways unimaginable just five years ago. Software patents have roiled the computer industry and alarmed developers of open-source programs. Meanwhile, displaying all the temperance of a methadone addict, Congress keeps handing more and more power to copyright owners.

The stakes are enormous. America's economic might, as Hollywood reminds us, arguably depends in large part on intellectual property law. But some of the entertainment industry's most cherished prizes, such as the Digital Millennium Copyright Act and the No Electronic Theft Act, raise troubling questions about free speech and private property rights.

Other proposals—such as Sen. Ernest "Fritz" Hollings' (D-S.C.) Consumer Broadband and Digital Television Promotion Act—go even further and impose government-mandated regulations on the U.S. hardware and software industries. The justification: piracy will decimate vital industries unless content is secured in a kind of impenetrable lockbox that would put Al Gore's campaign pledge to shame. "A lack of security has enabled significant copyright piracy which drains America's content industries to the tune of billions of dollars every year," Hollings says. "For example, the movie studios estimate that they lose over $3 billion annually."

Hollings has a point. Speedy Internet links, improved compression techniques, and fatter hard drives have dealt harshly with traditional views of copyright. Tens of millions of file-swappers are thumbing their noses impudently at legal proscriptions, and content owners fret that the ease of online distribution will reduce sales. They have reason to worry: As bandwidth increases and distribution technology improves, the price of intellectual property online may edge toward zero. Anonymous publishing systems promise to accelerate this trend.

Everyone likes stuff for free, of course, and piracy has always nibbled around the edges of publishers' and distributors' profits. But it's far simpler to copy an MP3 file than to photocopy a Tom Clancy novel, and digital copies—unlike their analog counterparts— do not diminish in value. Every copy has the same quality, which means that, if taken to its logical conclusion, widespread piracy could destroy the incentives to create valuable content.

By now it's clear that copyright holders have concluded the law alone is hardly sufficient to protect their work. Teenage pirates flout legal prohibitions, secure in the knowledge that there are too many of them to prosecute and they have few assets at risk in a civil suit. Overseas pirates are even less likely to be concerned about intellectual property laws, which aren't as strict as the ones in the United States. In response, just as tangible property holders rely not merely on the law but also on technology in the form of fences, locks, and safes to protect their property, copyright holders have started to do the same. "Digital rights management" is the catchall term for self-help technology, and everyone from Microsoft and Intel to AOL Time Warner is testing it out.

All of that is obvious enough. What is not so obvious is what government's proper role should be. Too often, debate has veered between two extremes: lobbyists from the entertainment industry seeking to regulate technology in hopes of limiting copying, and academics and self-described public interest groups seeking to regulate self-help technology in hopes of mandating "fair use." Both sides hope to enlist Congress—raising the possibility of interminable political battles that could shape the future of digital media more than the technology itself.

The business lobbyists' gains are well-known. The 1998 Digital Millennium Copyright Act banned "any technology, product, service, device, component, or part thereof" designed to bypass digital rights management schemes. The Walt Disney Company and Senator Hollings now want to implant anti-copying devices in all personal computers and electronic devices and most software. But fair-use proponents have not been idle. DigitalConsumer.org touts a six-point bill of rights promising Americans a right to copy and manipulate "content that they have legally acquired"—even if it is shielded by anti-copying technology. Similarly, Rep. Rick Boucher (D-Va.) has proposed regulating the sale of copy-protected compact discs. His reasoning, endorsed by a librarians' association: the new compact discs, already sold by some record labels, may not permit buyers to make fair use of their music.

Which approach is best? Can free-market methods relying on technological self-help supplant continued government intervention? Must future technologies follow standards to be set by the government? How can piracy be thwarted and reasonable uses of digital content be permitted? Are federal standards for software and hardware consistent with the cherished American idea of limited government?

There are no easy answers to those questions. Allowing the political process to make decisions is what James Buchanan, who won the 1986 Nobel Prize in economics for his public choice theory, warned us about decades ago. Although the free market is never a perfect judge of people's needs, politicians and bureaucrats in thrall to special-interest groups can do far worse.

I know of no better place to puzzle through these topics than the collection of articles that the Cato Institute has compiled for this book. Timely and learned, they unravel and explain one of the most important subjects that America's technology and entertainment industries are facing today. If you read this book today, you'll be a lot closer to understanding technology's future.

Declan McCullagh
Washington bureau chief
Wired News
April 2002

Introduction: The Great Intellectual Property Debate

Wayne Crews and Adam Thierer

Debates over the nature and scope of intellectual property law are centuries old, yet "new" at the same time. Over 200 years ago, America's founders struggled with the issue of intellectual property (IP) protection when they were authoring the Constitution. They arrived at a delicate balancing act contained in Article 1, Section 8, Clause 8, which gave Congress the power to "promote the Progress of Science and useful Arts, by securing for limited Times to Authors and Inventors the exclusive Right to their respective Writings and Discoveries."

Although inclusion of this line in the Constitution was an important sign that the founders believed strong utilitarian reasons existed for extending temporary legal protections to artistic and scientific creations, the language of this brief clause did not answer specific questions regarding such matters as the length of protection for various artistic or scientific creations, or what "fair use" or "prior art" was to mean, for example. Consequently, two centuries of legal wrangling have ensued as legislators, regulators, and jurists struggled to determine how best to achieve that balance.

Practically speaking, balancing has always been a messy process. Lengths of copyright and patent protection have always varied (although they have continuously expanded over time), and "fair use" and "prior art" have always been remarkably amorphous terms open to endless subjective interpretations and determinations. This has resulted in incessant bickering between creators and users.

Today in America, and indeed throughout the world, those ongoing tensions have seemingly reached a boiling point. In fact, it is fair to say that the debate over IP protection has become more contentious than ever before. There is increased awareness of the importance of the issue to both the creative community and the user community as the radical winds of technological change blow throughout the American economy. The "Napsterization" of just about everything digitizable—books, music, movies, and, of course, software itself—has brought copy protection issues to the forefront as never before, reenergizing the debate over such questions as:

- Why do we protect intellectual property at all?
- Do we really have "property rights" in our intangible creations the same way we have property rights to our homes or the land on which they rest?
- Are there more effective ways of incentivizing artistic creation and scientific discovery than through the use of copyright and patent laws that protect a limited monopoly?

Again, although these questions certainly are not new, the answers to them continue to prove remarkably elusive, perhaps more so than ever before.

IP and First Principles

Governments exist to protect property rights among other natural rights, but the property status of intangibles has always been unclear from a natural law perspective. Many natural law libertarians would agree with Ayn Rand that "Patents and copyrights are the legal implementation of the base of all property rights: a man's right to the product of his mind." Yet other natural law libertarians would claim that there is no such thing as a "right" to own intangible ideas and, therefore, the whole regime of limited grants of monopoly is a political construct that should be tossed aside. According to this line of thinking, the cost of protecting IP is just another cost of doing business, so why socialize it?

These same questions occupied our Founding Fathers, who constructed a *utilitarian* compromise to ensure that science and the useful arts would be promoted by offering limited terms of protection to ensure that innovators are rewarded for their intellectual creations. The Founders thus avoided the thorny issue of the natural law status of intangibles but made clear a view that some limited form of protection was necessary to encourage creative activity and commerce in the new republic.

And that was probably the best thing they could have done.

On one hand, a good argument can be made that in a world without any IP protection, some individuals would be discouraged from producing important goods or ideas (consider pharmaceuticals or genetically altered foods to feed hungry populations). A critic might claim that post hoc reasoning is at work here, but there is no denying the fact that there seems to be a strong correlation between strong IP protection and the industrial and commercial might of a nation. Moreover, those individuals who advocate the abolition of copyright or patent law should ask themselves why their same arguments and reasoning should not be applied to tangible property. Undercutting the roots of intellectual property law might undermine the foundations of all property law.

On the other hand, some creators seek (and often receive) excessive terms of protection—which seemingly go beyond any reasonable possibility of motivating creators, who often are deceased (think Mickey Mouse or the dispute over publication of the book *The Wind Done Gone*). Or they may seek to expand what is covered by copyright and patent law in the first place. One imagines record companies would assert the right to copyright the 12-bar blues chord progression if they could get away with it. Aggressive protection schemes often require an intrusive enforcement regime that can greatly discourage entrepreneurialism by others. That is especially the case in our modern, litigious society. For these reasons, terms of protection are being rethought over issues such as whether copyright should extend beyond the life of the author or whether "business methods" should be patentable.

So, succinctly stated, the problem we face when it comes to issues of IP and the Internet is how to balance artistic and entrepreneurial incentives with the interests of the larger community of users in an unhindered exchange of ideas and products.

The Internet Enters the Picture

With the rise of the Internet and a world of ubiquitous and instantaneous communications, revolutionary shifts are taking place in terms of how intellectual property is sold, used, and distributed. It's true that previous periods of technological innovation forced society to reconsider the proper balance of IP protections; indeed photocopiers, videocassette recorders, and other advances generated heated philosophical discussions and even some modifications in IP law. Nonetheless, so profound are the shifts brought about by the modern communications and computing revolution that many parties on both sides of this debate are wondering if IP law as now construed can or should survive.

IP skeptics posit that new digital technologies and other market developments have so fundamentally altered the nature of intellectual property that we need to consider radically abbreviating preestablished terms of protection or eliminating them altogether. "Information wants to be free!" is the rallying cry of many who claim allegiance to this school of thinking. These thinkers hold that information transmitted in electronic or digital formats cannot be "bottled up" and controlled by its creators once released into the public. Some IP skeptics equate efforts to do so with unworkable Soviet-style command-and-control mandates.

IP defenders fire back with claims that their intellectual property rights are under attack as never before, threatening their economic livelihood. They claim that the rise of the cyber-economy is placing incredible strains on the ability of creators to control the distribution of their products, making it less likely they will want to put anything in the public domain to begin with. They argue that new online technologies and digital computing systems are a particular threat to the creative community today given the potential infringing uses that they make possible for millions of Americans.

Not surprisingly, both sides are actively engaged in the legislative trenches, attempting to shift IP law in their preferred direction. This has brought the relatively arcane and quite complicated IP disputes to the attention of the public and the policymaking community as never before.

This debate is of particular interest to the Cato Institute and the market liberal movement in general, given that two cherished principles, property rights and free expression, are at stake. From a utilitarian perspective, libertarians value the importance of legal incentives that encourage artistic or scientific creation. And the movement is also fond of reminding policymakers of the paramount importance of private property rights to a free society.

But market liberals also advocate the free and unfettered expression and exchange of ideas in the marketplace and throughout civil society. The movement is skeptical of allowing coercion and political meddling to enter disputes that might be better left to voluntary interaction, contractual arrangements, and common law resolutions.

IP disputes have always involved the fundamental trade-off between these two principles. Consequently, the debate over intellectual property continues to divide politicians, policymakers, businesses, opinion leaders, and the public.

Organization of the Book

Given the remarkable spike in the public's interest in intellectual property matters, and recognizing just how bitter the ongoing disagreements within the libertarian movement on the issue had become, the Cato Institute convened a "Technology and Society" conference in Washington on November 14, 2001, to debate "The Future of Intellectual Property in the Information Age." Along with our cosponsors, *Forbes ASAP*, we brought together experts from the business community, academia, and Capitol Hill to square off on these complicated and controversial questions.

The result was a day of lively discussion and the collection of essays found in this reader. While these essays could not possibly resolve all the contentious issues raised by the digitization of music, movies, and books, they do provide a compelling framework for ongoing policy discussion on Capitol Hill, within academia, and throughout the general public.

Most of the chapters contained herein are drawn directly from the proceedings of the conference. Some reflect the informal nature of the panel format. A few additional articles for this book were assembled as well, because we felt the contributions of the writers would make for an even more compelling discussion. Of course, not every aspect of the intellectual property debate is covered in this volume. (In focusing largely on issues raised by the Internet, this book does not deal with other important issues such as trademarks and trade secrets.)

The book is divided into two main sections: theory and applications.

The Theory: What Rights Do We Have in Our Intangible Creations?

The theoretical arguments for and against copy protection in the Internet age, which are explored in Part I of the book, make for a fascinating debate. Tom Bell, an associate professor at Chapman University School of Law, argues that there really can be no "delicate balance" between creators and consumers, and that the best that can be hoped for is an "indelicate imbalance." This points to the possibility of considering new, market-based regimes that creators might employ to protect their content through extra-legal means in the future, thus enabling a "flight from copyright." One can legitimately reduce protections for what's created if creators opt out of traditional legal arrangements.

On the other hand, although also an advocate of market-based protections, Jim DeLong, a senior fellow at the Washington, D.C.-based Competitive Enterprise Institute, stresses the fundamental position that property rights occupy in our society. Many of the reasons for not protecting intangible property and relying on self-help apply to physical property too, he notes, but we don't use that fact to justify abandoning the regime. It isn't valid to point to "nonexhaustion" as the reason for not protecting intellectual property. The time one devotes to property creation, physical or not, is scarce, and most want their hard work protected. (Indeed, part of the outrage of robbery is the time consumed in one's life acquiring or creating the property that was stolen.) Important moral, economic, political, and even psychological rationales exist for protecting property.

Internet guru John Perry Barlow sees the 21st century as the stage for a struggle between open and closed systems. In his view, existing copyright beneficiaries are skewing the system to give themselves rights in near perpetuity, whereas he sees the alternative, the sharing of ideas, as a better model since resources aren't exhausted. Indeed, as he notes, even with rampant theft in software, software is still a top-five industry. Barlow, who was a lyricist for the Grateful Dead and is sympathetic to the sharing of music files, relates his experiences with sharing of music recordings at Grateful Dead concerts.

Finally, in a reprint of his seminal "Are Patents and Copyrights Morally Justified? The Philosophy of Property Rights and Ideal Objects," Cato Institute senior fellow Tom Palmer raises questions that terrify the major media companies but that are nonetheless important to ponder. Palmer rejects both the natural law and utilitarian justifications for government-compelled protection of intangible creations and argues that rights in the ownership of ideas threaten the liberty of individuals to act or express themselves freely. Palmer stresses that IP "rights" are based on an "artificial, self-created scarcity" unlike tangible property rights, which are based on legitimate scarcity, given that two people cannot use the same piece of tangible property at the same time. Intangible creations, however, can be used by many parties simultaneously, and efforts to restrict such uses ultimately violate the liberty of individuals to use their bodies as they wish.

Current Disputes in Intellectual Property Law

Part II explores the real world applications and consequences of copyright law, the disputes that make for the real meat of today's copy fights. This section of the book is further divided into four subsections: (1) how to reform IP law; (2) the specific debate over the remarkably controversial Digital Millennium Copyright Act (DMCA); (3) the question of what role digital rights management technologies can and should play in protecting copyrights; and, finally, (4) the increasingly contentious issue of "business method patents," which are generating heated debates in the "dot-com" sector.

Updating Copyright Law for the Digital Age

Rep. Rick Boucher (D-Va.), probably the most knowledgeable member of Congress on copyright matters, kicks off the second section of the book with an excellent overview of current IP disputes in Congress. Boucher makes the case that copyright and patent law has been corrupted and that the balance has tilted too far in favor of creators (or, more specifically, the middlemen who supposedly represent artists and creators). The DMCA and Internet business method patents are particularly troubling in this regard to Rep. Boucher. He lays out the case for reform on both fronts and discusses specific legislative measures that he feels will restore the proper balance to copyright and patent law.

Well-known Internet legal theorist David Post, a professor of law at Temple University Law School, points out in a fascinating discussion that part of the answer to resolving copyright disputes is to distinguish between property created "here" (in what other techies often refer to as "meatspace") that gets transferred over "there," into cyberspace, and property that gets created in cyberspace. Thinking about intellectual property in this way enables us to consider what a new regime might look like in the future as an increasing body of art is created for distribution in the cyber-sphere.

Wayne State University law professor Jessica Litman calls for revisions to copyright law that take into account new realities of the information age by "recasting copyright as an exclusive right of commercial exploitation." She would focus less on whether copies were made of a work, and instead focus more narrowly on assuring that copyright holders retain the sole opportunities for commercial exploitation of their work. Under this model, she points out, individual trading of song files would not be actionable, but perhaps Napster's facilitating of large-scale sharing would be because of its significant interference with rights-holders' commercial opportunities. Such an approach would put the law back in line with the public's typical understanding of the copyright bargain and fair use.

Finally, Drew Clark, a senior writer for *National Journal's Technology Daily*, wraps up this section and lays the foundation for the next by discussing "How Copyright Became Controversial." Clark argues that by adopting the DMCA a few years ago and by considering new digital rights management (DRM) mandates today, Congress has itself created a firestorm of justifiable opposition to the current copyright system.

The Digital Millennium Copyright Act

The Technology and Society panel discussions that addressed the DMCA and the question of circumvention of digital copy protections brought forth some interesting sparring.

Orin S. Kerr, an associate professor at George Washington University Law School, argues that the DMCA is a statute that libertarians should appreciate as "a respectable model for how to enforce intellectual property rights and contractual rights in cyberspace." Although uncertain about whether the law will be considered a success in the future, Kerr argues that "the Act reflects an intellectually coherent effort to protect copyrights and enforce contracts in an Internet age," and offers a potentially workable technological solution to a technological problem (the Internet's facilitating of breach of contract and copyright infringement).

Similarly, Emery Simon, special counsel with the Business Software Alliance, acknowledges that the anti-circumvention provisions of the DMCA may not strike a perfect balance, but they are nonetheless a sensible effort to achieve protection of copyrighted material given the new realities of digitization and the ease of theft. He regards efforts to characterize the law as unconstitutional as misguided. Moreover, he argues that it is not in the interest of profit-maximizing companies to behave in a manner that is going to restrict intellectual output and software research. In striking the balance, companies face market-induced incentives to avoid devising copy protection schemes so inconvenient or cumbersome that they go beyond the goal of deflecting piracy.

On the other hand, Mike Godwin, a policy fellow at the Washington, D.C.-based Center for Democracy and Technology, calls for assurances that noninfringing uses of materials and rights of fair use are preserved in the law. To Godwin, a key problem with the DMCA is that one's intent to infringe is not relevant; rather, a person engaged in the development or distribution of circumvention technology even for a benign purpose such as research or archiving is at risk of being held criminally or civilly liable. Fair use balances built into copyright law are undercut by the fact that there is no defense under the DMCA even if there is no underlying copyright infringement. Other developments, such as proposals to require digital rights management technologies in consumer devices, strike Godwin as efforts by the content industries to impose the costs of enforcing their interests on others.

Mitch Glazier, senior vice president of government relations and legislative counsel of the Recording Industry Association of America, notes that the digitization of content is forcing the industry and policymakers to confront new questions, such as what "reproduction" and "distribution" mean now. Even though there have been missteps and uncertainties remain for those developing business models on the Internet, agreements since the passage of the DMCA are leading to successes in the licensing of digital content. Many questions remain over how content providers will ultimately protect their shareholders' investments and their artists' creations. But the road is becoming clearer, and all—particularly consumers who ultimately determine what services survive—will benefit from the transformation.

Digital Rights Management

One of the more contentious disputes in the intellectual property arena today is over the appropriateness of technologies known as "digital rights management." These are technological tools that better copy-protect content using data encryption and other techniques.

Electronic Frontier Foundation staff attorney Robin Gross warns that such copy protection technologies can go too far—even further than existing legal protections—and erode fair use rights that individuals have come to expect, as well as pose a technical threat to free speech. She argues that while the Framers established copyright to provide an economic incentive for artists to create, the ultimate aim was to benefit the public. The rights of publishers and authors must be balanced with the rights retained by the public.

University of Texas professor of managerial economics Stan Liebowitz argues that, although content providers have cried wolf in the past over such developments as the photocopier and the videocassette recorder, digitization does appear to present a real threat to content companies. But digital rights management technologies present a way out of the woods. Although they won't prevent all copying, the imperative is to prevent massive unauthorized duplication, which does appear achievable. As to the criticism that such copy protections can trample fair use rights, Liebowitz points out that, given technologies such as micropayments, digital rights management will not restrict the output of intellectual property at all.

Putting a practical spin on a contentious economic and philosophical debate, Frank Hausmann, chairman and CEO of peer-to-peer file trading pioneer CenterSpan Communications Corporation (which acquired the Scour website, customer list, and other assets at bankruptcy auction in late 2000), argues that file-trading technologies can offer the security that content providers need, and with the right legal framework, fair use can be preserved as well. Hausmann also offers unique insights into the role—or lack thereof—of legal tools such as the first sale doctrine and compulsory licensing in an age of peer-to-peer computing and file sharing.

Business Method Patents

Many commentators have ridiculed patents for such seemingly "obvious" business processes as Amazon's "1-Click" and Priceline's "name your price" reverse auctions. Peter Wayner, author of several books on digital technology, in "How Can They Patent That?" asks the question that's on the minds of many—whether the business patenting process has gotten out of hand.

As it happens, the debate is quite nuanced, and what seems obvious may not be. Michael Nugent, a lawyer with the firm of Heller

Ehrman White & McAuliffe and former Citigroup general counsel for technology and intellectual property, demonstrates that business method patents that seem so novel to us today are actually nothing new; such patenting has a long history going back to the time of Abraham Lincoln.

Finally, Ron Laurie and Robert Beyers, attorneys with the law firm Skadden, Arps, Slate, Meagher & Flom, provide an exhaustive analytical framework for looking at business method patents to gauge the "obviousness" of new inventions. Their analysis of the current business method patent methodology suggests that some procedural improvements are necessary, but Laurie and Beyers argue that "most (if not all) of the cries of alarm regarding business method patents should subside if the PTO [Patent and Trademark Office] and the courts perform a proper substantive analysis of obviousness."

Potential Common Ground Solutions

Given that these chapters offer conflicting opinions and recommendations on the future of intellectual property, it may be difficult to draw definitive conclusions from this book. We would like to suggest, however, that this is a natural and quite healthy part of the ongoing IP debate.

But is there *any* common ground in this debate? Perhaps. All sides make some excellent points. Again, the debate is thorny because two important principles collide: legal protection for intangible works butts up against free expression and exchange of ideas. IP disputes have always involved the fundamental trade-off between these principles, but it would be a mistake to ask policymakers to advance one principle at the expense of the other. The following recommendations, while perhaps overly simplistic, provide at least some common ground solutions to this ongoing balancing act:

(1) *Take the principle "To promote the Progress of Science and useful Arts" seriously*—Reasonable people can legitimately debate the appropriate time periods over which works should be protected. Any term set in law will be arbitrary. But copyright protection that extends far beyond the life of the originator provides diminishing incentives for that person to innovate (even if one assumes he is innovating on behalf of yet-born descendants). Terms of protection may need to be rethought; indeed a new case in the Supreme Court

challenges the "Bono Act"—referred to by Stanford University law professor Lawrence Lessig as the "Mickey Mouse Protection Act"—which extended copyright protection terms to life of the author plus 70 years (up from 50 years).

The anger at the middleman is understandable: If you happen to be exploring, say, roots-country music, and want to sample some songs by the "singing brakeman" Jimmie Rodgers, you're not wild about paying BMG/RCA for the privilege, especially when the man has been dead 67 years. Many agree on the concept of the protection of property; the disputes often arise over how long property should be protected.

Adhering to the Constitution's goal of promoting the progress of science and useful arts, not unnecessary government monopoly, seems a sensible course. Copyright law can go beyond that if terms of protection are so extended that they can do little to "incentivize," but instead benefit a middleman. Rights owners certainly expend great energy on extending the legal monopoly granted by copyright. This is the widespread criticism of the Sonny Bono Act, where clearly the current rights-holders prevailed because new protections were given retroactively. The middleman—and heirs—continue to want to be paid. Decisions about how long they will be paid are always going to be arbitrary, but there seems little reason to provide retroactive legal protection decades after a creator is dead.

(2) Don't ban new technologies or business models to solve copyright or patent problems—In the raging file-sharing dispute, one side wants to ban or restrict file-sharing technologies that reduce copyright control. Meanwhile those who eagerly share copyrighted files often condemn experimental technologies by which copyright holders hope to shield works from reproduction, such as digital watermarking, enhanced encryption, and attempts to incorporate digital rights management into software or hardware. Some regard such efforts as threats to free expression (even though many in the next breath will assert that encryption, or watermarking can always be cracked). If companies go too far in locking up information, other companies (and consumers) have the option of dealing with less-restrictive entrepreneurs. Policymakers shouldn't ban any category of technology as the marketplace works through these difficult issues.

Digital rights management will never fully prevent copying but can make it inconvenient enough so that cracking encrypted songs isn't likely to be worth the trouble. Perhaps a 20-cent download that also includes liner notes, lyrics, a photo or two, and discount coupons on merchandise and concerts is a better deal than a free song.

Government coercion should not be used to "aid" the sharing of intellectual property. For example, some are calling for the imposition of compulsory licensing requirements on record companies. Such forced "contracts," with their accompanying government-set royalty fees (read "price controls") and regulatory dynamics, must be rethought for the sake of a nascent industry that needs to embrace voluntary deals.

Policymakers should not fall prey to calls for a quick fix to the transitional problems we are currently encountering by extending the compulsory license regime. That old order rests upon a notion of market failure. Digitization, at the very least, presents an opportunity to rethink whether such market failure even exists before extending the compulsory model. If technology is to contribute to solving the problems it has created, it must be given the chance. All sides should avoid injecting government coercion into the copyright resolution process as "Napsterization" proceeds. Perhaps technology can be a better means of managing copyright, in some applications, than law—even if law is in place as a backup.

It is worth noting that digital distribution does give producers, and artists, the option of avoiding the existing music companies and movie studios. Artists often feel ripped off, which is another fight within today's wide-ranging copyright debate. (MP3.com was one of those options—the artists-direct-to-the-customer model.)

Of course, if artists rather than middlemen control their copyrights, it won't end disputes over length of protection, but it could remove one layer of the dispute. With any luck, we are witnessing the transformation of copyright law as the current generation of post-Napster artists realize there may be better ways of protecting their intellectual creations than resorting to middlemen and legal arrangements. Technological solutions may be emerging that will offer artists and inventors the option of "opting out" of the IP legal regime entirely and instead relying upon new technologies and unique business models to protect their property and receive compensation for it.

(3) Remove government barriers to the marketplace's ability to protect intellectual property—To lessen the reliance on traditional copyright

protections, policymakers should ensure that government regulations don't stand in the way of private efforts by individuals to protect their intangible creations. To what extent are secrecy and privacy contracts among content creators enough? For example, overzealous antitrust enforcement might hamper collective private efforts to license songs, like the MusicNet and Pressplay services. Restrictive contracts that antitrust law might eye suspiciously could in fact benefit consumers by ensuring returns for producers. Indeed, some academics have suggested that regulation such as antitrust law may force the "need" for more intellectual property law and enforcement than would otherwise be warranted.

The Constitution clearly gives Congress the power to protect intellectual property. Yet the Internet invites new perspectives on the old models of IP protection. File-sharing technology clearly creates a problem, but an arguably transitory one involving the existing body of copyrighted work. In the post-Napster world, every musician and songwriter realizes there exist new methods for distributing and pricing products, meaning creative options for distributing and protecting future works are wide open.

Technology and new, post-Napster business models can play a role in allowing us to avoid the use of legal coercion. Technology may be able to substitute for law in many cases, and perhaps do a better job, just as barbed wire or an iron gate may be superior to a patrolman. Policymakers and artists should embrace these developments as an improvement over the litigious middleman model of the past and not seek to ban or restrict any technologies that facilitate this transformation.

PART I

THEORY: WHAT RIGHTS DO WE HAVE IN OUR
INTANGIBLE CREATIONS?

1. Indelicate Imbalancing in Copyright and Patent Law

Tom W. Bell

When we were kids, my brother and I quarreled at length about the color of the world. Our intractable dispute arose because my brother, David, favored blue, whereas I favored green. As proof that he had chosen the superior of the two colors, my brother claimed that the world had more blue in it. Being some four years younger and correspondingly smaller, I could not resort to David's favorite rhetorical device (the argument from pummeling). I instead had to rely on my half-pint wits. To his claim on behalf of the color blue, I thus replied: "Does not!"

"Does too!" came David's retort. "The sky is blue and so is the ocean."

"The sky isn't blue when it rains or at night," I parried, "and the ocean isn't blue—it's green. And the grass is green. And the trees are green, too."

You can well imagine where our colloquium on the world's color went from there: whether the sky was blue, black, or even (as I averred) deep purple at night; how to reckon the color of the sky *above* the clouds and, relatedly, how many airline passengers get window seats; which of us had better claim to the Red and Yellow Seas; whether the "Sea of Green" the Beatles sang of really existed; "does not"; "does too"; and so forth.

I relate this tale for two reasons. First, I want to publicly concede that my brother almost certainly had the better of our factual dispute. As a five-year-old in rural Virginia, I perhaps had good reason to think that the world sports predominately green hues. I've since learned, however, that we call Earth "the Blue Planet" for good reason. (It bears noting, though, that scientists recently discovered that "the current color of the *universe* is a sprightly green.")[1]

Secondly, and more important, that childhood argument over color illustrates an important aspect of contemporary arguments

1

over the proper scope of copyright and patent protection. Neither sort of argument could ever end by dint of quantitative measures. The necessary numbers do not exist and, even if they did, they could not alone suffice to settle the dispute in question. These types of arguments ultimately turn on questions of values—aesthetic in one case, ethical in the other—not on questions of facts.

Our ignorance about the relative amounts of blueness and greenness hardly mattered to me and my brother because we implicitly understood that our fight over facts served as a mere proxy for the ultimate, and ultimately irresolvable, issue: aesthetics. Ignorance of the relevant quantitative data *does* matter, however, to arguments over the proper scope of copyright and patent law. By all accounts, copyright and patent law aim to strike a "delicate balance" between public and private interests. By most accounts, moreover, and by the only convincing ones, the justifiability of copyright and patent protection relies on a showing that lawmakers have managed to at least approximate that balance.

But due to knowledge problems,[2] copyright and patent law has not and indeed cannot strike a delicate balance between public and private interests. Due to public choice problems,[3] lawmakers can at best achieve only a rather *in*delicate *im*balance between various private interests—namely, those private interests with sufficient clout to sway legislative deliberations.

Can the legislative process at least approximate *the real goal* of copyright and patent law, that of balancing public and private interests? That remains a difficult—and hotly contested—question. Merely to ask the question demonstrates the need to reevaluate the justifiability of state action protecting copyrights and patents. Copyrights and patents represent federal welfare programs for creators. As with other sorts of welfare programs, we may never know if copyright and patent work very well or even if they produce net benefits. But, as with other sorts of welfare programs, we should recognize copyrights and patents as evils—evils necessary at the best and susceptible to reform at the least.

Admittedly, some intellectual property theoreticians might object to the characterization of copyrights and patents as purely utilitarian devices for maximizing social utility. Such theoreticians characterize copyrights and patents as natural rights that vest in the creators of original expressions or novel inventions, respectively. To clear the way for the main topic—the indelicate imbalances struck by copyright and patent law—the next section offers a brief rejoinder to the natural rights argument for copyrights and patents. Then the paper discusses why copyright and patent law cannot demonstrably satisfy their utilitarian aims, and suggests what we should do about that problem.

Before turning to those arguments, allow me to clarify that I do not intend to analyze every sort of intellectual property. I focus here solely on copyrights and patents, which alone out of all intellectual property protections tout express authorization under the U.S. Constitution,[4] which thus arise almost solely under U.S. federal law rather than the laws of the several states, and which have little or no plausible claim to natural or common law foundations. Trademarks and trade secrets, the two other main types of intellectual property, present issues different from those covered by this paper and, thus, beyond its scope.

The Unnaturalness of Copyright and Patent Rights

The instrumentalism that pervades cases, legislation, and commentary on copyright and patent law leaves scant room for natural rights.[5] The Supreme Court has, for instance, described copyright as "the creature of the Federal statute"[6] and observed, "Congress did not sanction an existing right but created a new one."[7] In another case, the Court observed: "The patent monopoly was not designed to secure to the inventor his natural right in his discoveries. Rather it was a reward, an inducement, to bring forth new knowledge."[8] Nonetheless, a few commentators have argued that the propriety of copyrights and patents could and should rely on a Lockean labor-desert justification. That form of justification would run, in very brief, thus: 1) Because a creator owns himself, 2) he owns his labor and, thus, 3) those intellectual properties with which, by dint of his creative acts, he mixes his labor.[9]

That facially plausible extension of Locke's theory does not, however, withstand close scrutiny. The labor-desert justification of property gives a creator clear title only to the particular tangible item in which he fixes his creativity—not to some intangible wisp of the metaphysical realm.[10] It speaks only to the ownership of atoms, not to the ownership of bits. Locke himself did not try to justify intangible property.[11] Modern commentators who would venture so far beyond

3

the boundaries of Locke's thought, into the abstractions of intellectual property, thus ought to leave his name behind.

More pointedly, copyright and patent protection contradicts Locke's justification of property. By invoking state power, a copyright or patent owner can impose prior restraint, fines, imprisonment, and confiscation on those engaged in peaceful expression and the quiet enjoyment of their tangible property.[12] Because it thus gags our voices, ties our hands, and demolishes our presses, the law of copyrights and patents violates the very rights that Locke defended.[13]

At any rate, Locke's justification of the natural right to property runs little risk of convincing contemporary legislators or courts to forsake the prevailing utilitarian justification of copyright and patent. The Lockean labor-desert theory has only one realistic hope of influencing intellectual property law: via originalist interpretation of the U.S. Constitution.[14] Many judges find appeals to the original meaning of constitutional language, such as that embodied in the copyright and patent clause, quite persuasive.[15] We thus need to ask whether the Founders understood copyrights and patents to secure authors' and inventors' natural rights against unauthorized duplication. A careful review of the historical record indicates that the Founders almost certainly did not.[16]

Consider first the plain language of the Constitution's copyright and patent clause, which authorizes Congress to "promote the Progress of Science and the useful Arts"[17] The clause makes no reference to natural rights, instead offering only a utilitarian justification of copyrights and patents.[18] Consider second the available evidence of substantial discussion about the clause during the Philadelphia Convention or the state ratification debates: no such evidence exists.[19] Reconstructing the Founders' views on copyright and patent law thus calls, third and last, for us to consider their extra-legislative comments.

In *The Federalist Papers*, James Madison defended the power granted by the copyright and patent clause to Congress on grounds that,

> The utility of the power will scarcely be questioned. The copyright of authors has been solemnly adjudged, in Great Britain, to be a right of common law. The right to useful inventions seems with equal reason to belong to the inventors. The public good fully coincides in both cases with the claims of individuals.[20]

Note first that Madison's defense of the copyright and power sounds more in utility than natural rights. Note next that, intentionally or not, Madison misrepresented copyright's standing at common law, which had some years prior to his comments lost what little nonstatutory protection it ever enjoyed.[21]

Most importantly, however, note that notwithstanding Madison's reference to the "claims of individuals," he appears not to have held a natural rights view of copyrights and patents. The telling evidence appears in what he said—or rather what he did not say—in his correspondence with Thomas Jefferson about the copyright and patent clause. Jefferson wrote from Paris critiquing the proposed Constitution for failing to include a bill of rights, advocating in particular that it "abolish . . . Monopolies, in all cases. . . ."[22] Jefferson explained that "saying there will be no monopolies lessens the incitements [sic] to ingenuity . . . but the benefit even of limited monopolies is too doubtful to be opposed to that of their general suppression."[23]

Madison's reply gave ample credit to Jefferson's concerns and, more pointedly, nowhere defended the clause as a measure necessary to protect the natural rights of authors and inventors.[24] Madison's silence on that point would prove remarkable in any context.[25] In this case, though, writing to one of the foremost advocates of natural rights, in reply to his call for a bill of rights, and in defense of the copyright and patent clause, Madison's silence speaks tomes. Madison regarded copyrights and patents not as natural rights but as admittedly dangerous tools for advancing industrial policy, and ones of dubious efficacy at that.

As his comments to Madison indicated, Thomas Jefferson likewise regarded copyrights and patents as unnatural—and presumptively unwise—rights. His view of patents carries particular weight, as Jefferson served, in effect, as the first Commissioner of Patents.[26] Jefferson quite plainly regarded patents as utilitarian and statutory devices, describing "the exclusive right to invention as given not of natural right, but for the benefit of society. . . ."[27]

In sum, then, the argument for natural rights in copyrights and patents cannot claim the support of the plain language of the Constitution, judicial interpretation of that language, Locke's theory of property, or the Founders' views of copyrights and patents. On that evidence I conclude that copyrights and patents represent notable exceptions to the default rule that a free people, respecting common law rights and engaging in market transactions, can copy original expressions and novel inventions at will.[28] In that, I think I follow the Founders, who viewed copyrights and patents as exceptions to natural rights so extraordinary as to require explicit constitutional authorization.

The Statutory Failure of Copyright and Patent Law

Courts and commentators agree that copyright and patent represent statutory responses to a looming market failure—namely, the market's failure to provide adequate supplies of original expressions and novel inventions.[29] Why create copyright and patent rights? "To promote the Progress of Science and useful Arts,"[30] the Constitution explains. How do copyright and patent promote that end? By "securing for limited Times to Authors and Inventors the exclusive Right to their respective Writings and Discoveries," the Constitution's text continues.[31] The Supreme Court summed it up in *Mazer v. Stein*: "The economic philosophy behind the clause empowering Congress to grant patents and copyrights is the conviction that encouragement of individual effort by personal gain is the best way to advance public welfare."[32]

In other words, copyright and patent law provide emergency shelter to creations that, but for such special statutory protection, would have fallen between the common law's cracks and been left wandering unprotected through the market economy. Just as commentators call the special treatment that lawmakers afford to influential commercial interests "corporate welfare," we might thus call copyright and patent law "creators' welfare." Or, to draw a parallel with a type of welfare that, in contrast to corporate welfare, has seen bracing reform—the Aid to Families with Dependent Children (AFDC) program[33]—we might call copyright and patent protection "ACPE," for "Aid for Creators with Positive Externalities."

As that analogy suggests, we ought to withdraw copyright and patent protections when and if they prove redundant. Understand that by analogizing them to welfare I do not mean to dismiss copyrights and patents as utterly illegitimate. For one thing, copyright and patent law can lay just claim to using a fairly efficient means of incentivizing creators: the creation of fungible and divisible rights. For another thing, copyright and patent law tackles a very difficult problem—one the Founders thought salient and important enough to expressly address in the Constitution. But the analogy with welfare does serve to remind us that the legitimacy of copyrights and patents remains a contingent question of fact.

But here we face a problem: Notwithstanding ubiquitous claims that copyright and patent policy strikes a delicate balance between public and private rights,[34] thus maximizing social utility, it almost certainly does not strike such a balance. Indeed, it cannot. Political authorities cannot measure even the *economic* factors that would have to go into a calculation of the optimal level of copyright and patent protection.[35] Still less can they measure the myriad fluctuating and intangible ones, such as the Internet's effect on the production of new music or the social impact of parody.[36] Regardless of whether they could *measure* all the relevant economic, legal, technological, and cultural factors, moreover, politicians could not *balance* such incommensurable values.[37] The subject matter of copyright and patent law reaches so deeply into our lives that it has become not simply a matter of industrial policy, or even of information policy, but of social policy. Copyright law limits criticism of the Church of Scientology, for instance, while patent law raises the price of life-saving drugs. The intractable nature of those and related controversies ensures that no amount of open, sincere, and disinterested discourse will put copyright and patent law into delicate balance.

Does that sound discouraging? It gets worse. Public choice theory teaches that even if lawmakers could obtain the data necessary for delicately balancing all the public and private interests affected by copyright and patent law, it wouldn't matter.[38] Lawmakers would not use those data—or, more precisely, those data would not control the laws they make. Instead, lobbying by special interests would invariably ensure that copyright and patent law favors private interests over public ones. That is not to say that politicians are always corrupt or that democracies always fail; it means simply that politicians respond to the same incentives as the rest of us and that, consequently, democracies tend toward predictably biased outcomes.

Does "delicate balancing" rhetoric merit any place in copyright and patent jurisprudence? Copyright and patent legislation does reflect careful compromises struck between the various private parties that lobby for changes to federal law. As noted, however, any such truce among special interests does not and cannot delicately balance all the interests affected by copyright law. The influence of such rough-and-tumble politics merely ensures that copyright and patent law put public and private interests into an *indelicate imbalance*.

Toward Market Success in Protecting Original Expressions and Novel Inventions

What can we do about the apparently inexorable influence that ignorance and politics wield over copyright and patent law? We can, for a start, learn to recognize and resist how copyright and patent owners co-opt the rhetoric of property.[39] Such rhetoric proves especially attractive to those who have for so long courageously defended rights to tangible property.

True, copyrights and patents bear some of the attributes of real and chattel property. That they have nonnatural origins (arising solely by statute) and remain nonrivalrous in consumption (even if statutory protections render them somewhat excludable), means that copyrights and patents remain quite different from tangible property, however. The thief of your apple, house, or other tangible property violates your natural rights because you can no longer enjoy—or "consume"—those purloined goods. His consumption rivals yours. The copier of your copyright or patent, in contrast, leaves you at complete liberty to continue expressing your authorship or using your invention. He infringes only your statutory right to exclude others from those same benefits of consumption. Those who respect property rights should never forget that distinction, lest debates about the proper scope of copyrights and patents overextend and fatally dilute the very concept of property.

In addition, even though no one can tell whether copyright and patent have achieved that mythical "delicate balance" of public and private interests, we *can* tell when lawmakers have plainly put matters out of whack. Sentencing copyright infringers to death would, for instance, clearly go beyond the pale. Perhaps some current laws do too. The point here is not to settle such questions but rather simply to observe that imprecise knowledge should not preclude rough justice. Regardless of the merits of our childish debate over blue versus green, after all, my brother and I would have agreed that either of our favorites colored the world far more than, say, fuchsia.

Recalling the utilitarian foundations of copyright and patent law should encourage us to continually question its proper scope. At the very least, we should challenge the absurd argument that copyright and patent rights have become so important to the national economy that they must reach farther still.[40] To the contrary, the efficacy of copyright and patent protections demonstrates that market failure no longer looms and, thus, that they have reached the limits of their justification. Far from trumpeting the prodigious revenues, jobs, and exports that their clients generate, in other words, lobbyists for increased intellectual property protections should have to relate their clients' threadbare survival and imminent woe.

Still further, we should regard even extant copyright and patent protections skeptically. Perhaps creators would do just as well without such legal fripperies. We appear to suffer no shortage of creative perfumes,[41] recipes,[42] clothes designs,[43] furniture,[44] car bodies,[45] or uninhabited architectural structures,[46] even though U.S. law affords no effective protection to them *qua* original expressions or novel inventions.[47] Perhaps the same would hold true of subject matter now covered by copyrights or patents were their protections removed.

As set forth above, we cannot count on lawmakers to resolve such questions—or even to have much resolve in asking them. The problem of encouraging the creation and distribution of original expressions and novel inventions thus mirrors other difficult problems of social coordination; in no such case can we expect a central political authority to have the information and incentives necessary to identify and implement an efficient public policy. Here, as generally, we should insofar as possible rely on the decentralized enforcement of common law rights and remedies.[48] Although the common law cannot replicate copyrights and patents, those unnatural and purely statutory creations, it might nonetheless supplant them.

Whether and how the resultant "packet switched society," as I have elsewhere termed it,[49] will give rise to practices and institutions capable of supplanting copyrights and patents poses an interesting and difficult question. It seems reasonable to suppose that common law contract, tort, and property rules, buttressed by innovative institutions and technologies, could go some distance toward that goal. In place of copyrights, for instance, automated rights management systems could help protect an expressive work from unauthorized access and condition use of it on agreement to a "clickwrap" license.[50]

9

In place of patents, so-called "idea futures" or "decision markets" could reward research and invention by allowing people to "bet" for or against claims about future events.[51] Someone who had created a new cure for AIDS, for instance, could profit by shorting the market in claims about the disease's spread.

So go some plausible forecasts of how the market might respond had it greater incentives to protect expressive works and novel inventions. But we cannot really know what such a spontaneous order will achieve unless and until we free it to function. We thus face a preliminary problem: How do we get from here to there? In other words, how can we encourage the development of nonstatutory alternatives to copyright and patent law? Even if I had a complete answer to that question—which I do not—to relate it would surely exceed the bounds of this essay. I can, however, offer a few brief suggestions.

For reasons set forth above, public choice pressures make direct legislative attacks on the scope of copyright and patent law highly unlikely to succeed. That does not mean that statutory reforms offer no hope; it means simply that any such reform would have to pass muster with the various parties that lobby for more powerful intellectual property protections. I've elsewhere specified a very modest amendment to the Copyright Act, for instance, that might both win the support of such lobbyists and help encourage extra statutory protections of expressive works.[52]

It might also help drive the development of alternatives to copyright and patent were we to encourage practices more clearly demarcating the line between protected and unprotected creations. This would prove especially helpful in copyright law, where U.S. law by default grants protection to every fixed expression of authorship. I've thus argued for applying notices such as "Uncopyright," "Uncopr.," or even just "(¢)" to works that have been removed from, fallen out of, or never qualified for the Copyright Act's protections.[53] Such notices would encourage the growth of an "open" copyright system, one that respects and encourages movement across the Act's porous border.[54]

Beyond those measures, the best options for effectuating reform of copyright and patent law remain the standbys of reformers everywhere: long-shot legal claims, the diffuse effects of popular opinion, and long-term academic debates. Although that may sound dispiriting, I assure you from personal experience that it can prove a very engaging project. At the very least, the hard job of privatizing copyright and patent law promises to keep liberty-loving policy wonks motivated and busy for years to come.

Conclusion

Arguments over the proper scope of copyright and patent law resemble the argument between my brother and me in that both arguments wrongly assume knowledge of things unknown and unknowable. We can excuse such meta-ignorance in the case of two kids squabbling over the merits of their favorite colors. We cannot excuse it in the case of those who shape copyright and patent policy, however. The risks of simple ignorance, already too evident in copyright and patent policy, pale beside the risks of not knowing the limits of our knowledge.

Notes

1. Paul Recer, "Scientists Say Universe Is a Pale Green," Associated Press, January 10, 2002 (emphasis added). They arrived at this color by averaging all the colors from the light of 200,000 galaxies.

2. See, for example, Friedrich A. Hayek, *Individualism and Economic Order* (Chicago: University of Chicago Press: 1948), pp. 77–78. Hayek explains that the knowledge essential for central planning does not exist in concentrated form.

3. Public choice theory holds, in very brief, that because political actors respond to incentives in the same way that other humans do, we should not assume that political acts aim at promoting the public good. See, for example, James M. Buchanan and Gordon Tullock, *The Calculus of Consent* (Ann Arbor: University of Michigan Press: 1962); Mancur Olson, Jr., *The Logic of Collective Action* (Cambridge, Mass., Harvard University Press: 1965).

4. U.S. Const. Art. I, § 8, cl. 8.

5. See Mark A. Lemley, "Romantic Authorship and the Rhetoric of Property," *Texas Law Review* 75 (1997): 873, 879–95, reviewing James Boyle, *Shamans, Software, and Spleens* (Cambridge, Mass.: Harvard University Press, 1996). Boyle's collected cases, statutes, and commentary describe the instrumentalist philosophy underlying copyright and patent law.

6. *Fox Film Corp. v. Doyal*, 286 U.S. 123, 127 (1932).

7. Ibid.

8. *Graham v. John Deere Co.*, 383 U.S. 1, 9 (1966).

9. See, for example, Ayn Rand, "Patents and Copyrights," in *Capitalism: The Unknown Ideal* (New York: New American Library, 1967), p. 26; Wendy J. Gordon, "A Property Right in Self-Expression: Equality and Individualism in the Natural Law of Intellectual Property," *Yale Law Journal* 102 (1993): 1533; Alfred C. Yen, "Restoring the Natural Law: Copyright as Labor and Possession," *Ohio State Law Journal* 51 (1990): 517. See also Justin Hughes, "The Philosophy of Intellectual Property," *Georgia Law Journal* 77 (1988): 287, 296–331, exploring the uses and limits of the Lockean justification of intellectual property.

11

10. See Tom G. Palmer, "Are Patents and Copyrights Morally Justified? The Philosophy of Property Rights and Ideal Objects," *Harvard Journal of Law and Public Policy* 13 (1990): 851–55, distinguishing rights to tangible property from claims to intangibles.

11. For an argument from irony, consider this: The text that allegedly inspired a natural rights view of copyright among the Founders, John Locke, *The Second Treatise of Government*, in John Locke, *Two Treatises of Government*, ed. Laslett (1690, New York: Cambridge University Press: 1963), p. 299, appears not to have enjoyed copyright protection itself.

12. See Copyright Act of 1976, as amended, 17 U.S.C.A. §§ 502–11 (West Supp. 2001), for a description of remedies for copyright infringement; Patent Act of 1952, as amended, 35 U.S.C.A. §§ 283–88 (West Supp. 2001) (describing remedies for patent infringement). Note, however, that these two statutes do not afford equivalent remedies; the former generally offers more powerful ones. Most notably, U.S. patent law imposes criminal sanctions not for infringement per se but rather only for false patent marking, 35 U.S.C.A. § 292 (West Supp. 2001), and counterfeiting of letters patent, 18 U.S.C.A. § 497 (West Supp. 2001), and allows for seizure and forfeiture of infringing goods only with regard to imports, 19 U.S.C.A. 1337(a)(1)(B) (West Supp. 2001).

13. Tom G. Palmer, "Intellectual Property: A Non-Posnerian Law and Economics Approach," *Hamline Law Review* 12 (1989): 261, 281. See also Palmer, "Are Patents and Copyrights Morally Justified?" p. 827 (critiquing the Lockean argument for intellectual property rights on grounds that they "restrict others' uses of their own bodies in conjunction with resources to which they have full moral and legal rights."). But see Gordon, "A Property Right in Self-Expression," p. 1423, for a response to Palmer's argument with the Hohfeldian and positivist argument that "all entitlements limit each other."

14. Though originalists do not always take care to do so, one ought to distinguish between original meaning and original intent. Justice Antonin Scalia explains, "What I look for in the Constitution is precisely what I look for in a statute: the original meaning of the text, not what the original draftsmen intended." Antonin Scalia, *A Matter of Interpretation* (Princeton, N.J.: Princeton University Press, 1997), p. 38. Justice Scalia does well to favor original meaning over original intent. Our untrustworthy records of what transpired in the Constitutional Convention and in the states' ratifying conventions, not to mention the incoherence of ascribing intentions to deliberative bodies, should discourage attempts to divine the Founders' intentions.

15. See, for example, ibid., at 37–41.

16. I undertook a fairly comprehensive review of the evidence relating to copyrights in Bell, "Escape from Copyright: Market Success vs. Statutory Failure in the Protection of Expressive Works," *University of Cincinnati Law Review* 69 (2001): 762–74. Others have done much the same for patents. See, for example, Adam Mossoff, "Rethinking the Development of Patents: An Intellectual History," *Hastings Law Journal* 52 (2001) ("Regardless of the theoretical schema scholars have used to explain the history of patents, everyone agrees that natural rights theories played no part whatsoever in this story").

17. U.S. Const. Art I, § 8, cl. 8.

18. See H.R. Rep. No. 1494, 52d Cong., 1st sess. 2 (1892) ("There is nothing said [in the Constitution's Copyright and Patent clause] about any desire or purpose to secure to the author or inventor his 'natural right to his property'").

19. See Karl Fenning, "The Origin of the Patent and Copyright Clause of the Constitution," *Law Journal* 17 (1929): 109, 114 (reviewing the evidence and concluding

that the clause "apparently roused substantially no controversy either in the Convention or among the States adopting the Constitution").

20. James Madison, *The Federalist* No. 43.

21. Madison presumably relied on *Millar v. Taylor*, 4 Burr. 2303, 98 Eng. Rep. 201 (1769), in which the King's Bench read the Statute of Anne not to abrogate common law's protection of copyrights. But the House of Lords overruled that case five years later, in *Donaldson v. Becket*, 4 Burr. 2408, 98 Eng. Rep. 257 (H.L. 1774)—some thirteen years before Madison published *Federalist* No. 43. Madison's claim that copyright "has been solemnly adjudged, in Great Britain, to be a right of common law" therefore had as much truth as the modern claim that "slavery has been solemnly adjudged constitutional." In neither case would old bad law justify new bad law.

22. "Letter from Thomas Jefferson to James Madison," Paris, July 31, 1788, James Morton Smith ed., reprinted in *The Republic of Letters: The Correspondence between Thomas Jefferson and James Madison 1776–1826* ed., (New York: W.W. Norton, 1995), pp. 543, 545.

23. Ibid.

24. "Letter from James Madison to Thomas Jefferson," New York, October 17, 1788, ibid. at 562, 566.

25. That Jefferson did not raise a natural rights argument bears noting, too.

26. Jefferson, as secretary of state, effectively directed the three-member board that reviewed applications under the 1790 Patent Act. Edward C. Walterscheid, "Patents and the Jeffersonian Mythology," *John Marshall Law Review* 29 (1995): 269, 279–80. Some authorities also credit Jefferson as having authored the 1793 Patent Act. See for example, *Diamond v. Chakrabarty*, 447 U.S. 303, 308 (1980). Recent scholarship has somewhat mitigated that claim, however, making it appear more likely that Jefferson merely influenced that Act. See Edward C. Walterscheid, "The Use and Abuse of History: The Supreme Court's Interpretation of Thomas Jefferson's Influence on the Patent Law," *Journal of Law and Technology* 39 (1999): 195, 211–12.

27. "Letter from Jefferson to Isaac McPherson," Aug. 13, 1813, in XII Writings of Jefferson, supra note 5, p. 335.

28. As Justice Holmes explained of copyright law, and as he would no doubt have rightly said of patent law, too, it "restrains the spontaneity of men where but for it there would be nothing of any kind to hinder their doing as they saw fit." *White-Smith Music Publishing Co. v. Apollo*, 209 U.S. 1, 19 (1908) (Holmes, J., concurring).

29. See, for example, *Mazer v. Stein*, 347 U.S. 201, 219 (1954), describing copyright and patents as a response to market failure and analyzing them in cost/benefit terms; *United States v. Paramount Pictures, Inc.*, 334 U.S. 131, 158 (1948) (same with regard to copyrights); John R. Thomas, "Collusion and Collective Action in the Patent System: A Proposal for Patent Bounties," (2001) *University of Illinois Law Review* 2001 (2001): 305, 308–09 (describing patents as a response to market failure). Also see Brett Frischmann, "Innovation and Institutions: Rethinking the Economics of U.S. Science and Technology Policy," *Vermont Law Review* 24 (2000): 377–82; Wendy J. Gordon, "Fair Use as Market Failure: A Structural and Economic Analysis of the Betamax Case and Its Predecessors," *Columbia Law Review* 82 (1982): 1610–14; Stephen Breyer, "The Uneasy Case for Copyright: A Study of Copyright in Books, Photocopies, and Computer Programs," *Harvard Law Review* 84 (1970): 281; William M. Landes and Richard A. Posner, "An Economic Analysis of Copyright Law," *Journal of Legal Studies* 18 (1989).

30. U.S. Const. Art I, § 8, cl. 8.

31. Ibid.

32. 347 U.S. 201, 219 (1954).

33. The Personal Responsibility and Work Opportunity Act, Pub. L. No. 104-193 (1996) codified as amended at 42 U.S.C.A. § 600 *et seq.* (West Supp. 2001), replaced AFDC with the Temporary Assistance for Needy Families (TANF) program.

34. With regard to copyrights, see, for example, *Sony Corp. v. Universal City Studios, Inc.*, 464 U.S. 417, 429 (1984) (claiming that Copyright Act "involves a difficult balance between the interests of authors and inventors in the control and exploitation of their writings and discoveries on the one hand, and society's competing interest in the free flow of ideas, information, and commerce on the other hand"); *American Geophysical Union v. Texaco Inc.*, 60 F.3d 913, 917 (2d Cir. 1994) (referring to "delicate balances established by the Copyright Act"); *Recording Industry Association v. Copyright Royalty Tribunal*, 662 F.2d 1, 17 (D.C. Cir. 1981) ("'delicate balance' that Congress decreed in the Copyright Act"); *Morseburg v. Baylon*, 621 F.2d 972, 977 (9th Cir. 1980) ("'careful balance struck by Congress between those matters deserving of protection and those things that should remain free'"); David Nimmer et al., "The Metamorphosis of Contract into Expand," *California Law Review* 87 (1999): 17,19 ("'delicate balance' between the rights of copyright owners and copyright users"); Dennis S. Karjala, "Federal Preemption of Shrinkwrap and On-Line Licenses," *University of Dayton Law Review* 22 (1997): 511, 518.

With regard to patents, see, for example, *Bonito Boats, Inc. v. Thunder Craft Boats, Inc.*, 489 U.S. 141, 150–51 (1989) ("The federal patent system thus embodies a carefully crafted bargain for encouraging the creation and disclosure of new, useful, and nonobvious advances in technology and design in return for the exclusive right to practice the invention for a period of years."); *Saf-Gard Products, Inc. v. Service Parts, Inc.*, 532 F.2d 1266, 1270 n. 8 (9th Cir. 1976) (describing the "delicate balance between granting exclusive rights to developers of meritorious inventions and allowing general use of designs properly within the public domain."); John M. Golden, "Biotechnology, Technology Policy, and Patentability: Natural Products and Invention in the American System," *Emory Law Journal* 50 (2001): 101, 104 (claiming that patent law aims to strike a "delicate balance between two prongs of social desire: the desire to encourage initial invention and the desire to ensure the availability of that invention both for its initially intended use and for its use as a basis for further invention.").

35. See Jessica Litman, "The Public Domain," *Emory Law Journal* 39 (1990): 965, 997–98 (characterizing as an "unruly brawl" debate among economists about copyright's effects and concluding that in general "empirical data are not only unavailable, but are also literally uncollectible."); Yen, pp. 542–43 ("[T]he empirical information necessary to calculate the effect of copyright law on the actions of authors, potential defendants, and consumers is simply unavailable, and is probably uncollectible."). See generally Hayek.

36. See Trotter Hardy, "Property (and Copyright) in Cyberspace," University of Chicago Legal Foundation 1996 (1996): 257 (arguing that in the face of rapid technological change, "the high costs of group decision making ensure that the Copyright Act will be long out of date before it can be revised appropriately").

37. See George Priest, "What Economists Can Tell Lawyers about Intellectual Property," in *Research in Law and Economics: The Economics of Patents and Copyrights* 8 (1985): 19, 21 ("[E]conomists know almost nothing about the effect on social welfare of the patent system or of other systems of intellectual property."). See also Ludwig

Von Mises, *Liberalism in the Classical Tradition*, 3rd ed. (1962, 1985), pp. 70–75 (economic calculation cannot proceed absent price signals).

38. See generally James M. Buchanan and Gordon Tullock, *The Calculus of Consent* (Ann Arbor: University of Michigan Press, 1962); Mancur Olson, Jr., *The Logic of Collective Action* (Cambridge, Mass.: Harvard University Press, 1965).

39. See Lemley, pp. 895–904 (describing in cautionary terms a trend toward "propertization" of copyright, patent, and other types of intellectual property).

40. See, for example, Steven E. Siwek, *Copyright Industries in the U.S. Economy: The 2000 Report* (Washington: International Intellectual Property Alliance, 2000) (reporting on behalf of the International Intellectual Property Association that for the ninth straight year U.S. copyright industries ranked among the fastest-growing segments of the U.S. economy), www.iipa.com/copyright_us_economy.html.

41. See Pierre Breese, "Olfactory Measurement Methods Linked to Sensory Analysis, Designation and Comparison Tools for Use by the Legal Expert," www.breese.fr/guide/htm/parfum/cannes.htm (asserting that currently there is no intellectual property protection for olfactory creations apart from trademark law) (visited Novermber 12, 2001).

42. See U.S. Copyright Office, Form Letter 122: Copyright Registration in Recipes 1 (June 1999) ("Mere listings of ingredients as in recipes, formulas, compounds or prescriptions are not subject to copyright protection."), www.loc.gov/copyright/fls/fl122.pdf (visited November 12, 2001). Interestingly, recipes apparently represent the oldest known subject matter of intellectual property protection. See Steven L. Nichols, "Comment: Hippocrates, the Patent-Holder: The Unenforceability of Medical Procedure Patents," *George Mason Law Review* 5 (1997): 233–34 (reporting that c. 500 B.C. the Greek colony of Sybarius, in Southern Italy, afforded patent-like protection to recipes).

43. See Jennifer Mencken, *A Design for the Copyright of Fashion*, *B.C. Intellectual Property and Technology* 121201, ¶¶ 3–5 (December 12, 1997), www.bc.edu/bc_org/avp/law/st_org/iptf/ articles/content/1997121201.html, visited November 12, 2001 (detailing scope and reasons for noncopyrightability of fashion designs). Incredibly, the author argues for creating copyright protection in clothes designs even though she admits, "It is clear that the lack of copyright protection in the U.S., as well as the existence of protection in Europe, has not changed the ability of designers to create new garments each season. Nor has there been any adverse effect on the power of the public to purchase garments made by quality designers at reasonable prices."

44. See Craig Joyce et al., eds., *Copyright Law*, 5th ed. (Newark, N.J., and San Francisco, Calif., 2001), p. 200 (describing furniture as "largely untouched by the scheme of the copyright law, thanks to the 'useful articles' doctrine").

45. See Michael Peters, "Note, When Patent and Trademark Law Hit the Fan: Potential Effects of *Vornado Air Circulation Systems, Inc., v. Duracraft Corp.* on Legal Protection for Industrial Design," *Environmental Law and Technology Journal* 15 (1996): 126 ("[T]he relatively low level of outright invention in a new car design generally fails to meet the rigorous 'uniqueness' requirement of the design patent. Even when a design meets the technical requirements.... The process frequently takes longer than the typical market life of most products, rendering the patent useless.").

46. U.S. copyright protection of architectural works apparently extends only to habitable structures "such as houses and office buildings. It also covers structures that are used, but not inhabited, by human beings, such as churches, pergolas, gazebos, and garden pavilions." H.R. Rep. No. 735, 101st Cong., 2d sess. 20 (1990). It apparently

does not cover structures not intended for human occupancy, such as bridges, highway cloverleafs, and dams. Although in theory such structures could win patent protection, that appears in practice to have no influence on the creativity evinced in their design.

47. Although some of the works listed here could in theory win design patent protection under U.S. law, "the patent process has proved too rigid, slow, and costly for the fast-moving, short-lived products of mass consumption, and too strict in excluding the bulk of all commercial designs on grounds of obviousness." J. H. Reichman, "Legal Hybrids between the Patent and Copyright Paradigms," *Columbia Law Review* 94 (1994): 2432, 2460.

48. See generally Richard A. Epstein, *Simple Rules for a Complex World* (Cambridge, Mass.: Harvard University Press, 1995).

49. Bell, "Escape from Copyright," pp. 804–5.

50. See, for example, Tom W. Bell, "Fair Use vs. Fared Use: The Impact of Automated Rights Management on Copyright's Fair Use Doctrine," *North Carolina Law Review* 76 (1998): 557 (describing the functional features and legal impact of automated rights management systems), www.tomwbell.com/writings.html.

51. See, for example, Tom W. Bell, "Gambling for the Good, Trading for the Future: The Legality of Markets in Science Claims," *Chapman Law Review* 5 (2002) (forthcoming) (describing the functional features and legality of such markets), www.tomwbell.com/writings.html.

52. The proposed amendment would add the following subsection to § 301 of the Act: "(g) Nothing in this title annuls or limits any person's legal or equitable right to a work under the common law of any state if that party permanently abandons with respect to that work all rights and remedies under this title." For an explanation of why that might both appeal to the copyright lobby and promote the development of extra statutory protections of expressive works, see Bell, "Escape from Copyright," pp. 793–98.

53. Ibid., p. 802.

54. Ibid., pp. 801–03.

2. Defending Intellectual Property

James V. DeLong

Food Fights

Intellectual property (IP) is a fine topic for anyone with a bent for mischief. Because the views of the libertarian-leaning community are both fractured and vehement, at any Cato or Competitive Enterprise Institute gathering one can idly ask, "So, what do you think of Napster?" and sit back to enjoy the entertainment. This is special fun at lunch meetings, as anyone with fond memories of the food fight in *Animal House* will quickly understand. If you have forgotten that scene, you can rent the movie for about $3.00, thanks to a system of protecting intellectual property that enables video rental outlets to maintain large stocks of old classics.

Despite the virtues of protecting IP, as demonstrated by such pragmatic criteria as the easy availability of old movies, not everyone likes the institution. One camp of skeptics contains libertarian-oriented critics who accept the institution of tangible property as both morally compelled and socially vital but do not believe that intellectual property is supported by the same philosophical and practical considerations. They would not allow a creator to invoke the legal power of the state to exclude others from using his creation.[1] However, they would allow self-help, ranging from encryption to contract. Their objection is not so much to the idea of intellectual property as it is to the use of state power to enforce it.

Another camp might be called the anarchists. Their view seems to be that the intellectual property should be available to all, in no way subject to the control of the creator.[2] I have yet to read of anyone propounding the proposition that a creator has an affirmative duty to create and may not withhold his effort just because he has no mechanism for obtaining recompense for the effort, but I would not be surprised to see such an argument.[3]

The number of avowed anarchists is small, but they seem to me to have many fellow travelers in the academic world, closet anarchists who claim to favor intellectual property, in the abstract, if the rights of creators and the public are properly balanced, but whose policy prescriptions would in reality destroy IP as an institution. In *Universal City v. Corley*,[4] 48 prominent law professors endorsed the theory that encryption vitiates "fair use" doctrines that permit limited copying of IP and that the Digital Millennium Copyright Act (DMCA), which outlaws some encryption-cracking devices, is therefore unconstitutional.[5] Their view seems to encompass the proposition that encryption itself should be illegal because it extends protection of IP beyond the powers granted to Congress by the copyright clause of the Constitution.

The professors reject alternative methods of recognizing the interests protected by fair use doctrine, and do not consider at all whether the doctrine should be retooled for the digital age. For example, a strong argument for treating copying for academic use as fair use has always been that obtaining permission involves high transaction costs. Because the Internet reduces these costs, it undercuts this rationale and militates in favor of shrinking rather than expanding the scope of the fair use doctrine.[6] Realistically, an inevitable consequence of eliminating encryption would be to make all digitized property indefensible, which would amount to the destruction of intellectual property rights in anything that can be digitized. Since the professors are not stupid, it is fair to assume that they are aware of this consequence of their position, and that their dedication to fair use is in fact a cloak for a desire, or at least a willingness, to bring about this destruction.

That such views are found in academia is not surprising. Anyone who deals with issues of rights in tangible property knows that academia generally is permeated by hostility to property rights, usually justified by reference to environmental protection, smart growth, historic preservation, social justice, or some other abstraction.[7] Skepticism about IP is a logical extension of this distaste for property generally.

Another camp of skeptics focuses on the problems created by collisions between intellectual property rights and other values. Some measures designed to protect rights in IP, notably the DMCA, present serious First Amendment issues involving free speech, as in *Universal City v. Corley*, in which the defendant was charged with publishing a computer program that constituted a device for cracking encryption.

Other collisions can arise out of law enforcement or self-help efforts to defend intellectual property. Suppose, for example, that authorities or private parties hack into an individual's computer hard drive to see if it contains pirated material; the effort would present problems of search and seizure under the Fourth Amendment, of invasion of privacy, and of interference with business relationships. Even a firm supporter of IP rights can believe that they should be subordinated to other values in particular contexts. On the other hand, it is also possible for those who oppose intellectual property rights to seize on the need to protect other values as yet another weapon against IP in general. The Electronic Frontier Foundation,[8] which is the laboring oar in *Universal City v. Corley*, sees no grays at all. In any collision between IP and some other value, the other value wins.

One more position is also identifiable. Numbers of people who strongly support protection of intellectual property are happy to dilute rights in tangible property, at least when the tangible takes the form of real estate and the dilution carries a tag of environmental protection. (They would probably view differently any government effort to appropriate their retirement accounts.) This stance is not the product of a consistent philosophy, but it has a solid basis in the realpolitik of the modern world. Real estate has become less important as a producer of wealth and more of a consumption good. Intellectual property is an increasingly important source of wealth. Those whose economic position depends on IP defend it, even as they are indifferent to protecting rights in other forms of property not important to their economic well-being.

I have heard representatives of Hollywood-based entertainment industries—people who endorse "protecting endangered species," "wetlands preservation," "smart growth," and similar diminutions of property rights that serve the environmentalist cause—bemoan the lack of respect for property rights exhibited by the Napster generation. At one panel session, I finally got up, pointed out the incongruity, and asked: "Is it not possible that the Napsterites are only practicing what you taught them?" The remark was not well received, or even understood.

This phenomenon of picking and choosing among property rights also operates in the software industry. Think-tank staffers who regard the government's antitrust prosecution of Microsoft as an attack on intellectual property rights note wryly that Microsoft employees are major supporters of anti-property movements in the Northwest, and rarely see the connection between the government's quick willingness to appropriate Microsoft software and their cavalier attitudes toward the rights of owners of other types of property. These observers also believe that Microsoft's competitors are foolish to support the antitrust action, because success will provide a basis for continuing government efforts to take and reallocate other intangible assets that are important to the intellectual classes, such as 401(k) plans or telecommunications capacity.[9]

Not that the government needs much encouragement; it already regards telecommunications as subject to allocation by the government through "open access" and "must carry" rules.[10] Congress also arrogates to itself the right to reallocate intellectual property rights according to political whim— for example, recent legislation extended the copyright term of property that was about to fall into the public domain.[11] Washington scuttlebutt lays responsibility on the Disney Corporation, which was petrified about the expiration of copyright on some of its cartoon characters.

The analysis in this chapter addresses all these lines of thought, but its focus is on the views of the critics who defend tangible property while rejecting intellectual property. The other criticisms are taken up in passing. Similarly, the views of those who support intellectual property while disrespecting tangible property are addressed only by implication—it is not possible to make a coherent argument to this effect because arguments for IP are built on arguments for property generally, and any devotee of IP who ignores protection of tangible property is cutting off the roots of his own position.

Back to Basics: In Defense of Property

A fundamental reason for skepticism about the legitimacy of establishing property rights in the products of the mind is that consideration of IP tends to be divorced from thought about tangible property. This is evident in the legal profession, where both academicians and practitioners regard "property," meaning real property and other tangible goods, and "intellectual property" as distinct topics, with little cross-fertilization. The divorce seems to hold in economic discussion as well, and in general public discourse.

The roots of this division go back to the different origins of the different types of property in England, where tangible property was a creature of common law and copyright largely a creature of statute. For U.S. lawyers, the dichotomy is inherent in the Constitution. It is clear that "property" in tangible form has a legitimacy that pre-dates that basic charter. In the Fifth Amendment, which says that one may not "be deprived of . . . property, without due process of law" and "nor shall private property be taken for public use without just compensation," the drafters did not define "property," nor has Congress ever done so. A court deciding a case under the Fifth Amendment looks to state law to determine whether property exists.[12] Intellectual property is different. Although patents, copyrights, trademarks, and trade secrets long antedated 1787, to U.S. lawyers, including those who sit on the Supreme Court, patents and copyrights are a product of laws enacted pursuant to Article I, Section 8 of the Constitution, which gives Congress power "To promote the progress of science and useful arts, by securing for limited times to authors and inventors the exclusive right to their respective writings and discoveries." The lawyers tend not to look to any common law gloss on intellectual property lurking in the background, because, as the Supreme Court said:[13]

> The clause is both a grant of power and a limitation. This qualified authority, unlike the power often exercised in the sixteenth and seventeenth centuries by the English Crown, is limited to the promotion of advances in the "useful arts." It was written against the backdrop of the practices—eventually curtailed by the Statute of Monopolies—of the Crown in granting monopolies to court favorites in goods or businesses which had long before been enjoyed by the public. . . . The Congress in the exercise of the patent power may not overreach the restraints imposed by the stated constitutional purpose. Nor may it enlarge the patent monopoly without regard to the innovation, advancement or social benefit gained thereby. Moreover, Congress may not authorize the issuance of patents whose effects are to remove existent knowledge from the public domain, or to restrict free access to materials already available. Innovation, advancement, and things which add to the sum of useful knowledge are inherent

> requisites in a patent system which by constitutional com-
> mand must "promote the Progress of . . . useful Arts." This
> is the standard expressed in the Constitution and it may not
> be ignored. And it is in this light that patent validity "requires
> reference to a standard written into the Constitution." [Cita-
> tion omitted]

As a result, while definitions of tangible property may have some independent basis derived from preexisting common law and per-haps even from natural law, intellectual property is primarily the toy of Congress.[14] The legal consensus is that "aside from an early and sporadic influence, the notion that authors are entitled, as a matter of natural right, to a reward for their intellectual labor, let alone to a full proprietary right in their creative product, has been rejected repeatedly and in no uncertain terms by both Congress and the courts."[15] This legal reality forces lawyers to approach intellectual property issues in utilitarian-instrumental terms, devoid of illumina-tion from the rich history of thought about property in general.

My own view of IP is shaped by the evolution of my involvement in the topic, which blurred the distinction between tangible and intellectual property. For years, I worked on the law and policy of environmental issues and Environmental Protection Agency actions. Property rights is a logical segue from this, because property issues are at the core of many environmental topics, including wetlands, endangered species, zoning, land preservation, and historic preser-vation. In each of these areas, governments take property without payment through regulation.

Eventually, I struck a deal with a publisher to write a book about property rights.[16] As a by-the-way, my editor told me to put in a chapter on intellectual property. Reacting like most lawyers, my immediate response was, "Different topic; nobody treats tangible property and IP as part of the same whole."

But the editors insisted. And they were correct, because in fact the reasons for recognizing IP are much the same as the reasons for recognizing other forms of property, even though the historic evolution of the two types of property may have been distinct and even though a couple of important differences exist and create sub-stantial analytical and practical difficulties.

The concept of property is one of humanity's great inventions. It appears to be universal in human culture; the stories of noble savages who lacked a concept of ownership have been debunked, and the general rule is that if a resource is scarce or if it takes labor to convert it to a useful state, then humans will attach property rights to it. An Indian tribe would not recognize ownership rights in a buffalo running loose, but once shot it belonged to the hunter whose arrow brought it down.[17]

Property is one of the great foundation stones of civilization. It is the basis of the market systems and wealth accumulation that create economic progress, and thus cultural and spiritual progress. Material wealth may not be the highest goal of human life, but it is a prerequisite for other things that may be regarded as more exalted. When people talk of the excessive materialism of American life, it is fair to ask just what it is they want to give up: the electronic equipment that provides access to great music and theater at the touch of a button? The automobiles that provide the mobility and fantastic freedom of our professional and personal lives? The machines that allow us to spend about 3 percent of our collective time producing food rather than the 95 + percent required a couple of centuries ago?

Starting early in the 20th century, and at an accelerated rate after the New Deal 1930s, property rights fell into disrepute in academic and intellectual circles, and for several decades their advocates adopted a hangdog air of apology. Eventually, however, reality reasserted itself, and recognition of the importance of property to a free and prosperous society has recrudesced, due in no small part to the efforts of Cato, the Competitive Enterprise Institute, and similar institutions. At least two books, in addition to my own, have recently appeared that proudly defend the institution of property rights.[18]

The high-water mark of the anti-property movement—its Gettysburg—may have been 1972, when the Supreme Court was invited to state unequivocally that "property rights" occupied a lesser status than "personal rights." Given the set of the legal current at the time, this request was not frivolous. Many objective legal scholars would have given it excellent odds. The Court declined, emphatically:[19]

> The dichotomy between personal liberties and property rights is a false one. Property does not have rights. People have rights. The right to enjoy property without unlawful deprivation, no less than the right to speak or the right to travel, is in truth a "personal" right, whether the "property" in question be a welfare check, a home, or a savings account.

> In fact, a fundamental interdependence exists between the personal right to liberty and the personal right in property. Neither could have meaning without the other. That rights in property are basic civil rights has long been recognized. J. Locke, Of Civil Government 82–85 (1924); J. Adams, A Defence of the Constitutions of Government of the United States of America, in F. Coker, Democracy, Liberty, and Property 121–32 (1942); 1 W. Blackstone, Commentaries *138–40.

Since 1972, the Supreme Court has backed and filled and dithered, but the tide has turned. Starting in the 1980s, landowners actually began to win some regulatory takings cases under the Fifth Amendment in the Court, for the first time since the 1920s, and in 1998 a takings analysis was applied to a particularly high-handed retroactive congressional cash grab.[20]

Now, while property rights remain under attack in a multitude of specific contexts, at a general level the legitimacy and importance of the institution of property are universally recognized. Indeed, conventional wisdom is coalescing around an assumption that failure to recognize this importance is a symptom of dementia in a society.

Tenacious institutions, such as property, have deep roots. Richard Pipes, the eminent Russian scholar and author of *Property and Freedom*, notes that discussions of property "from the time of Plato . . . to the present" have involved four themes: concepts of morality, economics, politics, and psychology. (Pipes also noted that *Property and Freedom* is his only book that is not directly about Russia. But in a way, he said, it is very much about Russia, because it is precisely the absence of property that determines so much about that benighted place. The former USSR now acknowledges that progress depends on the expansion of property rights.[21])

Examining these themes, and expanding them a bit, produces the following rough and often-overlapping list of justifications for the institution of property.

Morality or Lockean Justice

This involves the familiar concepts of John Locke: Each person has the right to the fruits of his industry, and ownership is achieved by mixing one's labor with natural resources.

Interpreting and commenting on Locke is itself an industry and raises endless problems and complexities. However, the core idea

24

seems indisputable. After all, if you do not own the product of your labor, then who does? Only in slave systems do people lose this basic right. On examination, the disputes over Locke always seem to come down to the extent of the ownership right, not to whether it exists at all.

Economics

Economic arguments contain several subthemes:

- Incentives—people work hardest and produce the most when they produce for themselves.
- Investment—who would forego current consumption unless he got some future benefit, and the way to ensure investment is to give the investor a property interest.
- Allocation of resources—recognizing rights in property allows resources to flow to their most valuable uses as producers bid for them. Recognizing IP is an important signal that causes resources to flow into the production of intellectual goods as opposed to physical goods.
- Efficient administration—ownership decentralizes decisions so that they can be made at the level of local knowledge. Each of these is the subject of a complex body of analysis.

Politics

The existence of property rights diffuses power. If resources are not owned, they will be allocated by the rules of politics, not by rules of morality or economics. As the USSR showed, resource allocation is a powerful method of government control. It was not necessary for the Party to put people in jail or torture them. Rather, those who obeyed got decent apartments, educational opportunities, and jobs. Those who did not, did not.[22]

Another political theme concerns the functioning of a democratic polity. We are a long way from the Jeffersonian ideal of a nation of yeoman farmers, tilling fields that we own. But it remains difficult to refute the idea that a stable political system needs people with a stake in ensuring that its politics do not run off the rails, and that one of the best safeguards is to be sure that people own property and thus have something to lose. Certainly, at the local level, widespread property ownership in the form of homes seems to provide substantial stability and involvement in government.

The themes of economics and politics can also be combined. The long-term prosperity of the nation depends heavily on a system for making economic decisions that is divorced from the government. Socialist ownership of the means of production is a discredited concept, as is its cousin, industrial policy. Anyone not persuaded by the experience of the Soviets should examine the United States' own experiment in abolishing property and relying on government allocation of economic assets: the electromagnetic spectrum. In 1927, the airwaves were depropertized and given over to the agency that eventually became the Federal Communications Commission, which is micromanaged by the U.S. Congress at its most political.[23] The result has been continuing disaster. Nonprofit stations were driven off the air. FM broadcasting was ready for deployment in 1937 and delayed by the FCC until 1960. TV channels were left dark as the FCC favored a three-national-network structure. Cable television was stalled, satellite audio blocked, and cell phone use delayed. Only recently, low-power radio has been suppressed. It is a dreary tale for the most part of regulatory capture, sloth, and venality.

Government appropriation does not always take the form of outright appropriation. Regulation can also be used because, obviously, the identity of the holder of a piece of paper that says "Title" means little. Real ownership lies in having the right to decide how to use the property, against the claims not only of other citizens but of government itself. For those who heed the lessons of the 20th century, the proper respect for property rights is an indispensable bulwark of the market economy.

Psychology or "Personality"

Professor Pipes lists as the last great theme psychology—the idea that property enhances people's sense of identity and self-esteem. Another scholar identifies a more intricate treatment of this concept in Hegelian philosophy: "At the heart of Hegels' philosophy are his difficult concepts of human will, personality, and freedom. For Hegel, the individual's will is the core of the individual's existence, constantly seeking actuality (*Wirklichkeit*) and effectiveness in the world."[24]

A prosaic version of the arguments from psychology or personality is also available, one that crosses these concepts with economic arguments to create a hybrid. Property enhances not just the sense but the reality of personal autonomy and power. To exercise these, people must be able to pursue their own visions of how to conduct their lives, which means that they must have resources to support themselves while they do so, which means they must have property.

Even the most anti-bourgeois artist in a garret, totally contemptuous of the commercial world and its values, must have the economic means to obtain paint and canvas and to support herself, which means she must have access to property. At the least, she must have property rights in her own work.

Comparing "Plain Old Property" and Intellectual Property

These themes of Lockean Justice, morality, economics, politics, and psychology can be and have been explored at length and in depth. Each presents multiple layers of complexity, and the literature is vast. Interpreting John Locke is in itself a minor industry, and commenting on property rights in the context of economics is a major one.

For purposes of immediate analysis, the salient point is simple. Speaking broadly, the rationales for recognizing property rights apply to property in its intellectual as well as its tangible form.

The qualification "speaking broadly" is necessary because the intangible nature of IP does create some real and significant differences between it and "plain old property" (POP). Intangibility also creates some apparent differences that, on further analysis, are not significant.

The most obvious distinctions go under the rubrics of "nonexclusivity" and "nonexhaustion." The first means that possession and use of intellectual property are not limited to one person at a time. Only one entity can farm a plot of land or drive a car at any point in time, and multiple ownership will result in irreconcilable conflicts. If I sing a song, on the other hand, you can be singing it somewhere else at the same time without interfering with my "use." If I build a machine based on a novel idea, your construction of a similar machine based on the same idea does not at all affect mine.

Nonexhaustion means that the resource is not depleted by use. Even land, the quintessential symbol of permanence, loses its capacity to support crops and must be replenished. Veins of minerals run out. Capital goods wear out. Overgrazed pastures become bare dirt.

This depletion does not affect intellectual property because an idea exists forever. Your singing my song does not wear out the tune. Nor does your use of the idea underlying my patented invention destroy the idea.

The intangibility of ideas also means that they are easily transferred and used, which makes difficult the defense of property rights in them. My property right in my house is protected in part by the difficulty of stealing it. Even a portable item is protected by the requirement that anyone who wants to take it must be in physical proximity, which means that I must worry about only a small percentage of the billions of people in the world. This protection does not apply to intellectual property, especially in an age of instantaneous long-distance communication. IP can be copied by anyone who hears or reads it, and even by people who only hear it described. Policing also becomes difficult. Imagine the holder of the copyright on the song "Happy Birthday," which is indeed under copyright, trying to control all infringements.

There is no question that these differences between tangible and intellectual property have an impact on the basic arguments that support property rights as an institution, especially the Lockean and economic arguments. But, in one respect, the intangible nature of IP makes the Lockean case for recognizing it stronger than the case for recognizing physical property.

Lockean philosophy has trouble with a world in which natural resources are not unlimited. Locke recognized that labor had to be mixed with the blessings of the natural world to create the basis for property. For example, a farmer claimed land because of his investment in clearing it, draining it, and rendering it fit for cultivation. So, what happens when there is no more land to clear? In Lockean thought, the moral claim is limited to the situation in which there is "enough and as good" of the natural endowment so that others can also mix their labor with it. If the natural resource has been entirely taken, Lockeans have a problem.

Obviously, this is not a problem for intellectual property. The physical resources used to create it are not limited in any meaningful sense—there is no shortage of paper and ink, and much of the raw material of intellectual property is itself intellectual property, such as alphabets and systems of musical notation. Thus the enough-and-as-good dilemma does not exist.

The enough-and-as-good dilemma is particularly acute when one considers property over time. Given resource scarcity, as generations pass, the concept that X, however indolent he may be, is wealthy because his ancestors were industrious, while Y, deeply industrious, is poor because he lacks access to natural resources loses force. Lockean theory deals poorly with situations in which indolent Xs become rack-renting landlords while industrious Ys become poor tenants.

Again, this objection is weaker for intellectual property. Because the enough-and-as-good problem is avoided, any gap between haves and have-nots is less offensive. X's property does not keep Y from creating his own. And because intellectual property can be, and in the real world always is, limited in time, the intergenerational transfer problem is also limited. After some period, the idle progeny of the industrious lose their advantage.

One can also call on Lockean principles to contend against intellectual property on the ground that recognizing your dominion over an idea can inhibit my use of my physical property. If you patent a particular kind of plow, then the prohibition on my use of it constrains my actions on my own land.

This argument seems weak. No kind of property rights exist in a total vacuum, and uses of physical property are constantly adjusted in the light of conflicting rights. Your right to be free of offensive odors inhibits my right to use my land as a stockyard, for example, without violating Lockean principle. If intellectual property is an otherwise legitimate form of property, then the fact that its recognition inhibits uses of other property may present difficult practical problems of defining rights but does not constitute a fundamental objection.

The intangible nature of IP generates another, more complex argument. Opponents of IP may say that they fully recognize your right to use the products of your labor, whether these products are physical or mental. But only for physical property does recognition that the creator has a property right require that others be excluded from using the property. Given that only one person can use physical property, the creator has the superior claim.

For intellectual property, multiple use is possible, so recognizing the right of the creator to the fruits of his labor does not require that others be excluded. The laborer, after all, still has his creation, undiminished. Granted, other users are free-riding on his labor, but so what? The creator has lost nothing, and why should we recognize a right based on the desire to deprive others of something? The most famous statement of this view is a quotation from Thomas Jefferson: "He who receives an idea from me receives instruction himself without lessening mine—as he who lights his taper at mine, receives light without darkening me."[25]

This argument that free-riding is not a problem in the context of intellectual property has force only in the limited context of a society without barter or specialization of labor. When these elements are introduced, it weakens.

To illustrate this, imagine a situation involving tangible property. Suppose X is an expert arrow maker but a terrible stalker. He spends his time fletching, trading the arrows to better hunters in exchange for a share of the kill. They get good arrows, which enables them to kill more game, the arrow maker gets fed, and all are content.

If Y steals a batch of arrows from X, he does not deprive X of arrows to shoot. After all, X is producing more arrows than he personally can use, especially since he is not a good enough stalker to get close to a deer. What has been taken is his livelihood, or his ability to barter, or his time. X's Lockean right to exclude others from using the arrows he has created unless they pay him for the privilege encompasses a right to their exchange value, not merely to their use value.

If one makes the society in the example more sophisticated, and substitutes songs or ideas or literature for arrows, then the basic Lockean argument is still valid. It is the exchange value that matters, not just the use value. In fact, the parallel is very close indeed, because in a primitive society all the hunters have access to the same stock of wood. The special skill needed to make superior arrows is an intangible, a knack—quite similar, when one thinks about it, to products of the intellect. The finished arrows incorporate the knack the same way that a finished song incorporates the creator's ability.

This analysis segues nicely into consideration of the economic issues.

As noted, one argument for property is that ownership is necessary to ensure that resources are allocated to their most productive uses and not devoted to inferior purposes. This need provides a rationale for leaving the property rights in the hands of the indolent progeny of the industrious. They may be indolent, but they are also greedy, so if the highest return to the cleared land comes from farming, they will devote it to this purpose rather than to some inferior use. Society as a whole benefits from having properties devoted to their best use; therefore, establishing ownership as a mechanism to ensure that this happens makes overall economic sense.

This need for efficient allocation does not apply to intellectual property. A piece of IP can be used for a book, a movie, a play, a musical, a TV show, and any other uses one can think of without in the least subtracting from its capacity to be put to another use. A patented idea can be used as the basis for one machine, and then a thousand more constructed without in the least detracting from the first one.

This exception is important, with some analysts leaping to the conclusion that the lack of a need for rationing and allocation obviates all need for property in intellectual creations.

However, such a leap is reductionist because it assumes a static world in which the amount of property is fixed and property rights play no role in bringing new property into existence. In reality, we live in a dynamic world in which the amount of property that can be created is virtually unlimited and depends almost completely on the incentives for individuals to create it. The importance of incentive effects provides the justification for patent law, the creation of incentives not just to invent but to disclose inventions and make them into fodder for other creators and to convert ideas into commercially usable gadgets.[26]

Even intellectual property needs to be maintained—think of software—and administered. Innovation will spread more rapidly if inventors have incentives to find new uses for their creations and to open up new markets for them. Reportedly, 19th century thinker Herbert Spencer invented "an excellent invalid chair," and in an excess of charitable zeal declined to patent it. As a result, no manufacturer was willing to risk making it. If the chair failed, the manufacturer would bear the entire loss, whereas if it succeeded others would enter the market that the pioneer had developed and he would, again, be unable to recover the costs.[27]

Commenting on the industrial revolution, Douglass North, 1993 winner of the Nobel Prize in economics, concluded:

> [T]he social rate of return from developing new techniques had probably always been high; but we would expect that

31

> until the means to raise the private rate of return on develop
> ing new techniques was devised, there would be slow prog
> ress in producing new techniques. And, in fact . . . throughout
> man's past he has continually developed new techniques,
> but the pace has been slow and intermittent. The primary
> reason has been that the incentives for developing new tech
> niques have occurred only sporadically. Typically, innova
> tions could be copied at no cost by others and without any
> reward to the inventor or innovator. The failure to develop
> systematic property rights in innovation up until fairly mod
> ern times was a major source of the slow pace of technologi
> cal change.[28]

Furthermore, knowledge and technology steadily expand society's
production possibility curve, eroding the limits imposed by scarcity
of physical resources by making them more productive and by
inventing cheap substitutes for expensive raw materials. Until
recently, telecommunications consisted of the transmission of energy
through the electrons in wire made of copper. The fiber optic revolution made communication signals into photonic energy traveling
through glass, which is manufactured from silicon, a material much
cheaper than copper. Then advances in a technology called wave
division multiplexing exponentially increased the amount of information that can be transmitted through a fiber optic cable. Incentives
for production of intellectual property are growing more important
rather than less.

The economic argument is also illustrated by the example of the
fletcher. The thief, Y, makes everyone poorer, including his fellow
hunters. If X cannot make a living by making arrows that he trades
for game, then he will be forced to give up fletching and hunt his own
food. Everyone else will also be forced to return to a nonspecialized
system in which each makes his own arrows and does his own
hunting. This decreases both the absolute amount of game killed,
because the hunters must spend time making arrows, and the value
of the game that the hunters do kill, because it no longer has an
exchange value. Nor does Y actually do the hunters a long-term
favor if, after the theft, he shouts "arrows want to be free" and
passes his loot out to them, thus destroying the system for a shortterm gain. (Anyone who wants to connect this to Napster, feel free.)

However, an important caveat remains, which is that the differences in the economics of IP and POP must be adverted to. One cannot use them as a catch-all excuse to reject IP, but neither can one reflexively apply to IP all of the doctrines that we apply to POP. University of California economist J. B. DeLong comments:

> We don't know yet how to make the intellectual property system work for the coming e-conomy. Back in the Gilded Age, intellectual property was not such a big deal. Industrial success was based on knowledge, yes. But industrial success was based on knowledge crystalized in dedicated capital. Lots of people knew organic chemistry. Few companies—those that had made massive investments—could make organic chemicals.
>
> Now intellectual property is rapidly becoming a much more important source of value. And the political system's response seems to be to tighten up on intellectual property rights. To reinforce the rights of "owners" at the expense of the freedom of "users." The underlying idea is that markets work because everything is someone's property. Property rights give producers the right incentives to make, and users the right incentives to calculate the social cost of what they use.
>
> But with information goods, the social cost of distributing information is close to zero. Hence focusing on the rights of owners rather than the opportunities of users may not generate the fastest rate of economic growth, or the greatest wealth. It is far from clear that the political system will successfully handle the task of building the right intellectual property system for tomorrow.[29]

Moving beyond the realm of economics into the political and personal, the arguments for recognizing property that takes the form of intangible creations are as strong as the arguments for recognizing tangible property. Indeed, as mental products provide a larger proportion of the value created by our society, the arguments for respecting the importance of intellectual property become even more compelling. The political and personal benefits produced by the existence of property will be ephemeral unless the major sources of wealth are included in that category and kept free of arbitrary government action.

Conclusion

The arguments for putting IP within the same general framework as POP are persuasive. The two are not totally congruent, but the differences dictate that the definition of IP be adjusted to reflect its special characteristics, not that the basic concept be rejected.

The earliest references to protecting IP go back to Sybaris, a Greek colony in Italy around 500 B.C., but the first known patent statute was enacted in Venice in 1474. It included the same basic concepts that inform current patent policy: novelty, creativity, exclusivity, reduction of the creative idea to actual use and an embodiment in physical form, limited duration, and an explicit recognition of incentive effects.[30] United States jurisprudence is built around the same factors, adding only a number of limitations on the patentability of laws of nature, mathematical formulae, natural substances, methods of operation, and similar phenomena.

Analysis of these factors is beyond the scope of this paper, but they make good intuitive sense. Those of us who went to law school have been imbued with the "bundle of sticks" view of property rights, which teaches that ownership is not a single, immutable thing but a bundle of rights that can vary somewhat with time and circumstance. It is a reasonable metaphor, and it can be applied to intellectual property as well as physical. Because of its special characteristics, our society puts somewhat different sticks into the bundle than is the case for POP, but it is still a weighty bundle indeed.

Notes

1. See Tom G. Palmer, "Intellectual Property: A Non-Posnerian Law and Economics Approach, in Adam D. Moore, ed., *Intellectual Property: Moral, Legal, and Intellectual Dilemmas* (Lanham, Md.: Rowman & Littlefield, 1997), p. 179; N. Stephan Kinsella, "Against Intellectual Property," *Journal of Libertarian Studies* 15, no. 2 (Spring 2001): 1, www.mises.org/journals/jls/15_2/15_2_1.pdf.

2. See, for example, Richard Stallman, "Why Software Should Not Have Owners" (1994, last update September 15, 2001) www.gnu.org/philosophy/why-free.html. Professor Neil Weinstock calls those who adopt this position with respect to material distributable via the Internet "minimalists." Neil Weinstock, "Copyright and a Democratic Civil Society," 106 *Yale Law Journal* 283 (1996): 336–41, 372–75, and sources cited therein.

3. An analogy can be drawn to laws mandating preservation of historic properties. Initially, these forbade owners to alter property. However, in many cases a property is not a viable economic proposition if alterations are forbidden, because neighborhoods change and costs increase, and it becomes a cash drain on the owner. Owners respond by skimping on maintenance, naturally enough. This does not cause local officials to rethink the laws. Instead, they thunder against the evil owners and their "demolition by neglect," and promote new laws to compel owners to maintain the property for the public benefit. See the District of Columbia Prevention of Demolition of Historic

Buildings by Neglect Emergency Amendment Act of 1998, Bill 12754, September 17, 1998, www.dcwatch.com/archives/council12/12-754.htm.

4. 273 F.3d 429 (2d Cir. 2001)

5. 273 F.3d 429 (2d Cir. 2001), Brief *Amicus Curiae* in Support of Defendants-Appellants (January 26, 2001), www.eff.org/IP/Video/MPAA_DVD_cases/20010126_ny_lawprofs_amicus.html. Kathleen Sullivan, Dean of Stanford Law School, made the same argument, Electronic Frontier Foundation, Appeal Brief (Part V) (January 19, 2001), www.eff.org/IP/Video/MPAA_DVD_cases/20010119_ny_eff_appeal_brief.html.

6. For an excellent discussion of the issue, see *American Geophysical Union v. Texaco*, 802 F. Supp. 1, 23–26 (S.D.N.Y. 1992), *aff'd*, 60 F.3d 913, 930–31 (2d Cir. 1994).

7. See generally James V. DeLong, *Property Matters: How Property Rights Are under Assault—and Why You Should Care* (New York: Free Press, 1997).

8. www.eff.org.

9. See James V. DeLong, *The Battle over Property Rights Hits the Corporate Boardroom* (Washington: National Legal Center for the Public Interest, 1999), www.nlcpi.org/books/pdf/Briefly_july99.pdf.

10. The FCC's "Must Carry" rules require cable and satellite providers to carry the signals of local television stations without recompense. "Open Access" requirements force cable providers that provide Internet service to provide access to independent Internet service providers as well to the cable provider's own service. See William E. Lee, "Open Access, Private Interests, and the Emerging Broadband Market," Cato Institute Policy Analysis no. 379, August 29, 2000.

11. For example, Congress recently extended copyright for works that were about to fall into the public domain. See *Eldred v. Reno*, 239 F.3d 372 (D.C. Cir. 2001), petition for cert. filed.

12. See, for example, *Philips v. Washington Legal Foundation*, 524 U.S. 156 (1998).

13. See, for example, *Graham v. John Deere*, 383 U.S. 1 (1966). However, before statutory changes enacted in 1976, common law copyright existed for unpublished works. Upon publication, the common law right ceased and only statutory rights existed.

14. Trade secrets, a very important form of IP, are defined by state law rather than federal, and do indeed contain a large common law component. They are property for purposes of the Fifth Amendment, *Ruckleshaus v. Monsanto Co.*, 467 U.S. 986 (1984), but disclosure of trade secrets is governed by the law of torts. Trademarks, the fourth branch of IP law, are also based on federal law rather than state.

15. Weinstock, p. 307, note 97.

16. James V. DeLong, *Property Matters*.

17. Terry L. Anderson, *Property Rights and Indian Economies* (Lanham, Md.: Rowman & Littlefield, 1992).

18. Tom Bethell, *The Noblest Triumph: Property and Prosperity through the Ages* (New York: St. Martin's Press, 1998); Richard Pipes, *Property and Freedom* (New York: Alfred A. Knopf, 1999).

19. *Lynch v. Household Finance Corp.*, 405 U.S. 538, 552 (1972).

20. *Eastern Enterprises v. Apfel*, 524 U.S. 498 (1998).

21. "Putin Signs Key Land Code, Permitted Limited Sales of Land in Russia," abcNews.com, October 30, 2001, www.abcnews.go.com/wire/World/ap20011026_395.html. Sharon LaFraniere, "Cleaning Up Russia's Culture of Corruption," *Washington Post*, December 29, 2001, p. 18.

22. See Martin Cruz Smith, *Gorky Park* (New York: Random House, 1981).

23. Thomas W. Hazlett, "The Wireless Craze, the Unlimited Bandwidth Myth, the Spectrum Allocation Faux Pas, and the Punchlines to Ronald Coase's 'Big Joke'" (AEI-Brookings Joint Center for Regulatory Studies, Working Paper 01-02, January 2001), www.aei.brookings.org/publications/working/working_01_02.pdf.

24. Justin Hughes, "The Philosophy of Intellectual Property," in Adam D. Moore, ed. *Intellectual Property: Moral, Legal, and Intellectual Dilemmas* (Lanham, Md.: Rowman & Littlefield, 1997), pp. 107, 142.

25. Thomas Jefferson, Letter to Isaac McPherson, August 13, 1813.

26. See, for example, Donald S. Chisum et al., *Principles of Patent Law*, 2d ed. (New York: Foundation Press, 1998, 2001), pp. 58–90.

27. Ibid., p. 74.

28. Douglass North, *Structure and Change in Economic History* (New York: W.W. Norton, 1981), p. 164.

29. J. Bradford DeLong, "What Kind of Historical Turning Point?" Notes for a talk for the Global Business Policy Council Millennium Meeting, Phoenix, Ariz., January 13–16, 2000, www.j-bradford-delong.net/OpEd/virtual/phoenix.html.

30. Chisum, pp. 10–12.

3. Intellectual Property, Information Age

John Perry Barlow

Since the Telecommunications Reform Act of 1996, we have seen an extraordinary concentration of capital and access control and ownership of what they call "content" in the hands of a very few organizations. That process is continuing at a truly stunning rate. Five large institutions now control most of the world's entertainment and much of its scientific and technical intellectual property. They control broadcast media. They control cable networks. They control book and magazine publishers. They control Internet networks, and are moving rapidly to consolidate and extend that control on a global basis.

I'm not suggesting the answer is regulation. I try to stick to my beliefs. On the other hand, what we are doing with laws like the Digital Millennium Copyright Act is to give these media megaliths even more powerful tools for consolidation. The only real comparison I know is the control of information exercised by the Soviets. You may think that's hysterical, but totalitarianism works by creating a reality distortion field, self-iterating by the people themselves. Eventually it reaches a point where the people are no longer able to think anything that is not being put through the controlled media.

We've already reached a point where most of the policy that is made—not only in Washington but in most other capitals—is based on a map of the world that is created in Atlanta, Georgia. I do some consulting for the Central Intelligence Agency, which only recently discovered the information revolution. The last time I was in the headquarters building, I was taken through what you might call the nerve center of the U.S. intelligence community. There are five large screens on the wall; four of them were showing CNN, one was showing static. I'm not kidding. I don't think it was for my benefit.

How is it that we are willing to empower organizations with such authority over the ownership of ideas? If we're going to enter into an economy where the principal article of commerce is indistinguishable from speech, efforts to control that article of commerce will inevitably control speech. It's that simple. We are giving a kind of authority to that control, both in technology and in law. This is truly unprecedented.

Merely by digitizing something, it is now possible to claim things that have been in the public domain for decades. If you buy *Alice in Wonderland* in e-book format, among the things that you click through before you can activate it is a legal enjoinder from reading it out loud—because that's a form of reproduction. Now I have never seen a book that said I couldn't read it out loud, especially one for children. I think we're going a little too far. In fact, we're going a long ways too far.

So if we're not going to regulate the media monsters, we at least need to be very thoughtful about putting additional tools in their hands. We also need to be thinking about what happens when one generation of people imposes a set of business principles and understandings of how the world works on a new generation that does not share those views.

What's going on today in terms of the ownership of ideas is based on an industrial assumption—that there is a relationship between scarcity and value, just as there would be with toasters or automobiles or anything else of a material nature. If there is a proliferation of an informational good, the assumption continues, then each individual copy will naturally become less valuable.

As a practical matter, there is plenty of reason to doubt this. Information is not like physical goods. If I have a toaster and I sell it to you, I no longer have it. You can make toast in it. I can't. But if I have an idea and I sell it to you, I still have it. And not only does it not become less valuable to me, I can argue that it becomes *more* valuable. Now in the shared space between our two minds, new ideas can form around that first one—an ecology of ideas, in other words, no different from any other ecosystem.

Let's look at some examples. The Electronic Frontier Foundation's former counsel, Mike Godwin, has pointed out that Microsoft mostly failed, despite its best efforts, to impose copy protection. But that failure turned out to be crucial to Microsoft's ultimate success. People copied their software, flagrantly. It increasingly became the standard. And sooner or later, millions of people went out and bought it, if only by getting it preloaded on a personal computer.

How many of you can honestly say you have no unauthorized software on your computer? Let me guess: not many. Well that's the same answer I get when I ask a room full of copyright lawyers. And yet, software is the fourth-largest industry in the United States, soon to be the third. Microsoft has $36 billion in the bank. They're not exactly going broke. That's because the natural economics of the consumer software business are driven by an inverse of the scarcity-value relationship. Instead—as with most information goods—the direct relationship is between familiarity and value. Fame actually is fortune.

I remember when Jack Valenti (now president and CEO of the Motion Picture Association of America) was going around Washington saying things like "Letting the videocassette recorder into the United States would be like letting the Boston Strangler into the room with a young woman." The virginal character in question was the movie industry—you've got to love it. Then came the famous Betamax case—it's hard to believe now, but this actually had to go to court—in which videocassette recorders were finally allowed into the United States. And of course not only did it not kill off the movie industry, but video sales and rentals are now Hollywood's biggest single revenue source. Three-quarters of the movie industry's income comes from videos.

Today Jack Valenti is going around town again and saying "If completely unrestricted copying of film takes place online, then nobody will ever go see a movie again." They just don't get it.

On the other hand, there is an entire generation of younger people who do—all those millions of people who were using Napster, who find nothing morally repugnant about copying software from one another, or music or films or cartoons or anything else. There is no ethical dilemma for a 21-year-old college kid who gets some piece of information or entertainment off the Internet. For their own use— "not for commercial purposes," as the license agreements say. And yet we're now criminalizing that activity, in terms that I think are an absolute violation of the intent of the framers of the Constitution. I mean 125 years is a long time for a piece of information to be held in a monopoly. That's no longer a temporary monopoly, the 9 or 14 years the Founding Fathers had in mind when they created the American patent and copyright system. It's a permanent, state-enforced monopoly, for all practical purposes.

What's being created here is a system that breeds contempt for the law, but there's a more immediate point: We need to consider the longer-range social impact of trying to impose the notions of the industrial period on the denizens of the information age. As I alluded to earlier, information and ideas are life forms, and to reach their highest value they need to be free to mix with one another, as living things do in nature. Life grows out of difference. It thrives on energy differentials. The connections can be photons, they can be calories, they can be chemical differentials—the more complex and available they are, the more connections between those carbon-based chunks of code, the healthier the system becomes. The same applies to ideas, and yet now we have five organizations that make it increasingly difficult for ideas to mix it up. This is not healthy for anyone.

I love being able to go online and get things when I want them. The other night I was trying to find a poem by Allen Ginsberg—I wanted to read it to an audience in New York. I assumed I'd find it online somewhere, but there was not a single scrap of Ginsberg's poetry to be found. His publisher had done a very thorough job of seeing that Allen Ginsberg was not available. Now, I knew Allen Ginsberg and I just can't for the life of me imagine that's what he intended when he wrote those poems.

That brings up another fallacy. There is an assumption—a natural assumption if you're in the toaster business—that the only reason that people create is for the money. I don't think that's the case. I like being paid for my work, but most of the writers in the world do not get paid sufficiently for their work—which many of them don't own anymore anyway, the publishers do—to make it a worthwhile business on its own.

Look at the recording industry, where musicians sign contracts with record companies that will strip them of all of their intellectual property permanently. Ultimately 90 percent of the people on contract with one of the major labels end up owing the company money, from their advance. Some drummers are probably stupid enough to believe there's money in it, but most musicians are smarter than that. They want to be heard. They want to be heard and they want to be heard so badly that they're willing to sell their soul to Satan himself in order to be heard. And that increasingly is the only way that they can be heard by any kind of a broad audience, because five labels control 95 percent of what you hear.

Online Royalty Transfer, the organization that was set up last year to collect royalties for songs off the Internet, is being administered by an organization tied to the major labels, the Recording Industry Association of America. So if you want to get a royalty from your work online, whether you're signed with a major or not, you have to go through the majors. What they're doing, ultimately, is destroying the opportunity of the Internet to become the most fertile ecology of mind that has ever been created.

We are on the brink of a wonderful moment in human history, when anybody anywhere can express anything they want. And that anything—based on its uniqueness, robustness, clarity, whatever—has the possibility of spreading, at light speed, over the Net, to every other interested mind on the planet. That is, unless we continue our efforts to fence everything off, as we seem determined to do.

I ask you to consider what your role is—not in business, not in policy, not in whatever you're doing with your life at the moment. Think about what your ultimate role is. I'd suggest that what you ultimately are is somebody's ancestor, even if you don't have children yourself. Your basic human responsibility is to be a good ancestor, the best you can be. And I cannot imagine you will if you are denied the potential to know and to express everything you can.

When I left the cattle business, I was 40 years old. I didn't know a ROM chip from a cow chip, but I was really interested in the Internet, probably because I'd read Teilhard de Chardin. Teilhard was a French theologian who proposed that what was being built on this planet was a collective organism of mind. Something capable of keeping God company. Not that God needs it.

It's time that we took that act of faith as a society—opening up, rather than closing down—because the alternative is increasingly horrifying. The right to know is inferred by freedom of expression. Go out and do what you have to do to defend the right to know for your descendants.

4. Are Patents and Copyrights Morally Justified? The Philosophy of Property Rights and Ideal Objects

Tom G. Palmer

Introduction

Arguments for the right of property ownership are manifold. It is quite common for a single author to invoke a wide range of these arguments to support private property rights, as in John Locke's famous chapter on property in his *Second Treatise of Government.* Indeed, the convergence of varying and noncontradicting arguments on the same conclusion tends to make us more confident of that conclusion. It serves as a kind of "fail-safe" device in intellectual discourse: If five different but all plausible arguments lead to the same conclusion, we are generally more justified in accepting that conclusion than if only one of those arguments supported it.[1]

Intellectual property, however, is a different matter. Interestingly, the various leading arguments that normally buttress each other and converge in support of private property diverge widely when applied to intellectual property. For example, a theory wherein property is viewed as the just reward for labor (a "desert theory") might very well support intellectual property rights, while at the same time a theory in which property is defined as the concretion of liberty might not.

Most of the arguments discussed in this article, both for and against intellectual property rights, emanate from staunch defenders of a private property, free market system. That is not surprising, because those who strongly favor liberty and property are apt to see the concepts as intimately connected and are thus more likely to be very concerned with the theory and application of property rights. With respect to intellectual property, however, one should not be surprised if they come to differing conclusions. That happens because liberty and property in this context may be irreconcilable;

43

copyrights and patents seem to be property, but they also seem to restrict liberty. One would be hard-pressed, for example, to find two stronger defenders of liberty and property in 19th-century America than the abolitionist Lysander Spooner, and the Jacksonian editorialist William Leggett. Yet on the subject of intellectual property rights, each came to opposite conclusions: Spooner steadfastly championed intellectual property rights while Leggett advocated with equal force the unrestricted exchange of ideas. Although they came to opposite conclusions, each argued that his beliefs were consistent with his overall stance in favor of liberty, private property, and freedom of trade.[2]

Sometimes the best developed arguments in support of intellectual property rights are advanced by relatively marginal authors, like Spooner for example. This is because the great pioneers of the philosophy of property rights wrote before property rights for authors or inventors had become a popular issue; it remained for later figures to mold the arguments for intellectual property based on the property theories that had been developed earlier by more prominent thinkers. Consequently, while Locke, Hume, Kant, Hegel, and other philosophers will figure significantly in this article, attention will also be devoted to later interpreters, who applied the ideas of those and other great philosophers in new ways.

Intellectual property rights are rights in ideal objects, which are distinguished from the material substrata in which they are instantiated.[3] Much of this article will therefore be concerned with the ontology of ideal objects. That is because the subject of intellectual property, indeed, the very idea of exercising property rights over ideas, processes, poems, and the like, leads directly to speculation about how such objects are similar to or different from other objects of property rights, such as trees, land, or water flows. One cannot address how (or whether) such things ought to be made the objects of ownership without addressing their fundamental nature. To those who criticized the notion that ideas could be made into exclusive property, the political economist Michel Chevalier properly rejoined:

> After having fired off at patents this shot, so difficult to escape, the *Exposé des motifs* concludes by saying that all this is metaphysics on which it will not enter. An unhappy way of refuting itself; it is to fly from a discussion which the reporters had opened of their own accord. Should the legislator be ashamed of metaphysics? On the contrary, he ought

to be a metaphysician, for what would laws be in the absence
of what they call metaphysics; that is to say, recourse to
first principles. If the legislator does not consent to be a
metaphysician in this sense, he is likely to do his work badly.[4]

Thus, discussions in this article about the legal foundations of intellectual property cannot proceed without our taking up the ontological foundations of intellectual property.

Many defenses of intellectual property rights are grounded in the natural law right to the fruit of one's labor.[5] Just as one has a right to the crops one plants, so one has a right to the ideas one generates and the art one produces.

Another tradition of property rights argument bases itself on the necessity of property for the development of personality. Personality develops itself in its interaction with the world; without a sphere of property over which we exercise control, for example, moral responsibility is unlikely to develop. Property rights, in this tradition, may incorporate an "economic" aspect, but this approach is fundamentally distinguished from other conceptions of property rights. Rather than looking to moral desert, or to maximization of utility, or to the omnipresence of scarcity, personality-based rights theories begin with a theory of the person. Often harkening back to Kant's discussions of the nature of authorship and publication and to Hegel's theory of cultural evolution, personality-based rights theory forms the foundation of German and French copyright law. Several personality-based arguments will be considered in this article. As we shall see, some of these approaches provide a foundation for a more expansive form of intellectual property rights than do moral desert or utilitarian theories, extending, for example, to artists' inalienable "personal rights"[6] over their products.

Utilitarian arguments of various sorts can either support or undercut claims for intellectual property rights. Contingent matters of fact form an especially important part of the utilitarian structure. As I have written elsewhere on the utilitarian arguments for and against intellectual property rights,[7] I will limit myself in this article to a few brief remarks on that subject.

Attempts have also been made to derive intellectual property rights from the retention of certain tangible property rights. Thus, ownership rights to tangible objects are constituted by a bundle of rights that may be alienated or rearranged to suit contracting parties.

45

In selling or otherwise transferring a piece of property, like a copy of a book for example, some of those rights may be reserved, such as the right to make additional copies. The owner of the material substratum in which an ideal object is instantiated may reserve the right to use the material substratum for the purpose of copying the ideal object. This argument might be labeled the "piggy back" theory: the intellectual property right obtains its moral force from its dependence on a more conventional right of property.

I will take the opportunity in this article to present as clearly and fairly as possible each of those four kinds of property arguments. In turn, I will offer criticisms of each of those arguments' internal structures and then attempt to apply them to ideal objects. I will first take up the labor theory of property then the personality theory. I will address utilitarian concerns, but, as I have stated, only briefly. Also, I will discuss the attempt to derive intellectual property rights indirectly, that is, by "piggybacking" on rights to tangible property, and then conclude by presenting my own system that does not recognize copyrights and patents.[8]

I make no claims to an exhaustive taxonomy of property rights theories. Other important theories of property and other theoretical concerns are not dealt with here, because I have chosen to concentrate on those most relevant to the problem of intellectual property. Further, I will have little to say about the actual historical genesis of intellectual property; while intellectual property originated in grants of monopoly from the state and received its legitimacy from that source, the public debate over its legitimacy shifted radically in the late 18th century. As Fritz Machlup and Edith Penrose note, "those who started using the word property in connection with inventions had a very definite purpose in mind: they wanted to substitute a word with a respectable connotation, 'property,' for a word that had an unpleasant ring, 'privilege.' "[9] Given this shift in the popular conception of patents and copyrights, I intend to question whether they are *legitimate* forms of property.

Labor and the Natural Right to Property

Lysander Spooner was surely one of the most remarkable American men of letters of the 19th century. He was a constitutional scholar, a fervent crusader for the abolition of slavery, an entrepreneur who succeeded through competition in forcing the American postal service to lower its rates, a philosopher, a writer on economic matters, and more.

Spooner begins his book, *The Law of Intellectual Property: or An Essay on the Right of Authors and Inventors to a Perpetual Property in Their Ideas,*[10] by establishing the status of immaterial objects as wealth. "Everything—whether intellectual, moral, or material, however gross, or however subtle; whether tangible or intangible, perceptible or imperceptible, by our physical organs—of which the human mind can take cognizance, and which, either as a means, occasion, or end, can either contribute to, or of itself constitute, the well-being of man, is wealth."[11] That obviously includes ideas, which are often the objects of economic transactions. Property, as Spooner defines it, is "simply wealth, that is possessed—that has an owner."[12] The right of property is the "right of dominion," the right "which one man has, as against all other men, to the exclusive control, dominion, use, and enjoyment of any particular thing."[13]

Thus, according to Spooner's definitions, the ideas we have, as well as our feelings and our emotions, are our property. "If the ideas, which a man has produced, were not rightfully his own, but belonged equally to other men, they would have the right imperatively to require him to give his ideas to them, without compensation; and it would be just and right for them to punish him as a criminal, if he refused."[14]

The foundations of property, according to Spooner, are the acts of possession and of creation. Property is necessary to secure the "natural right of each man to provide for his own subsistence; and, secondly, . . . his right to provide for his general happiness and well-being, in addition to a mere subsistence."[15] Thus, while Spooner's account of the natural right to property, and especially of intellectual property, falls among the moral-desert arguments for property, it contains a consequentialist element: property is justified because it is a necessary means to the attainment of man's natural end. Having established that ideas are wealth and that all wealth is the product of intellect,[16] Spooner argues analogically that ideas are just as much property as tangible objects. If ideas pre-exist in nature and are merely discovered (as, for example, scientific principles or naturally occurring substances),[17] then "he who does discover, or first takes possession of, an idea, thereby becomes its lawful and rightful proprietor; on the same principle that he, who first takes possession of

47

any material production of nature, thereby makes himself its rightful owner."[18] On the other hand, if ideas are not pre-existing in nature, but are the products of an active intellect, then "the right of property in them belongs to him, whose labor created them."[19]

Spooner spends the rest of the book defending his argument against objections. Against the objection that ideas are incorporeal, he argues that other incorporeal entities can also be objects of property rights, such as labor, a ride, one's reputation and credit; even the right to property is itself inalienable property. To the objection that property rights in ideas cease on publication or communication of an idea to another (*"because that other person thereby acquires as complete possession of the idea, as the original proprietor"*[20]), Spooner responds that it falsely assumes that "if a man once intrust his property in another man's keeping, he thereby loses his own right of property in it."[21] Possession is not equivalent to the right of use, for "where one man intrusts his property in another man's possession, the latter has no right whatever to use it, otherwise than as the owner consents that he may use it."[22]

Against the objection that some ideas are social in nature, Spooner argues that the role of society in the production of ideas is nil. Ideas are created by individuals, and only individuals have rights to them. As Spooner counters, "Nothing is, by its own essence and nature, more perfectly susceptible of exclusive appropriation, than a thought. It originates in the mind of a single individual. It can leave his mind only in obedience to his will. It dies with him, if he so elect."[23] Even granting the truth of the objection, he asks, do we deny private ownership of tangible objects because their creators availed themselves of pre-existing knowledge, or cooperated with others in their production?[24]

Spooner also rebuts the objection that ideas are nonrivalrous in consumption; that is, that the use by one person of an idea does not diminish anyone else's use, and that ideas are therefore unsuitable candidates for the status of property, by showing its consequences if applied to tangible property, for:

> if it be a true principle, that labor and production give no exclusive right of property, and that every commodity, by whomsoever produced, should, without the consent of the producer, be made to serve as many persons as it can, without bringing them in collision with each other, that principle as

clearly requires that a hammer should be free to different persons at different times, and that a road, or canal should be free to as many persons at once, as can use it without collision, as it does that an idea should be free to as many persons at once as choose to use it.[25]

The key to Spooner's approach is to deny those defenses of property that rest on the joint operation of scarcity, the law of the excluded middle, and the desirability of avoiding violent conflict. He writes, "The right of property, or dominion, does not depend, as the objection supposes, upon either the political or moral necessity of men's avoiding collision with each other, in the possession and use of commodities. . . ."[26] Rather, "the right of property, or dominion, depends upon the necessity and right of each man's providing for his own subsistence and happiness; and upon the consequent necessity and right of every man's exercising exclusive and absolute dominion over the fruits of his labor."[27] Similarly, the argument that the propagation of an idea is like the lighting of one candle by another, illuminating the former without darkening the latter, would "apply as well to a surplus of food, clothing, or any other commodity, as to a surplus of ideas, or—what is the same thing—to the surplus capacity of a single idea, beyond the personal use of the producer— by which I mean the capacity of a single idea to be used by other persons simultaneously with the producer, without collision with him."[28]

A similar argument, but one that stops short of property rights in perpetuity, is offered by Ayn Rand. Rand states, "patents and copyrights are the legal implementation of the base of all property rights: a man's right to the product of his mind."[29] Patents and copyrights are moral rights, and not merely legal rights: "The government does not 'grant' a patent or copyright, in the sense of a gift, privilege, or favor; the government merely secures it—*i.e.*, the government certifies the origination of an idea and protects its owner's exclusive right of use and disposal."[30] Like many other advocates of intellectual property rights, Rand sees patents as the highest form of property: "the heart and core of property rights."[31]

In stopping short of granting to scientists and mathematicians rights to the facts or theories they discover, Rand relies on the same general moral principles as Spooner in her defense of the right to intellectual property, but adds a twist. Because of her focus on the

49

role of "productive work" in human happiness, she advocates limits on the temporal duration of intellectual property:

> [I]ntellectual property cannot be consumed. If it were held in perpetuity, it would lead to the opposite of the very principle on which it is based: it would lead, not to the earned reward of achievement, but to the unearned support of parasitism. It would become a cumulative lien on the production of unborn generations, which would immediately paralyze them. . . . The inheritance of material property represents a dynamic claim on a static amount of wealth; the inheritance of intellectual property represents a static claim on a dynamic process of production.[32]

Herbert Spencer, who testified on behalf of copyright before the Royal Commission of 1878, presented an argument for patents and copyrights based on moral desert.[33] "[J]ustice under its positive aspect," he argued, "consists in the reception by each individual of the benefits and evils of his own nature and consequent conduct"; therefore, "it is manifest that if any individual by mental labor achieves some result, he ought to have whatever benefit naturally flows from this result."[34] To the objection that the use of another's idea does not take property away from the originator of the idea but only allows its use, he responded, first, that "the use by others may be the contemplated source of profit," second, that a "tacit understanding" limits the rights transferred to "the printed paper, the right of reading and of lending to read, but not the right of reproduction," and, third, that patents and copyrights are not monopolies because monopoly is the use of force to constrain others in the use of what would "in the absence of such law . . . be open to all," while inventions and the like could not be said to exist before their creation.[35]

Lord Coke had defined monopoly as "an institution, or allowance by the king by his grant, commission, or otherwise to any person or persons . . . whereby any person or persons . . . are sought to be restrained of any freedom, or liberty that they had before, or hindered in their lawful trade."[36] Thus, reasoned proponents of patents and copyrights, an exclusive right over an innovation could not be a monopoly, because prior to its invention it was not a "liberty that they had before."[37]

Another labor-based moral desert argument has been advanced by Israel Kirzner.[38] Kirzner begins with the assumption that one is entitled to "what one has produced." His primary concern is to provide a justification for entrepreneurial profits. He asks whether that entitlement derives from the contribution to the production process of factors of production or from entrepreneurial activity. Following what he calls the "finders-keepers" rule, he argues that "a producer is entitled to what he has produced not because he has contributed anything to its physical fabrication, but because he perceived and grasped the opportunity for its fabrication by utilizing the resources available in the market."[39] He contrasts "ownership-by-creation" with "ownership-by-just-acquisition-from-nature" and argues that the former better justifies entrepreneurial profit because "until a resource has been discovered, it has not, in the sense relevant to the rights of access and common use, existed at all. By this view it seems plausible to consider the discoverer of the hitherto 'nonexistent' resource as, in the relevant sense, the creator of what he has found."[40] Clearly, if one were to substitute such an "ownership by creation" theory (or "finders-keepers") for "ownership-by-just-acquisition-from-nature," then the case for intellectual property rights would become much more plausible.

All of these lines of argument strongly emphasize the *moral* desert of the creator, inventor, or author.[41] They are consistent with the argument of John Locke in his *Second Treatise* that no one, so long as there was "as good left for his Improvement," should "meddle with what was already improved by another's Labour; If he did, 'tis plain he desired the benefit of another's Pains, which he had no right to."[42] When one has improved what was before unimproved (or created what before did not exist), one is entitled to the result of one's labor. One deserves it.

Objections to Labor-Based Moral Desert Theories

Arguments such as Spooner's and Rand's encounter a fundamental problem. While they pay homage to the right of self-ownership, they restrict others' uses of their own bodies in conjunction with resources to which they have full moral and legal rights. Enforcement of a property right in a dance, for example, means that force can be used against another to stop him from taking certain steps with his body; enforcement of a property right in an invention means that force can be used against another to stop him from using his hands in certain ways. In each case, an intellectual property right is a claim of a right over how another person uses her body.

As the pro-liberty journalist William Leggett, a leader of the Jacksonian Loco-Foco party and editor of the *New York Evening Post*, wrote,

> We do not wish to deny to British authors a right; but we do desire that a legal privilege, which we contend has no foundation in natural right, and is prejudicial to "the greatest good of the greatest number," should be wholly annulled, in relation to all authors, of every name and country. Our position is, that authors have no natural right of property in their published works, and that laws to create and guard such a right are adverse to the true interests of society.[43]

Leggett opposed copyright and patent rights for two reasons: First, he argued that intellectual property rights stifled the free spread of ideas and damaged the public interest.[44] Second, he argued that such rights were in reality statutory monopolies that infringed upon the rights of others to the ownership of their own bodies:

> Our position that an author has an exclusive natural right of property in his manuscript, was meant to be understood only in the same sense that a mechanic has an exclusive natural right of property in the results of his labour. The mental process by which he contrived those results are not, and cannot properly be rendered, exclusive property; since the right of a free exercise of our thinking faculties is given by nature to all mankind, and the mere fact that a given mode of doing a thing has been thought of by one, does not prevent the same ideas presenting themselves to the mind of another and should not prevent him from a perfect liberty of acting upon them.[45]

Leggett's argument, while containing strong consequentialist elements, rests on the intimate relationship between liberty and property:

> The rights of corporeal property may be asserted, without the possibility of infringing any other individual's rights. Those of incorporeal property may obviously give rise to conflicting claims, all equally well founded. . . . If you assert an exclusive right to a particular idea, you cannot be sure

that the very same idea did not at the same moment enter some other mind.[46]

Israel Kirzner's attempt to substitute "ownership-by-creation" for "ownership-by just-acquisition-from-nature" encounters difficulty because it leaves us with a mere assumption, that "a man deserves what he has produced," as a justification for property. However, entrepreneurial profits can be justified in other ways consistent with the theory of ownership-by-just-acquisition.[47] "Profits" are justified if they arise by means of Nozickian "justice-preserving transformations."[48] A rearrangement of property titles that emerged through a series of voluntary transfers, each of which was just, and which began on a foundation of just property titles, is itself just. If in the process profits or losses are generated, then those are just as well. The Kirznerian substitute, in contrast, suffers from a lack of grounding. "Because we produced it" is an inadequate answer to the question of why we deserve what we have produced.

These authors do not effectively deal with the important problem of simultaneous invention or discovery, which is often raised as an objection to positions such as those taken by Spooner and Rand. According to Rand:

> As an objection to the patent laws, some people cite the fact that two inventors may work independently for years on the same invention, but one will beat the other to the patent office by an hour or a day and will acquire an exclusive monopoly, while the loser's work will be totally wasted. . . . Since the issue is one of commercial rights, the loser in a case of that kind has to accept the fact that in seeking to trade with others he must face the possibility of a competitor winning the race, which is true of all types of competition.[49]

That response does not comport well with her earlier claim that intellectual property rights are natural rights that are merely recognized—not granted—by government; in this case a full monopoly is awarded by government to one inventor, while another with a claim equally valid in every respect except for a 10-minute lead time at the patent office is denied any right to exploit the invention.

Spooner offers a very different response to the problem:

> [T]he fact that two men produce the same invention, is a very good reason why the invention should belong to both; but it is no reason at all why both should be deprived of it.

> If two men produce the same invention, each has an equal right to it; because each has an equal right to the fruits of his labor. Neither can deny the right of the other, without denying his own.[50]

What if, however, one of the inventors were to give this right to the rest of mankind? As Leggett argued, in the case of authorship:

> Two authors, without concert or intercommunion, may describe the same incidents, in language so nearly identical that the two books, for all purposes of sale, shall be the same. Yet one writer may make a free gift of his production to the public, may throw it open in common; and then what becomes of the other's right of property?[51]

The same argument can be extended, of course, to inventions.

Liberty and intellectual property seem to be at odds, for while property in tangible objects limits actions only with respect to particular goods, property in ideal objects restricts an entire range of actions unlimited by place or time, involving legitimately owned property (VCRs, tape recorders, typewriters, the human voice, and more) by all but those privileged to receive monopoly grants from the state. To those who might argue that any form of property limits liberty in some way, Jan Narveson responds:

> This is to talk as though the "restrictions" involved in ownership were nothing but that. But that's absurd! The essence of my having an Apple Macintosh is that I *have* one, at my disposal when and as I wish, which latter of course requires that you not be able simply to use it any time you like; it's *not that you can't have one unless I say so.*[52]

My ownership claim over my computer restricts your access to that computer, but it is not a blanket restriction on your liberty to acquire a similar computer, or an abacus, or to count on your fingers or use pencil and paper. In contrast, to claim a property right over a process is to claim a blanket right to control the actions of others. For example, if a property right to the use of the abacus were to be granted to someone, it would mean precisely that others could not make an abacus unless they had the permission of the owner of that right. It would be a restriction on the liberty of everyone who wanted to make an abacus with their own labor out of wood that they legitimately owned. That is a restriction on action qualitatively different from the restriction implied in my ownership of a particular abacus.

The previous paragraph illustrates that intellectual property rights are not equivalent to other property rights in "restricting liberty." Property rights in tangible objects do not restrict liberty at all—they simply restrain action. Intellectual property rights, on the other hand, do restrict liberty.

Arguments from self-ownership, including Spooner's (but perhaps not Rand's), hinge upon the idea of liberty. As I argued above, there is no reason that a number of different arguments might not be marshalled in favor of property. Locke's argument for labor as the foundation of property has three principal pillars: First, having established the right to property in oneself, how can we determine when something has become "so his, *i.e.*, a part of him, that another can no longer have any right to it?"[53] The annexation of labor is the relevant point at which a thing becomes owned by becoming assimilated to one's body, the violation of which constitutes an infringement of liberty. Second,

> [God] gave [the earth] to the Industrious and Rational, (and *Labour* was to be *his Title* to it;) not to the Fancy or Covetousness of the Quarrelsom and Contentious. He that had as good left for his Improvement, as was already taken up, needed not complain, ought not to meddle with what was already improved by another's Labour: If he did, 'tis plain he desired the benefit of another's Pains, which he had no right to. . . .[54]

Third, "'tis *Labour* indeed that *puts the difference of value* on every thing . . . . [T]he improvement of *labour makes* the far greater part of *the value.*" Indeed, "in most of them 99/100 are wholly to be put on the account of *labor.*"[55]

These three arguments all lend support, each in a different way, to private property rights in land—Locke's primary interest in the chapter on property. They diverge when it comes to ideal objects, however. Although the second and third arguments lend support to intellectual property rights claims, the first emphatically does not. For Locke, self-ownership serves several important functions. First, it is the foundation of liberty; indeed, it is synonymous with liberty. Second, it allows Locke to respond effectively to Filmer's criticism of the consent theories of property set forth by Hugo Grotius and Samuel Pufendorf. If appropriation of common property rests on unanimous consent, Filmer knows of at least one person who would refuse his consent, thus knocking the struts out from under the entire edifice. Locke seeks to show "how Men might come to have a *property* in several parts of that which God gave to Mankind in common, and that without any express Compact of all the Commoners,"[56] that is, in a way that will avoid Filmer's otherwise fatal objection. By beginning with one tangible thing that is so clearly one's own that no one else can claim it—one's own body—Locke shows how property rights can legitimately emerge without requiring universal consent, thus sidestepping Filmer's objection.[57]

Locke sees this right of self-ownership as necessary for liberty. He explicitly rules out "voluntary slavery" (or absolutism along Hobbesian lines) and takes care to argue that our self-ownership is inalienable.[58] Indeed, the preface of the *Two Treatises*, in which he states that he hopes that his words *"are sufficient to establish the Throne of our Great Restorer, Our present King* William; *to make good his Title, in the Consent of the People, which being the only one of all lawful Govern-ments, he has more fully and clearly than any Prince in* Christendom,"[59] indicates that the arguments are intended to overthrow Stuart despotism and usher in an era of liberty. (Remarkably, one of the principal popular complaints against the Stuarts was their patent policy.)[60]

Ownership in ourselves is the foundation for ownership of alienable objects because they become assimilated to our bodies.[61] At a highly strategic point in his argument, Locke raises the following problem:

> He that is nourished by the Acorns he pickt up under an Oak, or the Apples he gathered from the Trees in the Wood, has certainly appropriated them to himself. No Body can deny but the nourishment is his. I ask then, When did they begin to be his? When he digested? Or when he eat? Or when he boiled? Or when he brought them home? Or when he pickt them up?[62]

Clearly, to force a man to disgorge his meal after he has eaten it would be to infringe his rights to his own body. But at what point does it become so intimately related to him, "so his, *i.e.* a part of him, that another can no longer have any right to it,"[63] that to take it from him would be an injustice? Locke settles on the transformation of the object through labor as the demarcation point:

> And 'tis plain, if the first gathering made them not his, nothing else could. That *labour* put a distinction between them and common. That added something to them more than Nature, the common Mother of all, had done; and so they became his private right.[64]

If the hinge to a Lockean labor theory of property, then, is ownership in ourselves (as I believe it is), the fact that Locke's two additional supplementary arguments point toward a form of "property" that would infringe on our ownership in ourselves (as copyrights and patents do) indicates that they should be detached from the argument from self-ownership as contradictory to it, in the case of patents and copyrights, at least. If one wished to insist on the justice of intellectual property claims, ownership rights in ourselves would have to be rejected as a foundation for property and independent arguments offered for rewarding moral desert based on labor. That is a difficult task, and one that has not been adequately undertaken, for reasons that Hume, Kant, and others have pointed out: desert has no principle, that is, no readily available and intersubjectively ascertainable measure.[65] Such an inherently subjective standard provides a poor foundation for the abstract and general rules that guide conduct in a great society.[66] In a great society, not all labor is rewarded;[67] and not all of the rewards to labor are in the form of property rights.[68]

Our ownership rights in ourselves are based on our natural freedom, and are indeed synonymous with it; they cannot rest on labor-based moral desert, as we are not the products of our own labor. But that is the subject of the next section of this article.

Personality and Intellectual Property Rights

The development of personality has been linked to property rights by a number of pro-property writers, notably the German classical liberal Wilhelm von Humboldt. In his seminal work, *The Limits of State Action,* von Humboldt declared that "[t]he true end of Man . . . is the highest and most harmonious development of his powers to a complete and consistent whole."[69] Further, he wrote:

> [R]eason cannot desire for man any other condition than that in which each individual not only enjoys the most absolute

> freedom of developing himself by his own energies, in his
> perfect individuality, but in which each external nature itself
> is left unfashioned by any human agency, but only receives
> the impress given to it by each individual by himself and of
> his own free will, to the measure of his wants and instincts,
> and restricted only by the limits of his powers and his rights.[70]

"Every citizen," writes von Humboldt, "must be in a position to act without hindrance and just as he pleases, so long as he does not transgress the law. . . . If he is deprived of this liberty, then his right is violated, and the cultivation of his faculties—the development of his individuality—suffers."[71]

Respect for property is intimately related to this self-development. "[T]he idea of property grows only in company with the idea of freedom, and it is to the sense of property that we owe the most vigorous activity."[72] Provision of security from external force is the proper end of government: "I call the citizens of a State secure, when, living together in the full enjoyment of their due rights of person and property, they are out of the reach of any external disturbance from the encroachments of others."[73]

This line of argument—deriving property from the requirements of personal development—seems in some ways a restatement of Locke's basic argument,[74] but with a different twist. Rather than emphasize the satisfaction of man's material wants and, through that, fulfillment of God's injunction to man in the Garden of Eden to prosper and multiply, von Humboldt emphasizes the development of human potential.[75] The key to both the Lockean and the Humboldtean arguments is ownership in ourselves, with state power severely constrained and limited to the protection of liberty. As J. W. Burrow notes, "[Humboldt's] view of the State's functions may not differ in practice from a natural rights theory of the traditional Lockean kind."[76]

In practice, the Lockean and Humboldtean liberty-based arguments for property are fundamentally the same, although the emphasis differs. At base, each is intimately concerned with freedom. Indeed, von Humboldt's argument against the validity of testamentary dispositions that go beyond mere transference of property titles to one's heirs shows the primacy of freedom in his theory:

> [A]s long as he lives, man is free to dispose of his things
> as he pleases, to alienate them in part or altogether—their

> substance, use, or possession; . . . But he is in no way entitled
> to define, in any way binding on others, what shall be done
> with his property after his decease, or to determine how its
> future possessor is to act. . . . [This] restricts that freedom
> which is essential to human development, and so runs
> counter to every principle we have put forward.[77]

That argument from personality offers little support for patents
and copyrights, and, like other arguments from ownership rights in
ourselves, would be more likely to undercut claims for intellectual
property rights.

A superficially similar, but in reality very different, argument
based on personality is offered by Hegel in his *Philosophy of Right*.[78]
Unlike von Humboldt's appeal to the development of personality,
the Hegelian argument sees property not only as a necessary condition for this development but as the manifestation of this development itself. In the *Phenomenology of Spirit*, Hegel emphasized that it
is through work that spirit comes to know itself.[79] In the *Philosophy
of Right*, a treatise on law, property fills the role of work. Notably,
the discussion of property culminates in patents and copyrights. For
Hegel, personality forms the foundation of any system of rights:
"Personality essentially involves the capacity for rights and constitutes the concept and the basis (itself abstract) of the system of
abstract and therefore formal right. Hence the imperative of right
is: 'Be a person and respect others as persons.' "[80]

Personality must be translated from mere potentiality into actuality, or, in Hegelian terms, from Concept (*Begriff*) to Idea (*Idee*).

> A person must translate his freedom into an external sphere
> in order to exist as Idea. Personality is the first, still wholly
> abstract, determination of the absolute and infinite will, and
> therefore this sphere distinct from the person, the sphere
> capable of embodying his freedom, is likewise determined
> as what is immediately different and separable from him.[81]

Hegel specifically eschews utilitarian justifications for property,
for "[i]f emphasis is placed on my needs, then the possession of
property appears as a means to their satisfaction, but the true position is that, from the standpoint of freedom, property is the first
embodiment of freedom and so is in itself a substantive end."[82]

The metaphysical grounding of this theory of private property is
straightforward: "Since my will, as the will of a person, and so as

a single will, becomes objective to me in property, property acquires the character of private property. . . ."[83] Personality does not simply require external objects for its development. Its development *is* its objectification through externalization of its will.

Occupancy, not labor, is the act by which external things become property: "The principle that a thing belongs to the person who happens to be the first in time to take it into his possession is immediately self-explanatory and superfluous, because a second person cannot take into his possession what is already the property of another."[84] This occupancy, or taking possession, can take three forms: (1) by directly grasping it physically, (2) by forming it, and (3) by merely marking it as ours.[85] It is the second of these forms of possession that is most interesting for our purposes. As Hegel remarks, "When I impose a form on something, the thing's determinate character as mine acquires an independent externality and ceases to be restricted to my presence here and now and to the direct presence of my awareness and will."[86]

Unlike Locke, Hegel does not see man as naturally free, and therefore as having natural or pre-political ownership rights in himself. It is only through the historical process of objectification and hence self-confrontation that one comes to be free: "It is only through the development of his own body and mind, essentially through his self-consciousness's apprehension of itself as free, that he takes possession of himself and becomes his own property and no one else's."[87]

When it comes to intellectual property, Hegel does not go nearly as far as his epigoni, such as Otto Von Gierke and Josef Kohler. Like Kant, Hegel offers great protection to literary works, but very little to the plastic arts. Kant argued for the protection of literary works in his essay, "On the Injustice of the Pirating of Books."[88] A brief digression on Kant's theory of copyright is appropriate here, after which we shall return to Hegel's treatment, and to its reformulation and extraordinary extension in more recent years.

In a chapter of his *Metaphysis of Morals* titled "*What Is a Book*," Kant identified the equivocal use of the term "book" as the source of the dispute over copyrights.

> The basic cause of an appearance of legality in something that is nevertheless, at the first inspection, such an injustice—as book piracy is—lies in this: that the book is, on the one

hand, a corporeal product of art (*opus mechanicum*), which can be copied (by him, who finds himself in legal possession of an exemplar of this product)—consequently has a real right therein; on the other hand, however, a book is also merely an address of the publisher to the public, which this publisher, without having the authorization thereto of the author, may not publicly repeat (*praestatio operae*)—a personal right; and now the error consists in this, that the two are confused with each other.[89]

Thus, a "book" is both the corporeal thing I hold when I read ("my book"), and also the address by one person to another (the "author's book"). Kant argued that a book or other literary product is not simply "a kind of merchandise," but an "*exercise of his* [the author's] *powers (opera)*, which he can grant to others (*concedere*), but can never alienate."[90] A copier, or infringer, offers to the public the thoughts of another, the author. That is, he speaks in the author's name, which he can properly do only with permission. The author has given permission, however, only to his authorized publisher, who is wronged when a book edition is pirated.

The extension of such a personal right beyond a real right is shown in the case of the death of an author prior to publication of his work:

> That the publisher does not conduct his business in his own name, but in that of another, is confirmed by certain obligations which are universally acknowledged. Were the author to die after he had confided his [manuscript] to the publisher for printing and the publisher had agreed to the conditions, still the publisher is not free. In default of heirs, the public has a right to compel him to publish it, or to give over the [manuscript] to another who may offer himself as publisher. For it had been a business which the author, through him, wished to carry on with the public, and for which he offered himself as agent. [H]e [the publisher] possesses the [manuscript] only on condition that he shall use it with the public in the interest of the author. If the publisher should mutilate or falsify the work after the death of the author, or if he should fail in producing a number of copies equal to the demand, then the public would have the right to require him to enlarge the edition and to exact greater accuracy, and, if he refused to meet these demands, to go elsewhere to get them complied with.[91]

61

Importantly, Kant limits those rights against copiers or mutilators to literary products and denies them to the plastic and representational arts.[92] Kant wrote:

> Works of art, as things, can, on the contrary, from a copy of them which has been lawfully procured, be imitated, modelled, and the copies openly sold, without the consent of the creator of their original, or of those whom he has employed to carry out his ideas. A drawing which some one has designed, or through another caused to be copied in copper or stone, metal or plaster of Paris, can by those who buy the production be printed or cast, and so openly made traffic of. So with all which anyone executes with his own things and in his own name, the consent of another is not necessary. For it is a work—an *opus*, not an *opera alterius*—which each who possesses, without even knowing the name of the artist, can dispose of, consequently can imitate, and in his own name expose for sale as his own. But the writing of another is the speech of a person—*opera*—and he who publishes it can only speak to the public in the name of the author. He himself has nothing further to say than that the author, through him, makes the following speech to the public.[93]

Thus, the key to Kantian copyright is speech; when no speech is present, no copyright accrues to the creator. Accordingly, Kant claimed consistently that translations or derivative works cannot be restricted by copyright: "He [an editor] represents himself, not as that author as if he were speaking through him, but as another. Translation into another language is also not infringement, for it is not the very speech of the author although the thoughts may be the same."[94]

Like Kant, Hegel argues that artistic reproductions are "so peculiarly the property of the individual artist that a copy of a work of art is essentially a product of the copyist's own mental and technical ability," while the reproduction of literary works or of inventions "is of a mechanical kind."[95] Hegel declared further that "this power to reproduce has a special character, viz. it is that in virtue of which the thing is not merely a possession but a capital asset."[96] The right of reproduction of inventions or literary works derives from their nature as capital assets, and not mere possessions. They yield an income stream, the diminution of which substantially diminishes the value of the capital.

The theories of personal rights and of personality set forth by Kant and Hegel have been extended in the last hundred years or so to embrace a range of rights to artistic productions far wider than they envisioned. Indeed, those alleged rights are not, like Anglo-American copyrights, fully alienable, but are, as the French 1957 Law on Artistic and Literary Property[97] declares, "perpetual, inalienable, and imprescriptible."[98] Substantial efforts have been made to import that notion into American law, much of them occasioned by the introduction of the technique of "colorizing" films originally produced in black-and-white.[99]

As developed under French law, four such personal rights are retained by artists: the right of disclosure, the right of attribution, the right of integrity, and the right of retraction.[100] Rather than offering a survey of some of the more *outré* results of this law, I will present instead a brief statement of its theoretical grounding.

Such rights entered the law (in France, at least, the place where they have received the greatest legal recognition) in court decisions governing the division of artistic property. In a 1902 case before the Court of Cassation, the court had to consider whether the ex-wife of an artist had the right to share in the commercial exploits of her husband's work.[101] The court ruled that she had a right to a share of the economic proceeds, but that this decision would not "detract from the right of the author, inherent in his personality, of later modifying his creation, or even suppressing it."[102]

Josef Kohler, author of an influential treatise on law, argued: "Personality must be permitted to be active, that is to say, to bring its will to bear and reveal its significance to the world; for culture can thrive only if persons are able to express themselves, and are in a position to place all their inherent capacities at the command of their will."[103] So far, this sounds familiar. But Kohler argued further:

> [T)he writer can not only demand that no strange work be presented as his, but that his own work not be presented in a changed form. The author can make this demand even when he has given up his copyright. This demand is not so much an exercise of dominion over my own work, as it is of dominion over my being, over my personality which thus gives me the right to demand that no one shall share in my personality and have me say things which I have not said.[104]

63

Damage to a work of art, even after ownership rights to it have been transferred to another party, constitutes damage to the personality of the creator; the work of art is an extension of the personality of the creator. Thus, according to Kohler, issuing an unauthorized, or *bowdlerized,* edition of an author's work, hanging red ribbons on a sculpture, or tearing down a piece of sculpture even so offensively ugly as Richard Serra's "Tilted Arc" (as was recently done in New York) all constitute damage to the personality of the creator.

In fact, the relationship between creator and creation is so intimate that when the personality of the former changes, so too can the treatment of the latter. Under article 32 of the French 1957 law, for example: "Notwithstanding the transfer of his right of exploitation, the author, even after the publication of his work, enjoys a right of modification or withdrawal vis-a-vis his transferee."[105]

The concept of personal rights has also been extended to encompass the so-called *droit de suite,* or inalienable resale royalty rights. According to this idea, a part of French law[106] and relatively recently adopted into law by several American states, a percentage of the resale profits beyond a certain level must be given to the original creator.

Objections to Personality-Based Intellectual Property Theories

At their foundation, personality-based theories of intellectual property suffer from a confusion about the ontological status of ideal objects and their relationship to their creators. If, as Hegel insists, "[a] person must translate his freedom into an external sphere in order to exist as Idea,"[107] this does not mean that that "translation" is constitutive of the person himself, nor that the artifacts resulting from that translation become inextricably bound up with the person. This is especially obvious in the case of such artifacts as a puff of smoke, a tracing in the sand, or a knot in a piece of rope. The smoke may dissipate; the tracing may be washed away by the tide; the knot may come undone; but in none of these cases is the personality of the creator diminished. Most claims on behalf of personality-based rights are confined to "artistic" creations. Thus, Rep. Edward J. Markey (D-Mass.) argues that: "A work of art is not a utilitarian object, like a toaster; it is a creative work, like a song, a poem, or a novel. We should not pretend that all connection between the artist and the creation is severed the first time the work is sold."[108]

Representative Markey, like the philosophers who have influenced him, has misunderstood the ontology of the work of art. The connection between "the artist and the creation" is indeed severed, not the first time the work is sold, but the moment that it is finished.[109]

Referents of discourse can enjoy various kinds of dependent being. They may, for example, be dependent upon another thing, as the brightness of a surface is "dependent" on the surface, or they may be dependent in another way, as a hand is dependent for its being on the body to which it is attached, although the hand and the body may become separated, unlike the surface and the brightness.[110]

Two senses of dependence are confused by advocates of personality-based intellectual property theories: the dependence of the art work on a human agent or agents for its *creation,* and the dependence of that same work of art on a human agent or agents for its continued existence. While a work of art obviously depends on its creator(s) for its creation, and is therefore a "translation of his freedom into an external sphere," once it is created it enjoys its own objectivity. The sign that an art work exists as an objectivity is that we can always return to it and find the same work. We do not experience a different work every time we see or read Shakespeare's *Othello.*[111]

Once created, works of art are independent of their creators, as should be evident by the fact that works of art do not "die" when their creators do. While no longer dependent on their creators, they nevertheless remain dependent on some human agency for their continued existence. The agents they depend on, however, are not artists but audiences.[112]

Romantic notions of creativity, which stress subjective experience and its expression, emphasize the sublime experience of the artist. The reproduction of this experience is what constitutes the artistic attitude. The artist recreates her own experience in the audience by means of artistic works or performances. But the concrete experience of the artist cannot be identical with the concrete experience of the audience—the readers, listeners, or viewers. In opposition to the romantic notions of art taken up in personality theories of intellectual property, with their emphasis on the subjective, Roman Ingarden argues that the identification of the work of art with its creator's subjective experiences would mean that "it would be impossible either to have a direct intercourse with the work or to know it."[113]

> The reason is that everything that would be directly accessible to us—except for the perceived characters—would be

only our ideas, thoughts, or, possibly, emotional states. No one would want to identify the concrete psychic contents experienced by us during the reading with the already long-gone experiences of the author. Thus, the work is either not directly comprehensible, or else it is identical with our experiences. Whatever the case, the attempt to identify the literary work with a manifold of the author's psychic experiences is quite absurd. The author's experiences cease to exist the moment the work created by him comes into existence.[114]

In addition, as Ingarden points out, we would have to ask how we could exclude from an author's experiences "a toothache he might have had in the course of writing," while simultaneously including in his work "the desires of a character . . . which the author himself certainly did not, and could not, experience."[115]

The fact that two of us can appreciate the "same" work (say, for example, a sonata), although we each undergo different perceptual experiences (you are in the front of the hall, I am at the back, etc.), indicates that the work enjoys at least an inter-subjective availability. We do not say that we went to two different performances, nor that we heard two different sonatas, simply because our perceptions (or impressions) were not entirely the same. The objectivity of Shakespeare's *Othello* consists in precisely this: that there is one *Othello* for all of us, rather than one *Othello* for each of us, or even one for each of our separate readings or viewings of the play.[116]

Each separate performance of *Othello* is a real event and as such is governed by property rights (the rights of self-ownership of the actors, the property rights of the theater owners, etc.), while *Othello* itself is neither a real event nor a real object. While the work of art does indeed originate in a definite time, as Ingarden notes:

> not everything which originates in a definite time must therefore be something real. . . . Every real object and every real event is, above all, something which exists or takes place *hic et nunc*. But . . . the categories of *here* and *now* cannot be applied to the musical work and its content. . . . What is it supposed to mean, for example, that Beethoven's sonata, *Opus* 13, is "here"? Where is "here"?[117]

The sameness, intersubjectivity, and objectivity of the work are intimately related. Without a manifold of appearances—like presentations and interpretations—the work cannot appear to us as "the same"; without appearing to us as the same, it cannot be intersubjective; and without intersubjectivity, it cannot be objective. In the dialectic of same and other, we cannot have the former without the latter; we cannot have "same" without "other." Thus, we cannot have the sameness of a work of art without a manifold of otherness in which its sameness can appear as an immanent pole of unity.[118]

Thus, a work of art enjoys its peculiar kind of objectivity only through a multitude of presentations and interpretations that provide the manifold within which it can appear as the same, not only to one interpreter but to many.[119] The special kind of objectivity enjoyed by art is called "heteronomy" by Roman Ingarden.[120] The art work is objective but "other ruled."

This situation of being "other ruled" arises from the dependence of the art work not only on the creative activity of the artist but—even more—on the activity of its audience. In order to exist as an art work, an object must have an audience that can appreciate it, that is, an audience with the appropriate capacities.[121] An audience of the tone deaf would be incapable of appreciating certain kinds of music; a group of Kalahari bushmen would be unlikely to appreciate a play by Molière; and an audience of modern Americans would probably not grasp the subtleties of Japanese "No" theater. A special competence is presupposed on the part of an audience for a work of art to be distinguished from a mere thing or event.

Thus, if special personal rights governing works of art are to be recognized anywhere, they should be in the audience, and not in the artist, for it is on the audience that the art work depends for its continued existence and not the artist. The concept of the *droit moral* for artists is completely misguided. It reveals a faulty appreciation of the relationship between artist, art work, and audience.[122]

If rights do exist to enjoy works unaltered from their original state, they inhere, as Kant noted, not in the artist (or author) but in the audience. A publisher who passed off as Shakespeare's *Hamlet* a work that was missing the soliloquy would be defrauding the audience; he would not be doing any harm to the personality of the late Mr. Shakespeare. If, however, the work were published as "Shakespeare's Hamlet, Minus Various Indecisive Parts," then the purchasers of the work would have no grounds for legal complaint.

Personality-based intellectual property rights attaching to manufacturing processes or algorithms lack any of the special ontological claims of personal rights for artists; the scientist may realize his freedom in his discoveries, the inventor in his inventions, but the personality of neither is harmed when their results are put to new uses.[123] Those claims to property rights as necessary to the realization of freedom reduce, then, to the argument of Wilhelm von Humboldt, which, as noted above,[124] is another version of the principal argument of John Locke. And that liberty-based argument, in its primary implications, is hostile rather than friendly to intellectual property claims, for such claims represent liberty restrictions on others in ways that tangible property rights do not.

As to the *droite de suite,* or inalienable resale royalty right, the economic consequences of that notion have been explored elsewhere.[125] It should suffice to point out that this resale royalty right benefits some established artists by awarding to them unearned windfall profits, while others suffer by having their freedom to negotiate over the schedule of payments coercively abridged. The prospect of having to part with a share of the appreciation of a work is capitalized into the sale price, meaning that the money received at the point of sale by the artist will be less.[126] In addition, like inalienable personal rights over art works, such "rights" reduce the moral agency of artists by restricting their rights to make contracts with others. The terms of the contract are fixed by others, and the contracting parties are constrained from freely transferring their property by contract.

The Basic Structure of Utilitarian Arguments and Intellectual Property Rights

As noted earlier, utilitarian arguments of a certain class can cut for or against intellectual property rights claims. As dealt with in much of the economics literature, for example, the utility gains from increased incentives for innovation must be weighed against the utility losses incurred from monopolization of innovations and their diminished diffusion. Some have argued that the first part of the comparison may be either negative or positive; patents or copyrights may actually decrease innovation rather than increase it.[127]

Thus, the specific situation matters a great deal in such arguments. But that kind of utilitarian argument does not exhaust the range of possible utilitarian approaches. Here, I will simply contrast arguments of that sort, which I will call "X-maximization arguments" (with "X" standing in for utility, wealth, or some other welfare-related maximand), with another sort of broad utilitarian concern: justice-as-order.[128] The former seeks to arrange property rights in such a way that some quantity is maximized; the latter seeks to create an overarching order within which human beings can realize their various ends without suffering from uncertainty arising from scarce resources, social conflict, and violent predation.[129]

X-maximization arguments over intellectual property rights hinge on contingent matters of fact. The relevant facts may change; technology, social practices, and other factors cannot be held constant in the real world.[130] Scarcity plays a vital role within such approaches. Innovations and research are scarce in the sense that they "use up" resources, and the allocation of those resources involves opportunity costs, that is, alternative uses of the resources that are foregone. The problem, then, is to allocate property rights—including intellectual property rights—in such a way that the greatest net "X" (utility, wealth, and so on) is produced.

The role of scarcity within the justice-as-order approach is equally important, but leads us in an entirely different direction. Rights to property are allocated precisely because the scarcity of resources means that, without legal demarcation and protection of rights, human beings would come into violent conflict over these resources.

That relationship between justice-as-order and property rights is what Hume is getting at when he argues that without property there is no justice:

> [T]ho' I assert, that in the *state of nature*, or that imaginary state, which preceded society, there be neither justice nor injustice, yet I assert not, that it was allowable, in such a state, to violate the property of others. I only maintain, that there was no such thing as property; and consequently cou'd be no such thing as justice or injustice.[131]

Scarcity in X-maximization arguments is the relevant factor in deciding whether intellectual property rights should be recognized, and if so, what form they should take. Scarcity in justice-as-order arguments is the relevant factor in determining when rights can or should be granted to resources over which humans may come into violent conflict. Intellectual property, however, does not have the "static" scarcity that tangible property has, and therefore does not qualify as a *locus* of property rights within justice-as-order arguments.[132] Two of us can think the same thought, sing the same song, or use the same method of making fishhooks without coming into violent conflict over the thought, song, or method. Justice-as-order is incompatible with intellectual property rights.[133]

Piggybacking on the Rights to Tangible Property

One final argument for intellectual property rights, or at least for copyright, deserves consideration before turning to the foundation of a property-rights system consistent with liberty. That is the argument that intellectual property rights can be justified as "piggy-back" rights, logical extensions of the right to own and control tangible objects. Thus, Murray Rothbard justifies what he incorrectly[134] calls "common-law copyright" as amounting to "the author or publisher selling all rights to his property *except* the right to resell it."[135]

Rothbard's argument implicitly rests on the distinction drawn by Kant between a "book" (or other object) as a material thing, and a "book" as the work that is instantiated in a material object but is capable of being instantiated in other such substrata ad infinitum.[136] He extends his argument beyond the realm of literature to include any artifact that incorporates or instantiates an ideal object, whether a mousetrap (its design or the process by which it was made), a map, or a dance step—which is always materially instantiated in some way, whether in a performance on some piece of property, or through a description in a book, film, or other device.

That would extend a copyright-type of protection to the subject matter of patents as well. Thus, argues Rothbard,

> Suppose that Brown builds a better mousetrap and sells it widely, but stamps each mousetrap 'copyright Mr. Brown.' What he is then doing is selling not the entire property right in each mousetrap, but the right to do anything with the mousetrap except to sell it or an identical copy to someone else. The right to sell the Brown mousetrap is retained in perpetuity by Brown.[137]

The fact that a property right can be conceived as a bundle of rights to a thing indicates that one right among the many may be retained by the original producer, in this case, the right to reproduce the item. Just as a piece of land may be sold, and certain rights retained (easements, building restrictions, etc.), so all the rights to a mousetrap could be sold except one, the right to copy it. That argument is not novel, and was in fact criticized by Kant and Hegel.[138] The separation and retention of the right to copy from the bundle of rights that we call property is problematic. Could one reserve the right, for example, to remember something? Suppose that I wrote a book and offered it to you to read but I had retained one right: the right to remember it. Would I be justified in taking you to court if I could prove that you had remembered the name of the lead character in the novel? Could the retention of the right to copy include the right to remember?

Suppose that I had memorized the book and then spoke the words aloud to another. Would I be violating a retained right to the tangible object?[139] What if I had heard another person recite the work and then wrote it down and published it? Would I be guilty of a violation of the creator's property rights by publishing a work that I had heard another recite? What if I recorded a broadcast on my VCR? Does the broadcaster own my television set and reserve the right to determine its use in recording signals that come over the airwaves?[140] If the answer is yes, then advocates of a "piggyback" copyright cannot base their argument simply on a retained right to tangible property, for this amounts to asserting a direct claim to the ideal object itself.[141]

Rothbard would have been far better off looking to the law of trade secrets rather than to the law of copyright as a foundation for a retained right, or for quasi-contractual legal exclusivity in the results of the creator's efforts. Under the law of trade secrecy, "trade secrets are not given protection against all the world, but only against one who has learned the secret by improper means or by virtue of a confidential relation."[142] Thus, if a secret, such as a manufacturing process, a design, or the internal operation of a device, is revealed to others who are not bound by contract or by a fiduciary relationship to keep the secret confidential, then the original proprietor of the secret has no grounds for legal action against others who would duplicate his product or otherwise use what was previously secret. If a chemist for the Coca-Cola Company were to reproduce the formula for Coca-Cola (a trade secret, unprotected by patent) on leaflets and drop them over New York City, the Coca-Cola Company would have uncontestable grounds for (drastic) legal action against the violator of their secret and any of his conspirators, but not against all those on whom the leaflets fell who proceeded to duplicate the firm's production efforts. Similarly, independent inventors would be immune from legal action. If the proprietor of the trade secret were unable to show that another user had improper access to his product, his production process, or some other relevant aspect of his business, then he has no legal claim against the independent inventor. Thus, an ideal object can be constrained within a contractual nexus by property rights, but once that ideal object has somehow escaped the nexus, it can no longer be restrained by force of law. Such an approach is fully consistent with the property rights regime set forth in the remainder of this article.

Justice and the Right to Property

Having offered criticisms of various property rights claims, it is incumbent upon me to offer an alternative argument that will establish property rights in tangible objects while denying them in ideal objects.

As noted above, liberty-based arguments for property rights are fundamentally hostile to intellectual property claims, for patent and copyright monopolies interfere with the freedom of others to use their own bodies or their own justly acquired property in certain ways. Establishing a liberty-based right to self-ownership would create the foundation for property in tangible objects while excluding property in ideal objects, for the latter amounts simply to controls placed on the use of our own bodies and on the use of our legitimately acquired property.[143]

The arguments of Locke and von Humboldt on the importance of ownership rights in ourselves and in tangible objects have already been discussed, so there is no need to review them further. What I do propose, however, is 1) that such rights have their foundation in nature and can without confusion be called natural rights, even though they emerge through a historical process and necessarily contain an element of the conventional and contingent (nature revealing itself through history); and 2) that self-ownership rights are consistent with justice-as-order (as discussed in the section on the structure of utilitarian arguments above).

The role played by scarcity in self-ownership theories is central, for the most obviously scarce of all physical resources is one's own

body. If justice has any meaning at all, it refers at least to the allocation of various rights to control physical resources. Such a system
of justice can emerge from a flow of historical events by an "invisible
hand" process, without diminishing its "naturalness." As Hume
remarks, "Tho' the rules of justice be artificial, they are not arbitrary.
Nor is the expression improper to call them Laws of Nature; if by
natural we understand what is common to any species, or even if
we confine it to mean what is inseparable from the species."[144] To
say that a law is natural is not, however, to affirm that it is self-
evident, or even that a sufficiently powerful deductive mind could
arrive at it. As Hume remarks, "Nor is the rule concerning the
stability of possessions the less deriv'd from human conventions,
that it arises gradually, and acquires force by a slow progression,
and by our repeated experience of the inconveniences of transgress-
ing it."[145] Practice, in social experience as well as personal, plays a
significant factor in the formation of ethics. ("Ethics" is, after all,
but a transliteration of the Greek word perhaps best translated as
"habit," that is, what is formed through practice.)

The fundamental question of who should have the right to control
one's body and, by implication, the products of one's labor, is, in
many respects, a problem of coordination. It is a problem of arriving
at a stable equilibrium solution in a "game" that has no *unique* stable
solution. Our bodies could be considered the property of the king;
some class of people could be owned by another; each of us could
be common property, in the sense that a social decision would be
made to determine every use of our bodies (participatory collectiv-
ism); or we could each be the owners of ourselves. Each of those
possible solutions has been tried at one time or another. Modern
society has tended to converge on the last, on self-ownership.[146]

What is it that might lead "players" in coordination "games" to
converge on self-ownership? In coordination problems there is a
natural tendency for players to converge on "obvious" solutions.
The pioneering work of Thomas Schelling has shown that players
in games with monetary payoffs for successful coordination tend to
converge on certain solutions.[147] As Schelling remarks, "A prime
characteristic of these 'solutions' to the problems, that is, of the
clues or coordinators or focal points, is some kind of prominence
or conspicuousness."[148] These conspicuous "clues" have come to be
known as "Schelling points."

We can find Schelling points in "property games" as well. In the case of ownership of our bodies, what can be more natural—more prominent—than the allocation of personal ownership rights to each person?[149] As Dectutt de Tracy affirms,

> [I]f it be certain that the idea of property can arise only in a being endowed with will, it is equally certain that in such a being it arises necessarily and inevitably in all its plenitude; for, as soon as this individual knows accurately itself, or its moral person, and its capacity to enjoy and to suffer, and to act necessarily, it sees clearly also that this self is the exclusive proprietor of the body which it animates, of the organs which it moves, of all their passions and their actions; for all this finishes and commences with this self, exists but by it, is not moved but by its acts, and no other moral person can employ the same instruments nor be affected in the same manner by their effects.[150]

Such an allocation may not make the best sense from a "social" perspective, that is, in terms of increasing the total utility of a group. But human beings typically are unable to make (and do not have to make) such God-like choices; our real choices are inevitably constrained by our own horizons. "Society" is not a single choosing entity, nor can it be considered as such.[151] The prominence of individuality and of our control of our own bodies naturally lends itself to a process whereby agreement is secured (it need not be explicit agreement) to respect rights to self-ownership and to the products of our labor. As Hume notes, "it must immediately occur, as the most natural expedient, that every one continue to enjoy what he is at present master of, and that property or constant possession be conjoin'd to the immediate possession."[152]

Let us make a distinction between goods that are simply given (if there are such goods) and goods that must be produced; one rule for allocating goods (such as equal division) might have a greater degree of "obviousness" when the goods are simply given than when they are produced; in the latter case the association of self to labor to product is more prominent.

Hume proposes a thought experiment: "Suppose a German, a Frenchman, and a Spaniard to come into a room, where there are plac'd upon the table three bottles of wine, Rhenish, Burgundy and Port; and suppose they shou'd fall a quarrelling about the division of them; a person, who was chosen for umpire, wou'd naturally, to shew his impartiality, give every one the product of his own country. . . . [T]here is first a natural union betwixt the idea of the person and that of the object, and afterwards a new and moral union produc'd by that right or property, which we ascribe to the person."[153] That seems to be a sensible solution that the three drinkers might also arrive at themselves.

Now suppose that the things to be divided must be produced by the three persons and are not merely found at hand. Is it not more reasonable to suppose that they will insist on a division of the product that recognizes the separate contributions of each, rather than, say, equal division or, as in the case of the wine, division by national origin? Further, let us suppose that the problem is faced, not by three laborers who know each other immediately and are engaged in a joint enterprise, but by members of an extended order who, while necessarily dependent upon each other for sustenance, have no knowledge whatsoever of each other.[154] Is it not even more reasonable to suppose that they will converge, not on some principle of even distribution, or of distribution to the most deserving (desert having, as noted earlier, no principle), but that each be awarded his "own" product, that is, what he produces? (In a market system, this need not bear any close relationship to the "amount of labor" that might have been expended, but to what can be claimed on the basis of self-ownership rights and mutually satisfactory agreements among contracting parties.)

Such a system of self-ownership and derived ownership of tangible objects provides the foundation for a society and economy based on contract,[155] as well as for justice-as-order. Property rights in ourselves and in alienable, material objects allow us to cooperate peacefully. They create an order within which people can pursue their separate or common ends.

By allocating resources through a property system we allow agents to negotiate (for example, through the price system) without resort to force in order to decide among potentially conflicting resources.[156] If a river can be used for boating, fishing, or swimming, but not for any combination of these three, then property rights and the market system that emerges from such rights allow parties that are potentially in conflict to use reason, rather than brute force, to decide how the river will be used.[157] As Adam Smith noted of the market exchange system,

> If we should enquire into the principle in the human mind on which this disposition of trucking [exchange] is founded, it is clearly the natural inclination every one has to persuade. The offering of a shilling, which to us appears to have so plain and simple a meaning, is in reality offering an argument to persuade one to do so and so as it is for his interest. Men always endeavour to persuade others to be of their opinion even when the matter is of no consequence to them.[158]

The function of property rights in such a liberal order, then, is not to maximize some maximand, but to allow human beings to cooperate in the allocation of scarce resources. Intellectual property rights, on the other hand, do not arise from scarcity but are its cause. As Arnold Plant observes,

> It is a peculiarity of property rights in patents (and copy-rights) that they do not arise out of the scarcity of the objects which become appropriated. They are not a consequence of scarcity. They are the deliberate creation of statute law; and, whereas in general the institution of private property makes for the preservation of scarce goods, tending (as we might somewhat loosely say) to lead us "to make the most of them," property rights in patents and copyright make possible the creation of a scarcity of the products appropriated which could not otherwise be maintained.[159]

Scarcity of that sort being central to the legitimation of property rights, intellectual property rights have no legitimate moral grounding.

Conclusion

Four possible theories of intellectual property rights have been examined: labor-desert, personality, utility, and "piggybacking" on rights to tangible property. In each case I have argued either that the particular arguments cannot be applied to ideal objects or that the arguments themselves are weak. That is not to deny that each contains some grain of truth, nor does that mean that they contribute nothing to our understanding of the moral foundations of property.

The idea of desert has an important place among our moral intuitions, although such moral intuitions may have their proper role in the moral order of the small group such as the family, and not in the extended order, where abstract rules prevail.[160]

If the foundation of the natural right to ownership is ownership in one's self, however, then claims to own ideas or other ideal objects conflict with this right to self-ownership, for such a claim is no less than a claim to the right to control how another uses his or her body. When one claims to own a dance step, for example, one claims that no one else can so move his or her body so as to perform this dance, and therefore that one has a right of dominion over the bodies of everyone else. Similarly, a copyright over a musical composition means that others cannot use their mouths to blow air in certain sequences and in certain ways into musical instruments they own without obtaining the permission of the copyright holder. Thus the real objects the copyright holder controls are the bodies and instruments of the other musicians. The same holds true of a patent governing the combination of a group of chemicals or the arrangement of the parts of a fishhook.

The theory of property that emphasizes personality also has something to add to our understanding of property. The development of personality and moral agency is certainly a good thing, and for full development it requires at least a minimal sphere of property. Aristotle recognized, for example, that liberality is impossible without property and liberty, the necessary conditions for the expression of that virtue.[161] But the more elaborate attempts to use this as a foundation for property, such as those of Hegel and his epigoni, suffer from serious philosophical difficulties. That is most notable when a theory of an inalienable *droit moral* for artists is built upon it. The relationship between artist, art work, and audience is a complex one, but it does not lend support to the idea that the work of the artist is an extension of the artist's personality, capable of being damaged in a way analogous to the bodily damage that could be inflicted on the artist. Personality and property are indeed related, as expressed by Richard Overton's statement: "To every individual in nature, is given an individual property by nature, not to be invaded or usurped by any: for every one as he is himself, so he hath a self propriety, else could he not be himself."[162] But such necessity of property for one to "be oneself" means preeminently self-ownership, which is a principle in conflict with intellectual property rights.

Utilitarian arguments also have a role to play in understanding the moral grounds of property rights. That people will be more productive and will generate wealth that can be enjoyed by all only when they can reap the rewards of their efforts is certainly true and has been recognized at least from the time of Aristotle's criticism of communism.[163] That is certainly an important consideration in judging whether private property is superior or inferior to state ownership. But to tailor legislatively the abstract rules of the extended order in an effort to reach predetermined results reveals a serious misunderstanding of the rule of (abstract) law, which aims at no definite result but which provides the framework within which just results can emerge. In contrast, the kind of utilitarian[164] account of law that has been characterized as "justice-as-order" does not seek to maximize some particular maximand, but to create an overarching order within which human beings can realize their various ends without coming into violent conflict over resources. As an empirical matter, we have good reason to believe that when individuals know what their property rights are, they will be more productive and prosperous than if such rights are uncertain. The key, therefore, in such a legal system is to avoid conflicts between rights.[165] Intellectual property rights, however, do create conflicts between rights to self and to tangible goods. Moreover, it is far from clear that intellectual property rights increase incentives for innovation rather than hamper them. (That last consideration is a matter for empirical investigation and cannot be decided on a priori grounds.)

The case for "piggyback" rights is also built around a hard kernel of truth. Various rights that resemble in some respects intellectual property rights, such as trade secrets, can indeed be built on the foundation of rights to tangible objects. But a trade secret is not a right against the whole world, as a patent is, but a right against those who interfere with rights to tangible goods or who violate legally binding contracts. A monopoly right restricting others, for example, from independently inventing and building a new contraption cannot rest on a foundation of contract, for contract presupposes consent and the point of intellectual property rights is that they bind non-consenting parties.

Finally, property has been examined as a means of realizing freedom and achieving social coordination, "justice-as-order." The foundation of such a system of social coordination is self-ownership, the "node" around which the conventions of property are constructed. Self-ownership is an "obvious" solution to coordination games and plays an important role in the historical development of natural law. Such "games" in real life are played because of the scarcity of resources. If goods were truly superabundant, there would be no need for property, for conflicts could not arise. The very nature of an economic good involves choice, however, and choice implies scarcity. That is most obviously true of our own bodies, which can be used as food for others, as objects to gratify the sexual lusts of others, or in any number of other ways. The problem for which self-ownership provides the answer is how to allocate rights over the most scarce of scarce resources, one's own body. The principle of self-ownership then, by analogy, provides the basis for ownership of objects that are not parts of our body.[166]

The key to all of this is scarcity. Without scarcity, an argument based either on the realization of freedom or on finding a solution to coordination games cannot generate a property right. Tangible goods are clearly scarce in that there are conflicting uses. It is that scarcity that gives rise to property rights. Intellectual property rights, however, do not rest on a natural scarcity of goods, but on an "artificial, self created scarcity." That is to say, legislation or legal fiat limits the use of ideal objects in such a way as to create an artificial scarcity that, it is hoped, will generate greater revenues for innovators. Property rights in tangible goods channel them into their most highly valued uses. The possibility for exchanging transferable property titles means that holders of property will constantly rearrange the titles in search of profit. Without scarcity this process would be unnecessary. But the attempt to generate profit opportunities by legislatively limiting access to certain ideal goods, and therefore to mimic the market processes governing the allocation of tangible goods, contains a fatal contradiction: It violates the rights to tangible goods, the very rights that provide the legal foundations with which markets begin.

Notes

This essay was written in the late 1980s and appeared in the *Harvard Journal of Law and Public Policy* 13, no. 3 (Summer 1990). Although in the intervening years I've improved my writing and my views on some important matters have evolved, I've made only a few cosmetic changes for this book. I've corrected some typographical errors in the original edition, modified for style a few exceptionally ugly sentences, and changed a few citations to direct readers to newer and more readily accessible editions of books. Other than those small changes, the essay is unchanged.

1. Randy Barnett, "Foreword: Of Chickens and Eggs—The Compatibility of Moral Rights and Consequentialist Analyses," *Harvard Journal of Law and Public Policy* 12 (1989).

2. See, for example, Lysander Spooner, "A Letter to Scientists and Inventors, on the Science of Justice, and Their Right of Perpetual Property in Their Discoveries and Inventions," in *The Collected Works of Lysander Spooner*, ed. Charles Shively (Weston, Mass.: M&S Press, 1971), and William Leggett, *Democratick Editorials: Essays in Jacksonian Political Economy*, ed. Lawrence H. White (Indianapolis: Liberty Press, 1984).

3. This catch-all category covers the subject matter of patents and copyrights, including those for algorithms, computer programs, manufacturing processes, inventions, musical or literary works, pictorial or other kinds of representations, sculptures, designs, and more. The relevant difference between such goods and tangible goods is that the former can be instantiated an indefinite number of times, that is, they are not scarce in a static sense, while tangible goods are spatially circumscribed and are scarce in both the static and dynamic senses of the term.

4. Michel Chevalier, "Patents for Inventions Examined in Their Relations to the Principle of Freedom of Industry, and That of Equality among Citizens," in *Copyright and Patents for Inventions*, ed. R.A. Macfie (New York: Scribner and Welford, 1883).

5. Natural rights arguments and utilitarian arguments (very broadly conceived) are close cousins. Utilitarian theories are explicitly consequentialist (and welfarist), while natural rights theories usually contain what Alan Ryan calls "a buried utilitarian assumption." (Alan Ryan, *Property* [University of Minnesota Press, 1987], p. 63). Such "buried assumptions" concern human flourishing or the attainment of a man's natural end. Those consequences are usually attained indirectly, through respect for general rights, or rules of conduct, rather than directly, as in most utilitarian theories. The sharp separation between natural rights and utility, or the common good, is, however, an artificial one and would certainly be foreign to any of the great natural law theorists.

6. Or *droit moral*, sometimes confusingly translated simply as "moral rights."

7. See Tom G. Palmer, "Intellectual Property Rights: A Non-Posnerian Law and Economics Approach," *Hamline Law Review* 12 (1989): reprinted in Adam D. Moore, ed., *Intellectual Property: Moral, Legal, and International Dilemmas* (New York: Rowman & Littlefield, 1997), pp. 179–224. That essay also reviews the history of intellectual property, considers the problem of whether common-law copyright extends after the act of publication, reevaluates the economics of public goods and property rights, and examines how markets for ideal objects without intellectual property rights function. For criticisms of my position, see Wendy Gordon, "An Inquiry into the Merits of Copyright: The Challenges of Consistency, Consent, and Encouragement," *Stanford Law Review* 41 (1989).

8. As will be shown, however, the approach I set forth would include trademarks and trade secrets as legitimate. Trademarks and trade secrets have roots in the common law and enjoy a contractual or quasi-contractual moral grounding.

9. Fritz Machlup and Edith Penrose, "The Patent Controversy in the Nineteenth Century," *The Journal of Economic History* 10, no. 1 (May 1950): 16.

10. Lysander Spooner, "The Law of Intellectual Property: or an Essay on the Right of Authors and Inventors to a Perpetual Property in Their Ideas," in *The Collected Works of Lysander Spooner,* Vol. III, ed. Charles Shively (Weston, Mass.: M&S Press, 1971).

11. Ibid., p. 13.

12. Ibid., p. 15.

13. Ibid., p. 15.

14. Ibid., p. 19. That assumes that a common right would necessarily entail a common right to access.

15. Ibid., p. 28.

16. See ibid., p. 27: "All that labor, which we are in the habit of calling physical labor, is in reality performed wholly by the mind, will, or spirit, which uses the bones and muscles merely as tools ... There is, therefore, no such thing as the physical labor of men, independently of their intellectual labor."

17. See Spooner, "A Letter to Scientists and Inventors," p. 10.

18. Ibid, p. 26. Note that this would go far beyond the traditional scope of the patent laws of the United States, which explicitly exclude discoveries of scientific or mathematical laws or of naturally occurring substances from patent protection. Recently, however, the U.S. Patent Office has been awarding patents to discoverers of useful mathematical algorithms, a trend that would surely have pleased Spooner.

19. Ibid., p. 27.

20. Ibid., p. 42 (emphasis in original).

21. Ibid., p. 42.

22. Ibid., p. 52.

23. Ibid., p. 58.

24. Ibid., pp. 61–64.

25. Ibid., p. 79.

26. Ibid., p. 81.

27. Ibid., pp. 81–82.

28. Ibid., p. 94.

29. Ayn Rand, "Patents and Copyrights," in *Capitalism: The Unknown Ideal* (New York: New American Library, 1966), p. 125.

30. Ibid., p. 126.

31. Ibid., p. 128.

32. Ibid., p. 127.

33. See Herbert Spencer, *The Principles of Ethics* (1893; Indianapolis: Liberty Classics, 1978), Vol. II, p. 121.

34. Ibid., p.121. Spencer specifically disavows reliance on utilitarian concerns. "Even were an invention of no benefit to society unless thrown open to unbought use, there would still be no just ground for disregarding the inventor's claim; any more than for disregarding the claim of one who labors on his farm for his own benefit and not for public benefit." Ibid., pp. 127–28.

35. Ibid., pp. 122–24.

36. Edward Coke, *The Third Part of the Institutes of the Laws of England: Concerning High Treason, and Other Pleas of Common, and Criminal Causes*, quoted in Stephen D. White, *Sir Edward Coke and "The Grievances of the Commonwealth," 1612–1628* (Chapel Hill: University of North Carolina Press, 1979), p. 119.

37. Robert Nozick argues on this basis that patents and copyrights do not run afoul of the "Lockean Proviso": "An inventor's patent does not deprive others of an object which would not exist if not for the inventor." Robert Nozick, *Anarchy, State, and Utopia* (New York: Basic Books, 1974), p. 182.

38. See Israel Kirzner, "Producer, Entrepreneur, and the Right to Property," in *Perception, Opportunity, and Profit* (Chicago: University of Chicago Press, 1979), pp. 185–99, and Israel Kirzner, "Entrepreneurship, Entitlement, and Economic Justice," in ibid., pp. 200–24. Kirzner does not apply the theory he advances directly to

intellectual property, but the implication of his argument would plausibly lead one to support patents and copyrights.

39. Ibid., p. 196.

40. Ibid., pp. 212–13.

41. Moral desert plays a powerful role in many theories of property. According to Lawrence C. Becker, "the concept of desert is constitutive of the concept of morality per se." Lawrence C. Becker, *Property Rights: Philosophic Foundations* (London: Routledge and Kegan Paul, 1977), p. 51.

42. John Locke, *Two Treatises of Government*, ed. Peter Laslett (Cambridge: Cambridge University Press, 1988), 2nd Treatise, Chapter V, §34, p. 291.

43. William Leggett, *Democratick Editorials: Essays in Jacksonian Political Economy*, ed. Laurence H. White, pp. 397–98. Interestingly, Leggett and Spooner not only agreed on the abolition of slavery, but also agreed that, if intellectual property rights are indeed natural rights, then they should be limited in duration. According to Leggett, "An author either has a natural and just right of property in his production, or he has not. If he has, it is one not to be bounded by space, or limited in duration, but, like that of the Indian to the bow and arrow he has shaped from the sapling and reeds of the unappropriated wilderness, his own exclusively and forever" (p. 398).

44. Ibid., p. 394: "If the principle of copyright were wholly done away, the business of authorship, we are inclined to think, would readily accommodate itself to the change of circumstances, and would be more extensively pursued, and with more advantage to all concerned than is the case at present."

45. Ibid., p. 399.

46. Ibid., pp. 399–400.

47. See Randy Barnett, "A Consent Theory of Contract," *Columbia Law Review* 86 (1986). The arrangements of property that result from transference of justly acquired property titles are themselves just, and if some arrangements mean profits for some and losses for others, the justice of the profits or losses is ancillary to the justice of the resulting arrangements of property titles.

48. Nozick, *Anarchy, State, and Utopia*, p. 151.

49. Rand, "Patents and Copyrights," p. 133.

50. Spooner, "A Letter to Scientists and Inventors," p. 68; see also Nozick, *Anarchy, State, and Utopia*, p. 182.

51. Leggett, *Democratick Editorials*, p. 402.

52. Jan Narverson, *The Libertarian Idea* (Philadelphia: Temple University Press, 1988), p. 77. For a liberty-based argument for property, see pp. 62–93. For another view, see David Kelly, "Life, Liberty, and Property," in *Human Rights*, ed. Ellen Frankel Paul, Fred D. Miller, Jr., and Jeffrey Paul (Oxford: Basil Blackwell, 1984), pp. 108–18.

53. Locke, *Two Treatises of Government*, 2nd Treatise, Chapter V, §26, p. 287.

54. Ibid., §34, p. 291.

55. Ibid., §40, p. 296.

56. Ibid., §25, p. 286.

57. "Though the Earth, and all inferior Creatures be common to all Men, yet every Man has a *Property* in his own *Person*. This no Body has any Right to but himself. The *Labour* of his Body, and the *Work* of his Hands, we may say, are properly his." Ibid.,, §27, pp. 287–88.

58. Ibid., 2nd Treatise, Chapter IV, §23, p. 284. "This *Freedom* from Absolute, Arbitrary Power, is so necessary to, and closely joyned with a Man's Preservation,

that he cannot part with it, but by what forfeits his Preservation and Life together. For a Man, not having the Power of his own Life, *cannot*, by Compact, or his own Consent, *enslave himself* to any one, nor part himself under the Absolute, Arbitrary Power of another, to take away his Life, when he pleases."

59. Ibid., p. 137.

60. See Christine MacLeod, *Inventing the Industrial Revolution: The English Patent System, 1660-1800* (Cambridge: Cambridge University Press, 1989).

61. See Samuel C. Wheeler, III, "Natural Property Rights as Body Rights," in *Noûs* 14, no. 2 (May 1980).

62. Locke, 2nd Treatise, Chapter V, §28, p. 288.

63. Ibid., §26, p. 287.

64. Ibid., §28, p. 288.

65. As David Hume notes, "'T'were better, no doubt, that every one were possess'd of what is most suitable to him, and proper for his use: But besides, that this relation of fitness may be common to several at once, 'tis liable to so many controversies and men are so partial and passionate in judging of these controversies, that such a loose and uncertain rule wou'd be absolutely incompatible with the peace of human society." David Hume, *A Treatise of Human Nature*, ed. P. H. Nidditch (New York: Oxford University Press, 1978), p. 502; see also F. A. Hayek, *The Fatal Conceit: The Errors of Socialism* (Chicago: University of Chicago Press, 1989), pp. 73–75.

66. Frank Knight has characterized the patent system as "an exceedingly crude way for rewarding invention," for "as the thing works out, it is undoubtedly a very rare and exceptional case where the really deserving inventor gets anything like a fair reward. If any one gains, it is some purchaser of the invention or at best an inventor who adds a detail or finishing touch that makes an idea practicable where the real work of pioneering and exploration has been done by others." Frank Knight, *Risk, Uncertainty, and Profit* (Boston: Houghton Mifflin Company, 1921), p. 372.

67. Indeed, often the greatest rewards go to those who have—in the usual sense of the word—labored the least. We may owe more to the laziest among us: to the person who was too lazy to carry loads by hand and came upon the idea of using a wheelbarrow, for example. Attempts to reduce such differentials in productivity to a substrata of undifferentiated labor are inherently doomed, as the failed attempt of Marxism indicates.

68. The reward to labor for inventiveness in marketing, for example, is greater sales or market share, not property rights in marketing techniques or (even less plausibly) in market share.

69. Wilhelm von Humboldt, *The Limits of State Action*, trans. J. Coulthard, ed. J. W. Burrow (Cambridge: Cambridge University Press, 1969), p. 16.

70. Ibid., pp. 20–21.

71. Ibid., p. 116.

72. Ibid., p. 39.

73. Ibid., p. 83.

74. See notes 53–67 and accompanying text.

75. As the English Leveller leader Richard Overton similarly argued, "To every individual in nature is given an individual property by nature, not to be invaded or usurped by any. For every one, as he is himself, so he hath a self-propriety, else could he not be himself; and of this no second may presume to deprive any of without manifest violation and affront to the very principles of nature and of the rules of equity and justice between man and man. Mine and thine cannot be, except this be.

No man hath power over my rights and liberties, and I over no man's. I may be but an individual, enjoy my self and my self propriety, and may right my self no more then my self, or presume any further; if I do, I am an encroacher and an invader upon another man's right—to which I have no right." Richard Overton, "An Arrow against All Tyrants," in Andrew Sharp, ed., *The English Levellers* (Cambridge: Cambridge University Press, 1998), p. 55.

76. J. W. Burrow, Editor's Introduction to von Humboldt, *The Limits of State Action*, p. xxxix.

77. Von Humboldt, *The Limits of State Action*, pp. 96–97.

78. See G. W. F. Hegel, *The Philosophy of Right*, trans. T. M. Knox (Oxford: Clarendon Press, 1952).

79. See G. W. F. Hegel, *The Phenomenology of Spirit*, trans. A. V. Miller (Oxford: Oxford University Press, 1977).

80. Hegel, *The Philosophy of Right*, p. 37. Knox (p. 315, n. 58) points to a similarity in the treatment of *Bildung* (loosely translatable as "education" or "spiritual development") in both Humboldt and Hegel. The difference is that whereas Humboldt saw the role of the state in the process of *Bildung* as "negative," that is, protecting citizens from violence but otherwise keeping out of the way, Hegel sees a positive role for the state in this process.

81. Ibid., p. 40.

82. Ibid., p. 42.

83. Ibid., p. 42.

84. Ibid., p. 45. Further, "[s]ince property is the *embodiment* of personality, my inward idea and will that something is to be mine is not enough to make it my property; to secure this end occupancy is requisite" (emphasis in original).

85. Ibid., p. 46.

86. Ibid., p. 47. This is the "mode of taking possession most in conformity with the Idea to this extent, that it implies a union of subject and object."

87. Ibid., p. 47. This process, as Hegel remarks in his notes, is the same as the dialectic of lord and bondsman described in the *Phenomenology of Spirit*. Remarkably, self-ownership emerges only at the end of a historical process of self-confrontation through possession of and transformation of the external world. The anti-liberal character of Hegel's approach is made most clear in his identification of the "Idea" of freedom (its concretion and synthesis with the content of its concept) with the state: "But that objective mind, the content of the right, should no longer be apprehended in its subjective concept alone, and consequently that man's absolute unfitness for slavery should no longer be apprehended as a mere 'ought to be', is something which does not come home to our minds until we recognize that the Idea of freedom is genuinely actual only as the state" (p. 48).

88. See Immanuel Kant, "Von der Unrechtmässigkeit des Büchernachdrucks," in *Copyrights and Patents for Inventions*, ed. R. A. Macfie (1883), p. 580.

89. Immanuel Kant, "Was ist ein Buch?" (trans. Tom G. Palmer) in Wilhelm Weischedel, ed. *Die Metaphysik Der Sitten* (Frankfurt am Main: Suhrkamp, 1977), p. 405.

90. Kant, "Von der Unrechtmässigkeit des Büchernachdrucks," p. 582.

91. Ibid., p. 584.

92. This may reflect the fact that Kant was a writer and not a sculptor.

93. Ibid., p. 585.

94. Ibid., p. 585.

95. Hegel, *The Philosophy of Right*, p. 54.

96. Ibid., p. 55.

97. *C. civ. art. 543, Code pénal [C.pén.] arts. 425–429* ("Law of March 11, 1957 on literary and artistic property"); see also "Loi du 11 mars 1957 sur la propriété littéraire et artistique," 1957 *Journal Officiel de la République Française* [J.O.] 2723, 1957 *Recueil Dalloz Législation [D.L.]102* (for amendments and cases interpreting the statute).

98. Ibid.

99. For an overview of the proposed legislation, as well as a discussion of the pros and cons of those proposals, see Donnelly, "Artist's Rights and Copyrights," 1 *Congressional Quarterly's 1 Res. Rep. 245* (1988); see also *Washington Post*, May 22, 1988, F1, col. 1.

100. See Edward Damich, "The Right of Personality: A Common Law Basis for the Protection of the Moral Rights of Authors," *Georgia Law Review* 23, no.1 (1988): pp. 6–25.

101. *Cinquin v. Lecocq*, Req. Sirey, 1900.2.121. note Saleilles (1902) (cited in S. Stromholm, *Le Droit Moral de l'Auteur* [1966], p. 29).

102. Ibid., p. 285.

103. Josef Kohler, *Philosophy of Law*, trans. Adalbert Albrecht (New York: A. M. Kelley, 1969), p. 80.

104. J. Kohler, *Urheberrecht an Schriftwerken und Verlagsrecht 15* (1907) (quoted in Edward Damich, "The Right of Personality," p. 29); see also Arther S. Katz, "The Doctrine of Moral Right and American Copyright Law—A Proposal," *Southern California Law Review* 24, no. 402 (1951).

105. *C. civ. art. 543, Code pénal [C.pén] arts. 425–429, art. 34*. Damich, however, argues that, due to difficulties presented by practical application and conflict with other rights, the right of retraction is "a 'dead letter' even in French Law." Damich, "The Right of Personality," p. 25.

106. *C. civ. art. 543, Code pénal [C.pén.] arts. 425–429* ("The authors of graphic or plastic works of art have, notwithstanding any transfer of the original work, an inalienable right to participate in the product of all sales of this work made at auction or through the intermediation of dealers.")

107. Hegel, *The Philosophy of Right*, p. 40.

108. Edward J. Markey, "Let Artists Have a Fair Share of Their Profits," *New York Times*, Dec 20, 1987.

109. That of course raises the question of when the work is finished. Who would know when it was finished? Would anyone else undertake to finish Schubert's "Unfinished Symphony"? The artist may indeed be in the privileged position of determining when a work is finished, but that does not privilege the subjective experience of the artist in the constitution of the art work as such.

110. The strategic differentiation between various kinds of dependence is elaborated in Edmund Husserl, "Investigation III: On the Theory of Wholes and Parts," in Husserl, *Logical Investigations*, trans. J. Findlay (London: Routledge & Kegan Paul, 1970), pp. 435–89; see also *Parts and Moments: Studies in Logic and Formal Ontology*, ed. Barry Smith (München and Wien: Philosophia Verlag, 1982).

111. I used the possessive—"Shakespeare's"—in describing that play to highlight the relationship of dependence that the work does have on its author. Shakespeare has been dead for centuries, while *Othello* lives on. One might say, however, that Shakespeare's mind remains active or still "lives" in *Othello*.

112. Of course, an artist may also be her own audience, but we are here speaking of ideal roles; one and the same person may fulfill various roles. When the term

"artist" is used, it will be understood that artist qua artist is meant, and similarly of other roles, such as "audience."

113. Roman Ingarden, *The Literary Work of Art: An Investigation on the Borderlines of Ontology, Logic and Theory of Literature*, trans. George G. Grabowicz (Evanston, Ill.: Northwestern University Press, 1973), p. 13.

114. Ibid., p. 13.

115. Ibid., p. 14.

116. That is what accounts for the nonrivalrous nature of the consumption of works of art and other ideal objects; their enjoyment by one person need not diminish their enjoyment by another. This also shows the difference between the concretion of a work, such as a performance, and the work itself. My enjoyment of a performance may diminish your ability to enjoy the same performance, perhaps because I block your view, but it does not exhaust or in any way diminish the work itself. It is for this reason that Thomas Jefferson denied any natural property right in ideal objects: "If nature has made any one thing less susceptible than all others of exclusive property, it is the action of the thinking power called an idea, which an individual may exclusively possess as long as he keeps it to himself; but the moment it is divulged, it forces itself into the possession of every one, and the receiver cannot dispossess himself of it. Its peculiar character, too, is that no one possesses the less, because every other possesses the whole of it. He who receives an idea from me, receives instruction himself without lessening mine; as he who lights his taper at mine, receives light without darkening me." Thomas Jefferson, "Letter to Isaac McPherson, Monticello, August 13, 1813," in Joyce Appleby and Terenu Ball, eds., *Thomas Jefferson, Political Writings* (Cambridge: Cambridge University Press, 1999), p. 580.

117. R. Ingarden, *Ontology of the Work of Art: The Musical Work, the Picture, the Architectural Work, the Film*, trans. Raymond Meyer with John T. Goldthwait (Athens, Ohio: Ohio University Press, 1989), pp. 35–36.

118. See Robert Sokolowski, *Husserlian Meditations: How Words Present Things* (Evanston, Ill.: Northwestern University Press, 1974), p. 99. ("Every 'cultural object' which requires a performance to be actualized—a musical composition, a play, dance, or poem—appears through a manifold of interpretations. All of them present the object itself, and the object is the identity within the interpretation."); see also Ingarden, *The Ontology of the Work of Art*, p. 36: "[H]ow does a literary work appear during reading, and what is the immediate correlate of this reading?. . . [A] distinction should be drawn between the work and its concretions, which differ from it in various respects. These concretions are precisely what is constituted during the reading and what, in a manner of speaking, forms the mode of appearance of a work, the concrete form in which the work itself is apprehended." Hans-Georg Gadamer, *Truth and Method*, ed. Joel C. Weinsheimer and Donald G. Marshall (New York: Continuum, 1982), p. 274: "Interpretation is not an occasional additional act subsequent to understanding, but rather understanding is always an interpretation, and hence interpretation is the explicit form of understanding." Rather than simply reproducing the experience of the artist, each member of the audience contributes a different interpretation—the way in which the work "speaks to us" and allows us to learn from it, rather than simply reproducing "in us" someone else's experience. That manifold of interpretations is what makes possible the special kind of intersubjectivity and objectivity that works of art enjoy. The manifold of interpretations provide the "other" that is the necessary condition for the appearance of the "same."

119. For the general approach to objectivity outlined here, see Edmund Husserl, *Formal and Transcendental Logic* (Hingham, Mass.: Kluwer Academic Publishers, 1978), pp. 232–66.

120. Ingarden, *The Literary Work of Art*, pp. 340, 349; for a discussion of the kinds of dependence and independence set forth by Ingarden, see Peter Simons, "The Formalization of Husserl's Theory of Holes and Parts," in Barry Smith, ed., *Parts and Moments: Studies in Logic and Formal Ontology*, pp. 135–42. Note that, while I have earlier used the term "ideal object" to cover all of the subject matter of copyrights and patents, Ingarden would limit that term to scientific discoveries, mathematical theorems, and the like (that is, typically to the subject matter of patents), and would consider works of art in a different category, since they come into being during a definite period of time and are not, unlike what he terms ideal objects, atemporal.

121. See Ingarden, *The Literary Work of Art*, pp. 336–55; see also Barry Smith, "Practices of Art," in *Practical Knowledge: Outlines of a Theory of Traditions and Skills*, ed. J. Nyíri and Barry Smith (London and New York: Croom Helm, 1988), p. 174: "Art works are dependent, now, not only upon the activities of their creators, but also upon certain correlated activities of an appropriately receptive audience. A shell, a leaf, or a relic of some lost civilization, existing in a world lacking every tendency toward appreciative evaluation, would be simply a shell, a leaf, or a lump of stone." Compare Nelson Goodman, *Languages of Art: An Approach to a Theory of Symbols* (Indianapolis: Hackett, 1976), p. 20: "The distant or colossal sculpture has also to be shaped very differently from what it depicts in order to be realistic, in order to 'look right.' And the ways of making it 'look right' are not reducible to fixed and universal rules, for how an object looks depends not only upon its orientation, distance, and lighting, but upon all we know of it and upon our training, habits, and concerns."

122. As a practical matter, one also faces the problem of identifying just who the artist is in any collaborative work. Testifying on the behalf of moral rights legislation, film director and producer George Lucas referred to film colorizers and others who alter art works as "barbarians." His colleague Stephen Spielberg insisted that "without the agreement and permission of the two artistic authors (the principal director and principal screen writer), no material alterations [should] be made in a film following its first, paid, public exhibition." See Tom G. Palmer, "Artists Don't Deserve Special Rights," *Wall Street Journal*, March 8, 1988 (quoting testimony that Spielberg and Lucas gave to a Senate subcommittee). But, by his own theory, is not Mr. Lucas (not to mention Mr. Spielberg) a barbarian? What of the art of the actors? Why should they submit to having their work distorted or left on the cutting room floor? And what of the lighting crew, and so on? Are not those other collaborators also artists? Why should only directors and screen writers enjoy such moral rights?

123. Whether they are harmed in the economic sense, by losing revenue, is another matter; as I have noted elsewhere, however, purely utilitarian claims on behalf of intellectual property rights are shaky, at best. See Tom G. Palmer, "Intellectual Property: A Non-Posnerian Law and Economics Approach".

124. See notes 69–77 above and accompanying text.

125. See, for example, Simon Rottenberg, "The Remuneration of Artists," in *Frontiers of Economics*, ed. Kenneth J. Arrow and Seppo Honkapohja (Oxford: Basil Blackwell, 1985), pp. 47–51; and Ben W. Bolch, William Damon, and C. Elton Hinshaw, "An Economic Analysis of the California Art Royalty Statute," *Connecticut Law Review* 10 (1978).

126. Those who prefer payment now to payment later, such as the many artists who sell their work "on the street," are harmed by such a requirement. As Ben W. Bolch remarks: "Many artists, 'starving' or not, want their money now, not tomorrow. Otherwise, they would 'invest' in the art by keeping it for themselves." Ben W. Bolch, "There Is No Just Price for Art," *New York Times*, Nov. 28, 1987.

127. By diminishing pre-patent cooperation among researchers, for example, or through diminishing opportunities for playwrights to emulate William Shakespeare, who rewrote Thomas Kyd's now forgotten play "The Spanish Tragedy" and gave us "Hamlet." See also Georg Bittlingmayer, "Property Rights, Progress, and the Aircraft Patent Agreement," *Journal of Law and Ecomomics* 30 (1988).

128. See Henry Sidgwick, *The Methods of Ethics* (Indianapolis: Hackett, June 1981), p. 440: "What Hume . . . means by Justice is rather what I should call Order."

129. Aristotle seems to have used both arguments in his dispute with Plato over the community of possessions. In his *Politics* he argued: "What belongs in common to the most people is accorded the least care: they take thought for their own things above all, and less about the things in common, or only so much as falls to each individually." Aristotle, *The Politics*, ed. Carnes Lord (Amherst: Prometheus Books, 1984), p. 57. That corresponds, more or less, to justice as "X-maximization." He addresses justice-as-order later. "In general, to live together and be partners in any human matter is difficult, and particularly things of this sort [owning common property]. This is clear in partnerships of fellow travelers, most of whom are always quarreling as a result of friction with one another over everyday and small matters. Again, friction particularly arises with the servants we use most frequently for regular tasks." Ibid., p. 60.

130. For a discussion of the impact of the printing press on a variety of matters, including intellectual property, see Elizabeth Eisenstein, *The Printing Press as an Agent of Change: Communications and Cultural Transformations in Early-Modern Europe* (Cambridge: Cambridge University Press, 1979).

131. Hume, *A Treatise of Human Nature*, p. 501 (emphasis in original).

132. Such objects, however, must be produced. In this sense they do share the kind of scarcity relevant to the X-maximization arguments.

133. As I shall argue at the conclusion of this article, justice-as-order is *consistent* with—indeed it is the genus for—the self-ownership, liberty-based argument for property that, as I have argued above, is *inconsistent* with patent and copyright.

134. Compare Howard Abrams, "The Historic Foundation of American Copyright Law: Exploding the Myth of Common Law Copyright,"*Wayne Law Review* 29 (1983).

135. Murray Rothbard, *The Ethics of Liberty* (Atlantic Highlands: Humanities Press, 1982), p. 144. (Rothbard seems to have made a slip here; he does not mean the right to "resell" the property but the right to copy it.)

136. See Kant, "Was ist ein Buch?"

137. Rothbard, *The Ethics of Liberty*, p. 123. Rothbard seems to have confused what is being made the subject of a property right. Clearly he cannot mean the right to *sell* the object, for then nothing that was copyrighted could be resold, and the market system would either grind to a halt or copyright would become a dead letter. He must mean the right to *reproduce*, rather than to resell. Note that the argument Rothbard presents in *The Ethics of Liberty* represents a shift from the argument presented in his early treatise on economics, *Man, Economy, and State: A Treatise on Economic Principles* (Los Angeles: Nash Publishing, 1970), in which he attacked patents as monopolies, but justified copyrights as a form implicit of contractual agreement

not to copy. (See especially pp. 654–55) Such an implicit agreement differs from the right *reserved* by the creator. "[T]he inventor could mark his machine *copyright*, and then anyone who buys the machine buys it *on the condition* that he will not reproduce and sell such a machine for profit. Any violation of this contract would constitute implicit theft. . . . " (p. 654; emphasis in original). Rothbard's more recent proposal at least avoids the most obvious problem with his earlier position: what right would the originator have against a copier who did not buy the item, but simply saw it, heard of it, or found it. There would be no agreement, implicit or explicit, on the part of such a copier, and hence no obligation to refrain from copying. The later "reserved right" position allows the right to be reserved regardless of who comes into possession of the object, although it might face difficulties in enforcing the claim against someone, who, say, recorded an illegally broadcast song or movie.

138. Kant's remarks deserve repeating: "Those who regard the publication of a book as the exercise of the rights of property in respect of a single copy—it may have come to the possessor as a [manuscript] of the author, or as a work printed by some prior publisher—and who yet would, by the reservation of certain rights (whether as having their origin in the author or in the publisher in whose favour he has denuded himself of them), go on to restrict the exercise of property rights, maintaining the illegality of reproduction—will never attain their end. For the rights of the author regarding his own thoughts remain to him notwithstanding the reprint; and as there cannot be a distinct permission given to the purchaser of a book for, and a limitation of, its use as property, how much less is a mere presumption sufficient for a weight of obligation?" Kant, "Von der Unrechtmässigkeit des Büchernach-drucks," p. 58. Hegel argues; "The substance of an author's or an inventor's right cannot in the first instance be found in the supposition that when he disposes of a single copy of his work, he arbitrarily makes it a condition that the power to produce facsimiles as things, a power which thereupon passes into another's possession, should not become the property of another but should remain his own. The first question is whether such a separation between ownership of the things and the power to produce facsimiles which is given with the thing is compatible with the concept of property, or whether it does not cancel the complete and free ownership on which there originally depends the option of the single producer of intellectual work to reserve to himself the power to reproduce, or to part with this power as a thing of value, or to attach no value to it at all and surrender it together with the single exemplar of his work." Hegel, *The Philosophy of Right*, p. 55.

139. It is important to remember that the retained right involved is a right to control a tangible object. No claim is made to a direct right to own the ideal object embedded in the tangible object. The control over this ideal object is an indirect consequence of a property right over a tangible object.

140. If an advocate of "piggyback rights" were to respond that the airwaves can and should be the objects of ownership, as some have argued, he would reveal a misunderstanding of the status of "the airwaves." One cannot own the broadcast spectrum, although one can have the right to use one's broadcasting or receiving equipment without interference from others. Thus, the first broadcaster over a frequency in a given spectrum area can have a legally recognized right to broadcast over a part of the electro-magnetic spectrum without interfering with another broadcaster. But if another broadcaster can send out a narrow beam signal within that spectrum that does not interfere with the first broadcaster's signal (and hence with his use of his tangible property), then the first should have no right to stop the

second. As Ronald Coase argues, assigning direct property rights over the broadcast spectrum is as sensible as assigning direct property rights over "the notes of the musical scale or the colors of the rainbow." Ronald Coase, "The Federal Communications Commission," *Journal of Law and Economics* 2, no.1 (1959): 33. In a private property system "if there were a market, what would be sold, is the right to use a piece of equipment to transmit signals in a particular way. The right in question would be a right over a tangible object, not over the immaterial broadcast spectrum." See also Milton Mueller, "Reforming Telecommunications Regulation," in Edwin Diamond, Norman Sandler, and Milton Mueller, eds., *Telecommunications in Crisis: The First Amendment, Technology, and Deregulation* (Washington: Cato Institute, 1983).

141. The general thrust of Rothbard's overall argument for property seems to be consistent with the "justice-as-order" notion, although he sometimes does not make the distinctions necessary in order to address intellectual property issues. Thus, Rothbard defends the property right in a sculptor's creation without distinguishing between the different ways in which the sculptor might own his "product," like ownership of the material artifact, or ownership of the form embedded in it: "[T]he sculptor has in fact 'created' this work of art—not of course in the sense that he has created matter—but that he has produced it by transforming nature-given matter (the clay) into another form in accordance with his own ideas and his own labor and energy. Surely, if every man has the right to own his own body, and if he must use and transform material natural objects in order to survive, then he has the right to own the product that he has made, by his energy and effort, into a veritable extension of his own personality." Rothbard, *The Ethics of Liberty*, p. 48.

142. Earl Kintner and Jack Lahr, *An Intellectual Property Law Primer* (New York: Clark Boardman Company, 1982), p. 168 (quoting *Carver v. Harr*, 132 N.J. Eq. 207, 209. 27 A.2d 895, 897 [1942]).

143. But see Wendy Gordon, "An Inquiry into the Merits of Copyright: The Challenge of Consistency, Consent, and Encouragement Theory," *Stanford Law Review* 41 (1989). Arguing against my earlier essay, which was critical of patents and copyrights (Tom G. Palmer, "Intellectual Property: A Non-Posnerian Law and Economics Approach"). Gordon agrees that intellectual property claims are restraints on other property rights but responds, in Hohfeldian and positivist fashion, that "all entitlements limit each other." (p. 1423).

144. Hume, *A Treatise of Human Nature*, p. 484.

145. Ibid., p. 490.

146. For a contrast in this respect between the ancient world and modernity, see Benjamin Constant, "The Liberty of the Ancients Contrasted with That of the Moderns," in *Political Writings*, ed. Biancarmaria Fontana (Cambridge: Cambridge University Press, 1988), pp. 308–28.

147. See Thomas Schelling, *The Strategy of Conflict* (Cambridge, Mass: Harvard University Press, 1960) pp. 53–58.

148. Ibid., p. 57.

149. See Thomas Hodgskin, *The Natural and Artificial Right of Property Contrasted*, (London: B. Steil, 1832; reprinted Clifton, N.J.: Augustus Kelley, 1973), pp. 28–29: "Mr. Locke says, that every man has a property in his own person; in fact individuality—which is signified by the word own—cannot be disjoined from the person. Each individual learns his own shape and form, and even the existence of his limbs and body, from seeing and feeling them. These constitute his notion of personal identity, both for himself and others; and it is impossible to conceive—it is in fact a contradiction

to say—that a man's limbs and his body do not belong to himself: for the words him, self, and his body, signify the same material thing. As we learn the existence of our own bodies from seeing and feeling them, and as we see and feel the bodies of others, we have precisely similar grounds for believing in the individuality or identity of other persons, as for behaving in our own identity. The ideas expressed by the words mine and thine, as applied to the produce of labour, are simply then an extended form of the ideas of personal identity and individuality." On the appreciation of the individuality and special status of other humans, see Edmund Husserl, *Cartesian Meditations*, trans. Dorion Cairns (The Hague, Netherlands: Martinus Nijhoff, 1960), p. 129. Husserl argues that the reason we do not simply consider others as things or as meat is that we apprehend that we exist in a community, with an *"[o]bjectivating equalization* of existence with that of all others."

150. Destutt De Tracy, *A Treatise of Political Economy*, trans. by Thomas Jefferson (1817; New York: August Kelly, 1970), p. 47.

151. James Mirrlees, "The Economic Uses of Utilitarianism," in *Utilitarianism and Beyond*, ed. Amertya Sen and Bernard Williams (Cambridge: Cambridge University Press, 1982), p. 71: "Roughly speaking, [in a society of identical individuals] the totality of all individuals can be regarded as a single individual. Therefore total social utility, the sum of the total utilities of the separate individuals, is the right way to evaluate alternative patterns of outcomes for the whole society. That should be the view of any individual within society, and therefore of any outside observer." This approach is subjected to withering criticism in Robert Sugden, "Labour, Property and the Morality of Markets," in *The Market in History*, ed. B. L. Anderson and A. J. H. Latham (London: Croom Helm, 1986) pp. 9–28. See also Robert Sugden, *The Economics of Rights, Co-Operation, and Welfare* (Oxford: Basil Blackwell, 1986), pp. 6–8, for a criticism of the "U.S. Cavalry Model" of moral philosophy and a presentation of an alternative based on the viewpoint of the individual decision maker. Sugden presents an extended argument about how property rights and other conventions can emerge spontaneously, without any centralized agency or guiding hand, and how they can gain in the process the moral approbation of the participants in the process, even though they may be "suboptimal" from some external perspective. I am deeply indebted to Professor Sugden's work for my own views on morality and property.

152. Hume, *A Treatise of Human Nature*, p. 503.

153. Ibid., pp. 509–10.

154. By "extended order" I mean what Adam Smith referred to as a "Great Society." That is a sort of order that extends beyond the small group to include individuals who, while part of the same economic or legal order, will never have any face-to-face relationships.

155. For further elaboration of this approach, see Randy Barnett, "A Consent Theory of Contract," and Randy Barnett, "Contract Remedies and Inalienable Rights," *Social Philosophy and Policy* 4, no. 179 (1986). As Barnett argues, a natural-rights self-ownership model leads not to absolutism and slavery (as Richard Tuck has argued in *Natural Rights Theories: Their Origin and Development* [Cambridge: Cambridge University Press, 1981]) but to inalienable liberty. Although Tuck has argued that self-ownership must imply that one could alienate all rights over oneself to a sovereign, Barnett argues that that rests on an ontological impossibility, the alienation of one's self from oneself. On the consent theory of contract and inalienable rights, see also von Humboldt, *The Limits of State Action*, pp. 94–95.

156. See Harold Demsetz, "Towards a Theory of Property Rights," *American Economic Review* 57, no. 2 (1967). Note that in Demsetz's model, scarcity—in the static sense—is central to the origin of property rights.

157. Lysander Spooner objects that the argument from avoiding "collision" would as clearly require "that a hammer should be free to different persons at different times, and that a road, or canal should be free to as many persons at once, as can use it without collision, as it does that an idea should be free to as many persons at once as choose to use it." Spooner, *The Law of Intellectual Property*, Vol. III, p. 79. That response ignores the fact that use of tangible objects *can* come into collision, even if at any particular moment they are not in collision. In addition, it ignores the fact that "nonuse," such as speculative withholding from the market, is as legitimate a use of one's property as is its active exploitation. Further, the "externalities-based" approach explains how property rights can emerge and change over time, as expanding populations, changing market conditions, and new technologies make possible forms of "collision" that were previously unknown. See Mueller, "Reforming Telecommunications Regulation," and Demsetz, "Towards a Theory of Property Rights."

158. Adam Smith, *Lectures on Jurisprudence* (Oxford: Oxford University Press, 1978), p. 352.

159. Arnold Plant, "The Economic Theory Concerning Patents for Inventions," in *Selected Economic Essays and Addresses* (London: Routledge & Kegan Paul, 1974), p. 56; see also F. A. Hayek, *The Fatal Conceit: The Errors of Socialism* (Chicago: University of Chicago Press, 1989), p. 6: "The difference between these [copyrights and patents] and other kinds of property rights is this: while ownership of material goods guides the use of scarce means to their most important uses, in the case of immaterial goods such as literary productions and technological inventions the ability to produce them is also limited, yet once they have come into existence, they can be indefinitely multiplied and can be made scarce only by law in order to create an inducement to produce such ideas. Yet it is not obvious that such forced scarcity is the most effective way to stimulate the human creative process."

160. See Hayek, *The Fatal Conceit*, pp. 11–21. We learn our mortality, Hayek argues, within the small group, notably the family, in which face-to-face interaction prevails. But we must also live in a world of strangers, in which "concrete, commonly perceived aims" cannot be assumed, nor can knowledge of the needs or abilities of others. "Part of our present difficulty is that we must constantly adjust our lives, our thoughts and our emotions, in order to live simultaneously within different kinds of orders according to different rules. If we were to apply the unmodified, uncurbed, rules of the microcosmos (i.e., of the small band or troop, or of, say, families) to the macrocosmos (our wider civilization), as our instincts and sentimental yearnings often make us do, we would destroy it. Yet if we were always to apply the rules of the extended order to our more intimate groupings, we would crush them. So we must learn to live in two sorts of worlds at once" (p. 18).

161. See Aristotle, *The Politics*, p. 61.

162. Overton, "An Arrow against All Tyrants," p. 55.

163. See Aristotle, *The Politics*, pp. 55–61.

164. I use the term here in a broad enough sense to include David Hume.

165. Of course, people of good faith sometimes do come into conflict, which is why we have courts of law to adjudicate disputes. To admit the possibility of such conflicts, however, is a far cry from seeing conflict as a built-in feature of social life.

166. Recall the discussion by John Locke regarding the question of when acorns that a person has eaten become his own: "so his, *i.e.,* a part of him, that another can no longer have any right to it." Locke, *Two Treatises of Government*, 2nd Treatise, Chapter V, §26, p. 287.

PART II

CURRENT DISPUTES IN INTELLECTUAL PROPERTY LAW

5. The Future of Intellectual Property in the Information Age

Rick Boucher

Intellectual property has deep roots in our law and, in fact, the United States Constitution expressly confers upon the Congress authority to adopt laws that will protect intellectual property rights for a reasonable period of time in order to encourage science and the useful arts. From the earliest days of this nation creative works have enjoyed the protection of federal law in recognition of the need to assure appropriate compensation to inventors, writers, and artists when the product of their creativity is commercialized.

In our country, there has always been a broad agreement that the law should recognize the rights of creators of intellectual property as an incentive to further the creation of original work. I share that belief. I am a strong defender of intellectual property and the rights of companies and individuals who have created works to receive fair compensation through the ability to limit the commercial use of that work in exchange for compensation for a limited period of time.

I also acknowledge the tremendous benefits that the products of American ingenuity, including inventions, literature, recorded music, and motion pictures, have conferred upon the American economy. These benefits are self-evident and they are broadly acknowledged.

I would also say that only through the compensation assurance that is provided by intellectual property laws can we expect these economic benefits to continue. Nowhere in the debate is there the slightest notion that intellectual property laws are not valuable. We have to begin the dialogue by acknowledging that they are.

American law has also historically contained a recognition of the rights of the users of intellectual property. When you whistle in the shower or when you sing a line from a romantic song to your husband or wife, you don't have to call the composer to get permission. The student at a public library doesn't have to get permission from the author of a book in order to make a copy on a photocopier of the one page from that book that the student needs to quote from in order to finish his term paper. These everyday uses of copyrighted works are permitted to users under the fair use doctrine, which enables reasonable use and copying of protected works for personal convenience.

The fair use doctrine keeps intellectual property laws in check. While acknowledging that creators of works should be reasonably compensated for commercial uses of their works, it keeps them from having monopoly control. The fair use doctrine was created by the courts as a way to give substance to First Amendment free speech rights.

Put simply, free speech doesn't mean very much if you have to get the prior permission of an intellectual property owner to use words in a series that may have appeared, perhaps coincidentally, in some copyrighted work. So the fair use doctrine was essential in the view of our American courts in order to give vitality to our precious freedom of speech.

It is the fair use doctrine that allows society to have an active discourse, while at the same time granting compensation rights to authors and artists. It is the oil that keeps the machine from seizing up. But the precious fair use right is under attack today as never before. The balance between the rights of the creators of intellectual property and the users of intellectual property is being recast in favor of creators in a manner that, if not checked, will fundamentally change the way that information is used in our society.

How the Digital Millennium Copyright Act Upsets the Delicate Copyright Balance

I am concerned about a number of recent developments in this regard, starting with the Digital Millennium Copyright Act (DMCA), which was enacted by Congress in 1998 largely at the behest of America's creative community. It was also the instrument of implementation in the United States of the World Intellectual Property Organization Treaty that a number of nations signed in 1996. It is, in my humble opinion, a broad overreach that severely limits fair use rights.

The Motion Picture Association of America, the Recording Industry Association of America, book publishers, and others representing content owners in the United States made an appealing claim when they first came to Congress in 1997 and suggested that the DMCA be adopted. They said that the roughly simultaneous arrival of digital technology and the Internet created twin threats that would result in broadly expanded piracy of protected works. They claimed that with digital technology, a copy of a copy of a copy retains the same clarity and integrity as the original of the work, and that digital technology differs dramatically from analog technology, in which each succeeding copy of the work degrades in quality.

They also claimed that, in the networked world, with expanded use of the Internet and the broad availability of Internet access, thousands of copies could be distributed around the world with the single click of a mouse. The creators of intellectual property complained that, with the arrival of digital technology and the Internet, their works were under greater threat of piracy than they had ever been before.

This was an appealing claim. And many of us believed that some change in intellectual property law was necessary in order to accommodate these twin threats. The question was: To what extent should Congress respond and how broad should the new protections be? Frankly, what should have been an extensive debate on that very subject turned out not to be a debate at all. And so the DMCA was adopted with almost no modification.

So powerful was the claim of vulnerability to piracy that Congress, in passing the DMCA, granted unprecedented rights to copyright owners, which, unless changed, will cede to the intellectual property owner total control over the work. The new rights go well beyond providing defenses against piracy and beyond what is necessary to assure adequate compensation to the intellectual property owner. They forecast a time when the content owner can monopolize the use of the work, and when what is available today in the library for reading and limited copying under fair use will be available for reading and limited copying only under pay-per-use.

The most troubling provision in the DMCA is Section 1201(a)(1). That section declares that it is a criminal offense to circumvent a technological protection measure that guards access to a copyrighted work. It matters not why the circumvention occurs; circumventions that are designed to further piracy or to enable piracy are punished as a crime. All other acts of circumvention, for whatever purpose, are also punished as a crime, with the same force of the law and the same penalties. Circumventing a technological protection measure for the purpose of exercising fair use rights is punished as a crime under Section 1201(a)(1).

A time will come in the not too distant future when most of what libraries get from record companies, from movie companies, and from publishing houses will come in the form of digital media. And those digital media can easily be protected by a password, which is going to be given to the librarian who will act as a gatekeeper and collect whatever fee the content owner exacts as a condition for allowing the password to be used. It will be a simple encryption of some kind. But the law says, however simple it is, it can be placed as a gate in front of this copyrighted work. And then people who today would go get a book off the shelf and copy one page in order to produce a term paper will be able to do that in the future only when they pay a fee. Fair use now would be available only under pay-per-use in the future.

I am also concerned about another development—the copy protection of compact discs (CDs). Most of the record companies have announced that they intend to introduce into the U.S. market, perhaps even by the end of this year, demonstration versions of CDs that are copy-protected. This means that you can play the CD in a regular CD player, but if you put it in your computer, depending on which mechanism is used to copy-protect, it may not play.

Under no circumstance would you be permitted to engage in the time-honored fair use application of space-shifting. In space-shifting a person rearranges the tracks on a commercially produced CD and transfers them to his own blank CD so that he can listen to the music that he wants to hear in precisely the order in which he wants to hear it. That is a classic fair use. The Supreme Court, about 20 years ago, in the case of *Universal Studios v. the Sony Corporation*, held that time-shifting was fair use. Time-shifting is the practice of putting a tape in the videocassette recorder and recording a television program when it airs so that you can see it later, at a time of greater convenience to you. The Supreme Court upheld that this represented a classic fair use.

It's hard to imagine that the same doctrine that holds that to be fair use would not hold space-shifting on CDs to be fair use as well.

And yet that fair use application is threatened by what we now see as the intended introduction into the United States of copy-protected CDs so that people could not use the music they purchase to create a CD that has the tracks they want. Under Section 1201(a)(1), anyone who tries to do that is guilty of a crime.

I can absolutely assure you that, within a matter of weeks of copy-protected CDs being introduced into the U.S. market, you will be able to go down to the college bookstore and buy a T-shirt that will have written across it the code that will enable you to circumvent the technological protection measure. This is already being done for digital videodiscs (DVDs); people are producing T-shirts that have a code printed on them that cracks DVD protection systems.

I think Section 1201 overreaches. It extends to the copyright owner monopoly control. It is not necessary to assure fair and reasonable compensation. It is an effort to give the creative community monopoly control over the use of the work.

In 1998, when the DMCA was being debated in the House Judiciary Committee, of which I am a member, I offered amendments at that time that would have restricted the scope of Section 1201. It would have said that it is only a crime if you circumvent for the purpose of infringing a copyright. That is what 1201 should say. And I intend to introduce legislation shortly that will restrict Section 1201's application to those instances in which the circumvention is for that purpose—for infringing the copyright. Other acts of circumvention, whether to exercise fair use rights or for other benign purposes, would then not be criminal conduct.

What has changed since 1998? A number of things have changed that give me reason to believe we have an opportunity now to pass this necessary change in Section 1201(a)(1). First of all, in 1998, there was very little public debate about any of these provisions. The public was not paying much attention to what Congress was doing in enacting these measures. The user community was not well enough organized to thwart the overreach that the DMCA accomplished.

A lot has changed in the meantime. There is now a growing public perception that Section 1201(a)(1) is a threat to user rights. *Newsweek* magazine, for example, recently had a full-page commentary on the subject. There have been other examples of the popular press talking about the overreach of Section 1201(a)(1). National Public Radio has done a series of programs, and plans more, on the problems that will be created for the flow of information in society if this provision is not changed.

The other reason I have some confidence that we can succeed this time around is that the user community is much better organized. Organizations such as the Digital Media Association and the Digital Future Coalition have grown dramatically in strength since 1998. These are organizations that publicly defend user rights. I would encourage you to visit those Web sites and learn about what they do. We can also use your support in Congress as we seek to reaffirm user rights and the classic balance between intellectual property rights and user rights that our law has historically contained.

Business Method Patents

Another area in which I find this classic balance between the rights of users and the rights of creators to be moving alarmingly in the direction of creators is that of business method patents.

Patents historically were awarded only for mechanical inventions. In order to get a patent, you actually had to have a working model of whatever it was you wanted to protect. And you would take that to the patent office, and a patent examiner would look at it and say, "Yes, that sure looks unique to me; here is your patent." So you had to show that you had invented something. You had to have a physical manifestation of whatever work you were trying to protect.

A lot has changed since those early days, and some of the changes have been necessary. But with regard to business method patents, the change is rampant. Mere concepts of doing business can now entitle you to get a patent. Entire fields of commerce are being walled off through the protection of the patent law and assigned as a property right to an individual who has created a concept about a way to do business.

For example, Priceline has gotten a patent on the "name your own price" approach to marketing products, notwithstanding the fact that reverse auctions have been known almost since the creation of commerce thousands of years ago. A reverse auction is exactly what Priceline does, but it got a patent on using a "name your own price" theme on the Internet in order to engage in the sale of a product. This has proven to be detrimental to other companies that would like to use it. Travelocity, for example, the number one Web site for travel reservations, has to pay a royalty to Priceline whenever it uses the "name your own price" approach.

Here is another example: Charitable giving on the Internet was patented as a practice, as a method of doing business. And then the person who got that patent immediately sued the Red Cross, which—guess what—solicits charitable contributions on the Internet. This is an overreach of the patent law, and the time has come to change it.

I am concerned that if we do not change the award of business method patents, we are going to see entire fields of commerce walled off, and then the patent law will accomplish exactly the opposite of its intended result. The patent law is designed to encourage innovation by giving limited protection for a limited period of time to the originators of works as an incentive to create more works. But by walling off entire areas of commerce, business method patents do just the opposite. They inhibit competition because they make it impossible to compete in that space. And by inhibiting competition, they broadly provide a disincentive to innovation.

Rep. Howard Berman (D-Calif.) and I have proposed legislation that would say that something is not novel simply because a known and recognized practice is transported from the physical world to the Internet. The reason that Priceline got its patent, the reason that charitable giving on the Internet was patented, was that something that was well known in the physical world was transported to the Internet and that supposedly made it novel. But the Patent and Trademark Office was of a different view.

A practice is not made novel because it is carried out in a new medium. Simply placing something on the Internet that is known, and known and well understood in the physical world, does not make it novel. But the Patent and Trademark Office was of a different view.

Second, we would provide an opportunity for the PTO to get better information about the current state of the art. The PTO is directed not to award a patent if the subject of the patent is also the subject of "prior art." That is the term of art that is used. But the PTO at the present time does not have very good access to that information. It searches its own database, but because many of these patent applications are not published and we don't know that a patent application is pending, the general public does not have the opportunity to educate the PTO about the existence of prior art.

We would provide that opportunity by requiring that the patent applications be published, and then providing a formal proceeding whereby the patent examiner would receive information from the public about the prior art.

We would then establish a formal opposition proceeding after a patent has been issued. The European Union has an opposition proceeding today, as does Japan. But the United States does not. If you want to challenge a patent once it is issued in our country, you have to go to court. And you have to persuade the court, through a very high standard of proof, by clear and convincing evidence, that the patent examiner was wrong in issuing the patent. And so, even if the majority of the evidence indicates that the patent should not have been awarded, that there was prior art, you are not entitled to win. You have to have overwhelming evidence that there was prior art in order to win.

That is such a high barrier that only rarely is a patent overturned through such a challenge in court. We need a formal administrative opposition proceeding, and we need a standard of proof that reflects reality—and that is merely a preponderance of the evidence that the patent should not have been awarded.

Our bill is strongly opposed by the people who formally represent intellectual property interests in the Congress—the American Bar Association's IP section and the intellectual property owners—who are the most frequent witnesses called before our subcommittee on any matters relating to patent law. It is a rare day indeed when someone who represents user rights is even invited to testify in the Congress.

Online Music in a Post-Napster World

In the post-Napster world Internet users who have become accustomed to downloading music from the Web have two basic and legitimate expectations. One is that music will be available on the Internet for permanent downloading—meaning that when it's downloaded to the hard drive it will stay on the hard drive in perpetuity, until the user decides to erase it. The other is that the music that is downloaded will be portable, meaning that it can be transferred from the hard drive to an MP-3 portable player, a CD, or other kinds of portable devices. That is what people were used to when Napster was alive and kicking.

What is not, in my opinion, a reasonable expectation is that the music will be available for free. Unless compensation flows to the creator of the product, there is not going to be any more product. I think most Americans fundamentally understand this and are willing to pay a reasonable fee if they can get something that meets their legitimate expectation of its being a permanent download and something that is portable and not tethered.

Frankly, I think the only defense that the record companies are going to have against the new generation of peer-to-peer services—the generation that moves beyond Napster, that doesn't have central servers, that is not subject to suit because there is literally nobody to sue—is to make available themselves on the Web the very product that the consumer legitimately expects to be able to receive for a reasonable fee: portable and permanent downloads. But instead of doing that, the record industry is attempting to monopolize distribution of the product on the Web and to dictate the format in which whatever is distributed on the Web will be distributed. It is attempting to monopolize, through MusicNet and Pressplay, the two sites on the Internet that are being formed by the companies that own 80 percent of the world's inventory of recorded music, threatening the day when we will have a vertically integrated duopoly for the distribution of music on the Web.

At the same time, the industry is seeking to dictate the format in which this music will be distributed. The downloads will not be permanent. They will only reside on the hard drive as long as the purchaser continues to pay a monthly subscription fee or in some other way continues to compensate the record company over time; and the downloads will not be portable, they will be tethered.

I don't think these products are, over the long term, going to be acceptable in the market. I think the recording industry is going to find itself, with regard to these new services, rather powerless to respond, because people are simply going to go to Gnutella or FreeNet or some other place to get products that meet their legitimate expectations of permanence and portability. I think the industry eventually will see that. I hope they see it sooner rather than later.

I and my colleague Chris Cannon (R-Utah) have introduced a bill on this subject. We call our bill the Music Online Competition Act (MOCA). Our goal is to provide a caffeine injection for the delivery of music over the Web.

We do a couple of things in this bill that I think are important, including provide a right to make backup copies. If you go on the Web and buy music and put it on your hard drive, you ought to be able to make a backup copy as a prudential measure. My hard drive has crashed occasionally; I suspect that yours has as well. When that happens, you shouldn't have to go back to the Web and pay a fee again in order to restore that music to your hard drive. Common sense suggests that you ought to make a backup copy, and the law ought to accommodate that need.

Current law is curious. It allows you to back up the software that you use in order to put the music on the hard drive. If you are using the RealPlayer or RealJukebox software, for example, you can make a backup copy of that without infringing copyright. But if you try to make a backup copy of the data you have put on your hard disk by using that software, that is a copyright violation. You ought to be able to do both. You ought to be able to back up the music just like you back up the software. Our bill would allow that.

We also provide a mechanism for clearing the rights of songwriters, composers, and publishers. That doesn't work very well under existing copyright law. The major record labels, as well as those we would like to see competing with them and distributing music on the Internet, need this change in the way copyrights are cleared when those copyrights are owned by publishing and composer and songwriter interests.

The most important provision in our legislation is the nondiscrimination provision. It would say that if a record company licenses an affiliated entity the right to distribute its inventory of music on the Internet, it must license other companies that come to it with an offer of the same terms and conditions. So the terms that are extended to the first licensee would be available to competitors who would like to distribute music on the Internet.

There are a number of precedents in the law for doing this. If we don't do it, I am concerned that we are going to have the companies that own 80 percent of the world's music dominating the distribution of music across the Internet and using their copyright interests as a way to leverage a business in a whole other market—the market for distributing the product.

The Justice Department has launched a broad and full-scale antitrust inquiry on whether the launch of MusicNet and Pressplay, which are owned by the companies that own 80 percent of the world's recorded music, constitutes an antitrust violation. I was glad to see the Justice Department's intervention in this matter. The fact that the Justice Department is so interested lends credence to the notion that Chris Cannon and I have put forward—that the law should provide a clear nondiscrimination right for those who seek to compete in distributing music across the Internet.

6. His Napster's Voice

David G. Post

By now, everybody knows the Napster story. Napster, a clever little Internet application invented by a 19-year-old college dropout right out of central casting, is quite simple. It works, more or less, as follows. You download the Napster software. You run the software on your computer. It scans your hard disk and compiles a directory of the names of the music files it finds there. It then sends that directory—not the files themselves, just the *list* of file names—back to Napster's "home" computer, the Napster server, where it is placed into a database, along with the directories of all of the other Napster users who have gone through the same process (70 million or so at its peak).

The next time you (or any of the 70 million) log onto the Internet, your computer, in addition to doing whatever else it is doing, sends a message to the Napster server: "User John Doe here—I've just logged on to the Internet, and my 'Internet Protocol address'—the number my Internet Service Provider has assigned to me so that I can send and receive messages over the Internet—is [255.255.4.11]."[1] The Napster server updates the database with this information, so that, in addition to the names of the music files on each Napster user's hard disk, it now contains information about whether each user is, or is not, currently logged on, and the Internet address of all users who are currently online.

So far, so good. If you then find yourself, on some dark and lonely night, desperate to hear, say, Bob Dylan's version of the Stanley Brothers' classic "Rank Stranger," you send a query to the Napster server: "Does your database list any machines that have a copy of this song? If so, can you please provide me with the list of those that are currently logged onto the Internet—with their IP addresses, if you don't mind?" When the server sends you back that list, the Napster software conveniently lets you send a message directly to any of those machines—because you have their IP addresses you can easily contact them—requesting the file in question; a copy of the file is then transmitted directly from that remote machine to yours.

This simple application was, at least according to some reports, the fastest-growing software application in the (relatively short) history of personal computers.[2] To use it is an intoxicating experience, a glimpse at the extraordinary—the almost unimaginable—power of a truly global network, of the planet's collective mind: If information exists, *anywhere* on earth, you can find it and you can use it. That is a very powerful notion, one that has been lurking around in human consciousness ever since the Library of Alexandria, if not before. We all heard talk, back in 1995 or thereabouts, about the coming of the "celestial jukebox," the instantly downloadable library of songs that would be available at the click of a mouse. Most people, I think it is fair to say, pictured this in Library-of-Alexandria terms: there really would be some big *box*, housed in the basement of an office building in L.A., that we would all be dialing into, some machine with a zillion songs stored on it, owned and operated by Time/Warner, or Sony Music, or EMI, or BMG, or all of them together.

But lo and behold, it didn't happen that way. *The network is the jukebox.* Aha! Like many great ideas, this one is so simple that in retrospect it seems obvious. Why go to the immense trouble and expense of gathering and cataloguing all of the material into a single library? The library already exists—at least bits and pieces of it—scattered in a million different places; it comes into being the moment everyone is given the keys to everyone else's library. A string of code—relatively simple and straightforward code, I'm told—does the trick; the entire network becomes your personal, searchable hard drive.

This is all, of course, old news, last year's headlines. Napster, like some cyberspace algal bloom, or supernova, exploded on the scene, had its 15 minutes of fame (including a *Time* magazine cover story), and burned out some time last year, when a California federal district court shut it down because of copyright violations[3] and the Ninth Circuit Court of Appeals upheld that action.[4] Time to move on to the next new thing and whatever legal puzzles *it* presents to us.

But perhaps we should pause for a moment. One of a law professor's jobs is, on occasion, to resist the temptation to move too quickly, to slow the debate down so we can figure out exactly where we are, how we got there, and where we might be going. Napster's not old news—at least we shouldn't treat it as if it were old news. There are some hard questions here about how copyright law is going to function on the global network, questions that will be with us for a very long time. The Napster case represents one small (though important) excursion into a deep, dark forest. Napster-like functionality will surely reappear in thousands of different guises—it's too powerful for it to be otherwise. We will see many variations on the legal problems it poses, and we will need to understand the ways in which those different variations are the same as Napster (for copyright purposes) and the ways in which they may be different (for copyright purposes).

The "Is"

To start thinking about the relationship between "peer-to-peer" file-sharing technologies (like Napster) and copyright law, we need to distinguish the "is" from the "ought," the "descriptive" from the "prescriptive"—the question "*does* copyright law currently make Napster's activities unlawful?" from the question "*should* copyright law make Napster's activities unlawful?"[5]

Is Napster, Inc., infringing copyright? Although the answer, we all know, is "yes"—at least that's what the headlines ("Napster Loses!") told us when the Ninth Circuit issued its ruling in 2001—the question is a tricky one, for one simple reason: Napster itself never actually makes, and the Napster server never actually stores or redistributes, "copies" of any copyrighted files. All that Napster copies and stores is the (uncopyrightable) list of files already on each user's hard drive. Napster users may, it is true, use Napster's database in order to make infringing copies of copyrighted works[6]—but what makes Napster liable for the infringements of its users? Is the screwdriver salesman liable because his customer chooses to use the screwdriver to burglarize a house?

The record company plaintiffs were, needless to say, aware of this little complication. In their suit, they acknowledged that Napster was not "directly" liable for copyright infringement; instead, they claimed that Napster should be held responsible for the infringing activities of Napster *users* under the doctrine of "contributory copyright infringement."

109

The doctrine of contributory copyright infringement, which dates back to the early part of the 20th century, holds that one who "materially contributes" to the infringing conduct of others with knowledge of the infringements can be held liable for them. The Supreme Court put its imprimatur on the doctrine in 1984, in the "VCR case" (*Sony v. Universal Studios*).[7] *Sony* was similar, at least superficially, to the Napster case; there, too, entertainment industry plaintiffs brought a claim of contributory copyright infringement against the purveyors of a new copying technology—in that case, the videocassette recorder (VCR)—that was being used to make infringing copies of the plaintiffs' copyrighted works (television broadcasts and movies).[8]

The court in *Sony*, however, ruled in favor of the defendant VCR manufacturers, holding that they were *not* contributorily liable for the infringements of VCR users. The rule that the court enunciated was this: manufacturers and distributors of technology that has "substantial *non*-infringing uses"—technology that can be used for lawful copying activities in addition to its potential infringing uses—cannot be held liable under the doctrine of contributory infringement for users' infringing conduct. Because the VCR was used by many people for "time-shifting" televised broadcasts to more convenient viewing times, for example—an activity the court found to be a noninfringing "fair use"—Sony (and the other VCR manufacturers) could continue to distribute VCRs to their customers without permission from (or payment to) the holders of copyright in those broadcasts.

"We're just like the VCR manufacturers," Napster claimed; Napster also has "substantial non-infringing uses," and should therefore be free from copyright liability to the holders of copyright in the music Napster users were distributing to one another.[9] There is, after all, a great deal of original music being written out there for which the authors do *not* assert their rights to prohibit copying and distribution but in fact encourage it; go to MP3.com if you don't believe that. Sharing *those* files is not infringement of copyright. Napster can be used for the transfer of those files, in—at least potentially—substantial numbers.

The district court disagreed: Napster is *not* like the VCR manufacturers, because the noninfringing uses of Napster are *not* substantial—"minimal," in the court's words—in comparison to its infringing uses.[10] The court held that only "substantial or commercially significant use" of the Napster service was "the unauthorized downloading and uploading of popular music, most of which is copyrighted"[11]; other uses—for instance, the "authorized promotion of independent artists, ninety-eight percent of whom are not represented by the record company plaintiffs"—are "not substantial enough" to bring Napster within the protective confines of the *Sony* defense.

The ruling was not just a defeat for Napster; it was, potentially, a crippling blow for the future development of peer-to-peer file-sharing technology. Developers beware: no matter how powerful the sharing technology you come up with, it is your responsibility to make sure that your users are not exchanging copyrighted information—or, at least, to ensure that a more "substantial" part of their activity is devoted to lawful copying activities. No mean feat.

Many of us thought that part of the district court's ruling was plain wrong on this score, and when the Ninth Circuit heard Napster's appeal, it did too. The appeals court reversed the district court on this point; it said that the district court had "improperly confined the use analysis to current uses, ignoring the system's capabilities,"[12] placing "undue weight on the proportion of *current* infringing use as compared to current *and future* noninfringing use."[13] Napster cannot, the Ninth Circuit ruled, be held liable "merely because the structure of its system allows for the exchange of copyrighted material"[14]; to hold it liable "simply because the network allows for infringing use would . . . violate *Sony* and potentially restrict activity unrelated to infringing use."[15] Napster can be held contributorily liable for the infringing conduct of its users only if (a) the copyright holder "provide[s] the necessary documentation" containing "specific information which identifies infringing activity" to give the defendant *"actual* knowledge that *specific* infringing material"[16] is being transmitted using its system; (b) the defendant has the ability "to block access to [its] system by the suppliers of the infringing material," and (c) it "fails to purge such material from [its] system."[17]

This ruling, to be sure, was of scant comfort to Napster itself, because the court went on to find that the record companies *had* given Napster "actual notice" of infringing activity by Napster users, having identified "more than 12,000 infringing files" that had appeared in Napster's database; Napster, therefore, *did* have *"actual* knowledge that *specific* infringing material" was being transmitted using its system.[18] Because it also had the ability "to block access to [its] system by the suppliers of the infringing material," and had "fail[ed] to purge such material from [its] system,"[19] the injunction against its continuing operation was allowed to stand.

But the ruling was, nonetheless, of critical importance for the future development of these technologies. It placed the initial burden on the copyright holders themselves; the plaintiffs had to identify the *specific* infringing files being shared over the Napster system, the names of the copyright holders, and a "certification that [they] own or control the rights allegedly infringed"[20] before Napster can be deemed liable for the exchange of those files by its users. That is not a trivial burden, as evidenced by the continued wrangling between the parties after the Ninth Circuit ruling concerning the precise way that the record companies can sustain that burden.[21] More importantly, though, while it may have shut the door forever on Napster itself, it left other doors open for the development of other kinds of peer-to-peer file-sharing technology. The rule the court formulated—no liability for developers and distributors of these technologies without both *"actual* knowledge that *specific* infringing material"* is being transmitted using their systems and the ability "to block access to [their] systems by the suppliers of the infringing material"—virtually assures the continued development and deployment of systems that will accomplish the peer-to-peer magic without those characteristics. Napster was liable because it maintained a central database of song listings (and therefore had the ability to remove offending material once it was identified as such by the record companies). Predictably, many second-generation peer-to-peer technologies—gnutella, morpheus, and FreeNet technologies, for example[22]—design around this legal impediment, allowing peer-to-peer sharing without the need for central databases.

It ain't over, like the man says, till it's over.

The "Ought"

If that, then, is the "is," what about the "ought"? What *should* copyright law say about Napster? Is this the copyright law we want? How do we figure *that* out?

The first task, when faced with complicated and difficult questions like this one, is to try to unpack them into their difficult, and their not-so-difficult, components, to tease apart the complicated thicket of legal questions into those that are easy (the answers to which we all might be able to agree on quickly), and those that are hard (the answers to which will be more difficult to come by). This will allow us to focus on the latter and to begin the task of figuring out what to do about them.

Here's an easy question. Suppose we were trying to come up with a copyright law applicable *only* to information created and distributed on the global network: what would that law look like? Suppose, just for argument's sake, that there was an impenetrable boundary between the world of atoms—"Over Here"—and the world of bits—"Over There"—and that information *cannot move* across that boundary, that information can appear Over There only if created Over There and vice versa.

I am well aware that this is a fantasy, that there is no such boundary, that information moves easily back and forth from analog to digital to analog, from cyberspace to realspace and back. That is, indisputably, reality. Knowledge, though, as Kierkegaard said, sometimes consists of "translating the real into the probable"[23]; let's indulge in this thought experiment and put reality aside for the moment—there will be plenty of time to reintroduce it later. If we pretend that there *is* such a boundary, what copyright law would we think would be best Over There, on the *other* side of the border?

An easy question? I think it is—at least it is if you look at copyright rights as "instrumental" rights. From an "instrumentalist" perspective, the rights bestowed by copyright law are not "natural rights" that must, in that sense, appear in any just legal system; rather, they are rights that are granted for one very specific purpose: to increase society's overall stock of creative works. Thomas Jefferson's remains the clearest and most elegant formulation of the position:

> It has been pretended by some ... that inventors have a natural and exclusive right to their inventions, and not merely for their own lives, but inheritable to their heirs. But while it is a moot question whether the origin of any kind of property is derived from nature at all, it would be singular to admit a natural ... right to inventors. ...
>
> Stable [property] ownership is the gift of social law, and is given late in the progress of society. It would be curious then, if an idea, the fugitive fermentation of an individual brain, could, of natural right, be claimed in exclusive and stable property. *If nature has made any one thing less susceptible*

113

than all others of exclusive property, it is the action of the thinking power called an idea, which an individual may exclusively possess as long as he keeps it to himself; but the moment it is divulged, it forces itself into the possession of every one, and the receiver cannot dispossess himself of it. Its peculiar character, too, is that no one possesses the less, because every other possesses the whole of it. He who receives an idea from me, receives instruction himself without lessening mine; as he who lights his taper at mine, receives light without darkening me.

That *ideas should freely spread from one to another over the globe,* for the moral and mutual instruction of man, and improvement of his condition, seems to have been peculiarly and benevolently designed by nature, when she made them, like fire, expansible over all space, without lessening their density in any point, and like the air in which we breathe, move, and have our physical being, incapable of confinement or exclusive appropriation.[24]

Ideas, in other words, "cannot, *in nature,* be a subject of property."

Society may give an exclusive right to the profits arising from them, as an encouragement to men to pursue ideas which may produce utility, but this may or may not be done, according to the will and convenience of the society, without claim or complaint from any body.[25]

This "instrumentalist" view is by no means universal; many European copyright regimes, for example, are founded on the opposite presupposition, the notion that copyright exists primarily to protect authors' natural rights—the "droit moral," as the French put it. I make no attempt here to persuade you that the instrumentalist view is the better one—my point is just that it is the instrumentalist view that underlies U.S. copyright law.

As we all learn in Copyright 101, U.S. law gives legal protection to creative expression in order to induce creative activity—in the words of the U.S. Constitution, "to promote the progress of Science and the useful Arts"[26]—giving creators an incentive to produce new works of authorship by promising them an opportunity to profit from their labors via a property right, and hence a market, in their works. We tolerate the "monopoly" that we grant to these creative artists because, and to the extent that, it is a means to that end. We seek in our copyright law the right balance, the optimum point, between protection that is "too strong" (i.e., protection that reduces creative output by making it difficult for authors to borrow from previously created works) and protection that is too weak (i.e., protection that does not give authors enough of an incentive to invest the time and energy required into producing works of value).

So, back to our (supposedly) easy question: how much copyright protection do we need to induce creative activity Over There, on our hermetically sealed global network?

To answer this question, we would like to know what cyberspace would look like as a "copyright-free zone." Fortunately, we have been conducting—inadvertently, to be sure—a little natural experiment over the past decade or so to help us answer this question. We know how much creative activity we'd get if there were little or no copyright protection in cyberspace, because there has been, in effect, little or no copyright protection in cyberspace. As the recording industry itself keeps reminding us, copyrights are routinely flouted on the global network, copyright "piracy" is rampant Over There; nobody in his right mind would voluntarily make information available on the global network in the expectation that copyright law will protect that information (and any lawyer who has been advising clients otherwise is probably guilty of malpractice).

So a "copyright-free" cyberspace would look much like what cyberspace looks like today.

And what does it look like? It looks to me like the greatest outpouring of creative activity in a short span of time that the world has ever seen. The Internet itself, let us not forget, is only a quarter century or so old, and it has been all of eight years since the World Wide Web was loosed upon an unsuspecting world. I can't prove that (any more than I could prove its opposite, that we would have seen *more* creative activity had there been more legal protection for that activity). All I know is that cyberspace keeps growing and growing; more and more stuff keeps appearing, in new guises and new shapes; there are more and more people trying to give me information to place in my computer than I have room for. Look at my desktop: real time stock quotes, the weather in five preselected cities, news headlines from Reuters and the Associated Press, the complete works of Thomas Jefferson, the latest scores from the English Premier League, maps of the city of my choice, maps of the distribution of information in cyberspace, powerful search tools, and more. I'm one click away from a lot of pretty interesting stuff—all at a marginal cost to me of zero. And all this *without* any substantial legal protection for that information.

It was fortunate that we actually conducted this natural experiment because without it the conventional wisdom would have assured us that it could never happen. Without any incentive to create provided by strong property rights, we surely would have said, there will be no creative activity out Over There. Cyberspace will become, and remain, just a vast wasteland.

But somehow that's not what happened. Perhaps we don't understand everything there is to understand about the need for intellectual property protection. Perhaps the world is trying to tell us something, that this is a new kind of place where things that worked well in the world of atoms don't work so well. Perhaps in *these* special circumstances—in a medium built upon the ability of machines to copy and to disseminate information at previously unimaginable speeds, with previously unimaginable efficiency, and at a previously unattainable low cost—there are other ways that creative activity can be stimulated.

Eben Moglen of Columbia Law School puts it more elegantly (and colorfully):

> In a world of digital products that can be copied and moved at no cost, traditional distribution structures [that] depend on the ownership of the content or of the right to distribute are fatally inefficient.[27]
>
> As John Guare's famous play has drummed into all our minds, everyone in society is divided from everyone else by at most six degrees of separation.[28] Let's not concentrate on the precise number, but on the fact it reveals: the most efficient distribution system in the world is to let everyone give music to whomever they know who would like it. When music has passed through six hands under the current distribution system, it hasn't even reached the store. When it has passed through six hands in a system that doesn't require the distributor to buy the right to pass it along, . . . it has reached several million listeners. This increase in efficiency means that composers, song-writers and performers have everything to gain from making use of the system of unowned or anarchistic distribution. . . .
>
> "Incentives" is merely a metaphor, and as a metaphor to describe human creative activity it's pretty crummy. [T]he

better metaphor arose on the day Michael Faraday first noticed what happened when he wrapped a coil of wire around a magnet and spun the magnet. Current flows in such a wire, but we don't ask what the incentive is for the electrons to leave home. We say that the current results from an emergent property of the system, which we call induction. The question we ask is "what's the resistance of the wire?" So Moglen's Metaphorical Corollary to Faraday's Law says that if you wrap the Internet around every person on the planet and spin the planet, software flows in the network. It's an emergent property of connected human minds that they create things for one another's pleasure and to conquer their uneasy sense of being too alone. The only question to ask is, what's the resistance of the network? Moglen's Metaphorical Corollary to Ohm's Law states that the resistance of the network is directly proportional to the field strength of the "intellectual property" system.[29]

We can surely discuss *why* all this is happening (and have an interesting discussion in the process), but it seems to me very difficult to deny that it *is* happening.

Thinking about cyberspace as a copyright-free zone[30] might not come naturally to most of us, but it sure comes naturally to my kids (and probably to yours, too). And remember: they get to write the rules soon. As the plaintiff record companies put it in their brief to the Ninth Circuit, "If the perception of music as a free good becomes pervasive, it may be difficult to reverse."[31] Indeed.

What good, though, is any of this talk? A "bordered cyberspace" would flourish without strong copyright protections: So what? What if it were true, *if* there were an impenetrable boundary between Over There and Over Here, that we might not need much in the way of intellectual property protection Over There in order to induce creative activity Over There? There is no such border; what good is it to talk as if there were? Where has this little thought experiment gotten us?

Further along than it might appear, I suggest. Thinking about the question in this way doesn't make the problems disappear, but it does turn them into *different* problems. There *is* a "Napster problem," but it is not that people are using the remarkable new tools at their disposal in this remarkable new place to accomplish previously

117

unimaginable feats of information sharing and information redistribution; *that is not a problem at all, that is the solution to a problem,* the problem of finding better ways to get more information more quickly to more people.

The "Napster problem" is not that information is being shared but that information is being *smuggled*—across the border, from realspace to cyberspace (and, somewhat more metaphorically, from the past to the future). The problem is created by the permeability of the boundary, by the ease with which people can transfer information from Over Here—the songs, say, of Jerry Lieber and Ben Stoller,[32] or Metallica[33]—and move it Over There, onto the global network, where it can be placed into the remarkable and remarkably efficient Over There distribution system.

The RIAA is at least partially correct: There *is* something unfair about this. We made a bargain with Lieber and Stoller: Write and publish your songs, and you will be compensated each time a copy is made of a recording of each of those songs. They kept their end of the bargain, and now we're breaking ours.

Solving the "Napster problem," then, might not necessarily mean figuring out ways to impose an unnecessary copyright regime on the information circulating on the global network; it might mean figuring out ways to reduce the incidence of smuggling, and/or to compensate those whose works are being smuggled, across the border into cyberspace. It means focusing our attention on devising ways that copyright can continue to do its work (if and where it is needed) and can disappear (if and where it is not).

What we need—and what, if I were working for the RIAA, I'd focus my efforts on—are ways to build better borders, tools for making the boundary between realspace and cyberspace more impermeable. It sounds like a task that is either ridiculous or impossible, but it is neither. We actually once had a very nice little "border-construction tool"—it was called the "copyright notice requirement," a requirement that information had to bear an identifying label if it was to be protected. Unlabelled = unprotected. It would be far, far easier to patrol the border if protected information were labeled in this way.

Oddly enough, though, we got rid of that labeling requirement some time ago—just, some might argue, when we needed it most.[34]

Cryptographically based protection schemes to prevent unauthorized access to, and movement of, information are another kind of

border-construction tool, another means of creating more impermeable boundaries between the worlds of protected and unprotected
information. If Metallica wants to "lock up" its performances in
completely unbreakable cryptographic envelopes, and charge me
outrageous prices to access them, I say: more power to them. A
clearer boundary between protected and unprotected information
universes will allow us to see—not just to speculate about, but
actually to observe—the extent to which copy protection really *is*
necessary to stimulate creativity. I happen to think that the world
of unprotected information will grow much more luxuriantly than
its counterpart, that precisely because creativity *will* flourish where
reuse and redistribution are most widely permitted we'll find it less
and less necessary to spend time on the other side of *that* border.

But I might be wrong about that; perhaps accessing the really
good stuff will require a trip across the line. Time will tell—but it
will tell.[35]

Another place I'd look if I were trying to solve this problem is to
Charles Dickens.[36] Dickens, it turns out, was as angry about border
permeability and copyright smuggling as Metallica or Lieber and
Stoller are. Dickens' works, too, were being taken without his permission across a border—the border between the United Kingdom and
the United States—and, over on the Other Side, they were being
freely reproduced and distributed without compensation to him.
Interestingly enough, it wasn't even truly "smuggling," because U.S.
copyright law, in the 19th century, gave absolutely *no protection
whatsoever* to works created Over There, on the other side of the U.S.
border. It was, in other words, perfectly lawful to bring Dickens'
works across the U.S. border and to reproduce and distribute them
at will. (Sound familiar?)

International copyright relations have always reflected a simple
opposition between net copyright exporters (favoring reciprocal recognition of foreign copyrights) and net copyright importers (resist-
ing such recognition). In Professor Paul Goldstein's words, "If Country A imports more literary and artistic works from Country B than
it exports to Country B, it will be better off denying protection to
works written by Country B's authors even if that means foregoing
protection for its own writers in Country B."[37] The first copyright
exporters (like Great Britain and France) were happy to offer protection to the works of foreign authors, provided *their* authors were

given reciprocal protections. The United States, on the other hand, was in its early days primarily an *importer* of copyrighted works, and U.S. copyright policy was designed precisely to promote the development of infant copyright industries within the United States. Providing copyright protection *only* for American authors would, it was widely believed, work to the advantage of the growing American publishing industry, because American publishers could publish cheap versions of foreign (especially British) works since they were not obligated to pay royalties to the (foreign) authors when they did so.

These protectionist provisions of the U.S. Copyright Act were relatively uncontroversial for the first 40 years or so, and the American publishing industry did in fact grow (at least partly due to these protections). Dickens and other prominent British authors did not take kindly to their treatment at the hands of the Americans, and they complained bitterly, and quite publicly, about the injustice of this arrangement.[38] As the 19th century proceeded, however, *domestic* voices began to be heard in support of the recognition of foreign copyrights. The first formal proposal to recognize international copyright and to remove the discrimination against foreign authors was made in 1837 by Senator Henry Clay—one of America's most influential Congressmen and a future Presidential candidate—in the much-publicized "Clay Report." Clay argued that *American* interests were harmed, not benefited, by the absence of recognition for foreign copyrights; whatever benefits American *publishers* might be reaping by virtue of the ability to reprint foreign works at low cost, Clay suggested, was offset by the benefits that American *authors* would reap by an extension of copyright to the works of foreigners. Soon thereafter, many of the most distinguished American authors and artists—including Louisa May Alcott, William Cullen Bryant, George William Curtis, Ralph Waldo Emerson, Horace Greeley, Oliver Wendell Holmes, William Dean Howells, Henry Longfellow, Harriet Beecher Stowe, and John Greenleaf Whittier—began to speak out on behalf of copyright protection for their foreign counterparts.

It sounds like a paradox: What did American authors have to gain by an extension of copyright protection to the works of their counterparts—their competitors—in other countries? The answer is twofold.

First, American authors were finding that *their* works, though protected by copyright in the United States, were hard-pressed to compete with inexpensive editions of foreign works; Why pay a dollar for the work of American authors like Herman Melville or Nathaniel Hawthorne when you can get the latest Dickens or Trollope for half that price or less? Second, U.S. authors found that they were being harmed by discriminatory treatment directed against them in foreign markets; other nations were—understandably—reluctant to give copyright protection to American authors when the United States was denying copyright protection to their authors, and American authors were accordingly frustrated in their attempts to market their works overseas.

This battle was fought where all battles about policy in a democratic society are fought: in the court of public opinion. The American people (and the U.S. Congress) ultimately were persuaded that Dickens' copyrights should be respected Over Here. In 1891—101 years after enactment of the first U.S. Copyright statute—the U.S. Congress passed the International Copyright Act, granting, for the first time, protection to foreign works.

The moral of the story? Border construction is a long and complicated process, unlikely to satisfy those looking for a quick fix. Only when Napster users believe that it is in *their* interest to grant recognition to the "foreign" copyrights held by Lieber and Stoller will they do so. Only when there is a constituency for reciprocal copyright recognition Over There, among cyberspace's new Hawthornes, Melvilles, and Emersons, will we see it. There may be things we can do to speed that process up; taking our cue from Dickens, a policy of nonrecognition of *cyberspace* copyrights here in realspace, for example, under which we might deny copyright protection Over Here for software and systems developed Over There, might be an interesting place to start.

I can't solve this problem; I can only point out that it's there. Borders are always as real as we want them to be, and the future is (always) just beginning.

Notes

Thanks to Shannon Burke for research assistance with this article. A version of this paper is forthcoming in the *Temple Environmental and Technology Law Journal*.

1. For nontechnical discussions of the Internet Protocol addressing scheme see, for example, A. Michael Froomkin, "Wrong Turn in Cyberspace: Using ICANN to Route around the APA," *Duke Law Journal* 50 (2000): 17 (personal.law.miami.edu/~froomkin/articles/icann-main.pdf); David J. Loundy, "A Primer on Trademark Law and

Internet Addresses," 15 *John Marshall Journal of Computer and Information Law* 15 (1997): 465 (www.loundy.com/JMLS-Trademark.html); Jonathan Weinberg, "ICANN and the Problem of Legitimacy," *Duke Law Journal* 50 (2000): 187; Milton Mueller, "Technology and Institutional Innovation: Internet Domain Names," *International Journal of Communications Policy* 5 (2000): 1; Jay P. Kesan and Rajiv C. Shah, "Fool Us Once Shame on You—Fool Us Twice Shame on Us: What We Can Learn from the Privatizations of the Internet Backbone Network and the Domain Name System," *Washington University Law Quarterly* 79 (2001): 89.

2. Simon Crerar, "Websites of the Year," *Sunday Times* (London), December 31, 2000; News in Brief, *Chicago Sun-Times*, September 12, 2000, p. 3.

3. *A&M Records, Inc.* v. *Napster, Inc.*, 114 F. Supp.2d 896 (N.D.Cal. 2000), *aff'd*, 239 F.3d 1004 (9th Cir. 2001) (hereinafter "*Napster* I").

4. *A&M Records, Inc.* v. *Napster, Inc.*, 239 F.3d 1004 (9th Cir. 2001), *aff'g*, 114 F.Supp.2d 896 (N.D.Cal. 2000) (hereinafter "*Napster* II").

5. "Is" and "ought" questions are related to each other, of course; the meek may not inherit the earth, but the next generation surely will, and one characteristic of a democratic society is that the "ought" sometimes becomes the is, that processes exist whereby people can bring the law as it is into closer conformity with what they believe it should be.

6. There are a number of contrary arguments that can be made, based on either the "fair use doctrine" or other provisions of the Copyright Act, that Napster users themselves are not infringing copyright when they share music files for their own "personal use," but we can pass over those arguments for the time being.

7. *Sony v. Universal Studios*, 464 U.S. 417 (1984), supct/cases/464us417.htm.

8. The entertainment industry had launched a public campaign to suggest that the VCR was about to destroy the very foundations of the industry, that tumbleweed would soon be blowing through the streets of Hollywood if the VCR were not brought under control. See Glynn S. Lunney, Jr., "Reexamining Copyright's Incentives-Access Paradigm," *Vanderbilt Law Review* 49 (1996): 483. They were, in fact, wrong; the industry learned how to live with that technology (and its "substantial non-infringing uses") quite comfortably. And notice, too, this nice twist: Sony, Inc., is pitching a 2–0 shutout thus far—having won both as one of the copyright *defendants* in *Sony v. Universal* and as one of the copyright *plaintiffs* in *A&M Records et al. v. Napster*.

9. The briefs and court opinions in the *A&M v. Napster* litigation can be found at www.napster.com/pressroom/legal.html and at www.riaa.com/Legal.cfm.

10. Napster I, 114 F. Supp. 2d 896 at 912 (2000).

11. Ibid.

12. *Napster II*, 239 F.3d at 1021.

13. Ibid. (emphasis added) (citing *Vault Corp. v. Quaid Software Ltd.*, 847 F.2d 255 (5th Cir. 1988).

14. *Napster II*, 239 F.3d at 1021 (citing *Sony Corp. v. Universal City Studios, Inc.*, 464 U.S. 417 (1984)).

15. Ibid., p. 1021.

16. Ibid., pp. 1021–22 (emphasis in original).

17. Ibid.

18. Ibid.

19. Ibid., pp. 1021–22 (citing *Religious Technology Center v. Netcom On-Line Communication Services, Inc.*, 907 F. Supp. 1361, 1371 [N.D.Cal. 1995]).

20. Order filed in March 2001 by the Northern District of California complying with the Ninth Circuit Opinion at 2, *A&M Records, Inc.* (No. C 99-05183 MHP, MDL No. C 00-1369 MHP), news.findlaw.com/cnn/docs/napster/napster030601ord.pdf.

21. As of this writing (February 2002), the Napster litigation has been suspended at the request of both sides, to allow the parties to continue settlement discussions and to avoid what Recording Industry Association of America General Counsel Cary Sherman called "more burdensome" litigation. Matt Richtel, "Judge Grants a Suspension of Lawsuit on Napster," *New York Times*, January 24, 2002, p. C4.

22. See David P. Anderson and John Kubiatowicz, "The Worldwide Computer," *Scientific American*, March 2002, pp. 40–47, and references therein, for a general description of a variety of different peer-to-peer file-sharing technologies, including gnutella (www.gnutella.com and www.gnutellaworld.com), Freenet (http://freenet-project.com), Mojo Nation (www.mojonation.com), KaZaA (www.kazaa.com/en/index.htm), and Morpheus (www.musiccity.com). According to various reports, these services quickly exceeded Napster's popularity at its peak. See Matt Richtel "Free Music Service Is Expected to Surpass Napster," *New York Times*, Nov 29, 2001, p. C4. Shortly after the Ninth Circuit ruling in the Napster case, the RIAA launched a series of lawsuits against a number of these services as well. See Scarlet Pruitt, "Recording, Movie Industries Sue Napster Progeny," www.cnn.com/2001/TECH/industry/10/07/recording.sues.idg/ (October 7, 2001).

23. See W. H. Auden, ed., *The Living Thoughts of Kierkegaard* (New York: New York Review of Books, 1952): p. 113.

24. Thomas Jefferson to Isaac MacPherson, August 13, 1813, reprinted in Thomas Jefferson, *Writings* (New York: Library of America, 1984), p. 1286; see www.geocities.com/tjletter/ home.html for an annotated version of this letter.

25. Ibid.

26. U.S. Constitution, Art. I, Sec. 8 ("The Congress shall have Power . . . to promote the Progress of Science and the useful Arts, by securing for limited Times to Authors and Inventors the exclusive Right to their respective Writings and Discoveries").

27. Eben Moglen, "LiberationMusicology," www.thenation.com/doc.mhtml?i = 20010312&s = moglen. Moglen continues:

Hundreds of potential 'business models' remain to be explored once the proprietary distributor has disappeared, no one of which will be perfect for all artistic producers, but all of which will be the subject of experiment in decades to come, once the dinosaurs are gone. . . . [The] wholesale defection from the existing distribution system is about to begin, leaving the music industry—like manuscript illuminators, piano-roll manufacturers, and letterpress printers—a quaint and diminutive relic of a passé economy.

28. See Duncan Watts, *Small Worlds* (Princeton, N.J.: Princeton University Press, 2001), for a summary of recent research on "small world" network phenomena.

29. Eben Moglen, "Anarchism Triumphant: Free Software and the Death of Copyright," emoglen.law.columbia.edu/publications/anarchism.html.

30. Early suggestions that cyberspace might function best as a copyright-free zone came from John Perry Barlow, "The Economy of Ideas," *Wired*, March 1994, p. 84, and Jessica Litman, "Revising Copyright Law for the Information Age," *Oregon Law Review* 75 (1996): 19, 30.

31. Brief of Plaintiffs/Appellees at 32, *A&M Records, Inc. v. Napster, Inc.*, 239 F.3d 1004 (9th Cir. 2001) (Nos. 00-16401, 00-16403); news.findlaw.com/cnn/docs/napster/riaa/napster09082000. pdf.

32. Lieber and Stoller were two of the plaintiffs in the *A&M v. Napster* litigation, as well as two of America's greatest songwriters, the authors of such classics as "Love Potion Number Nine," "Yakety Yak," "Charley Brown," "On Broadway," "Spanish Harlem," "There Goes My Baby," "Stand By Me," and "Jailhouse Rock." See nfo.net/.CAL/tl3.html.

33. Metallica took a particularly aggressive public stance against Napster. See, for example, "Metallica Unmasks Music-Swapping Fans," May 4, 2000, www.usatoday.com/life/cyber/tech/review/crh110.htm.

34. As a condition of its accession to the Berne Convention on Artistic and Literary Property, the United States prospectively eliminated the copyright notice requirement from its domestic law on March 1, 1989. See Copyright Act, Sec. 401 (17 U.S.C. Sec. 401, as amended) ("Whenever a work protected under this title is published in the United States or elsewhere by authority of the copyright owner, a notice of copyright as provided by this section *may* be placed on publicly distributed copies from which the work can be visually perceived . . .") (emphasis added); see, generally, *Nimmer on Copyright*, Sec. 7.02 ("Statutory Formalities").

35. The Napster litigation may actually bring us closer to accomplishing that goal, precisely because of the nuances introduced by the Ninth Circuit. The perception of music as a free good *has* become pervasive; that's the good news. The record companies wanted a ruling that would have declared peer-to-peer file-sharing technology unlawful until the border was properly constructed. That's what they got from the district court, in effect: a ruling that peer-to-peer systems could not operate lawfully unless and until Napster could demonstrate that its users were not sharing copyrighted information. But that's not what they got from the Ninth Circuit. What they got from the Ninth Circuit was a ruling that placed the burden on them—on the copyright holders—to identify the specific instances in which the border had been breached.

36. This argument is presented in more detail in David G. Post, "Some Thoughts on the Political Economy of Intellectual Property: A Brief Look at the International Copyright Relations of the United States," www.temple.edu/lawschool/dpost/Chinapaper.html. It is taken primarily from Thorvald Solberg, "The International Copyright Union," *Yale Law Journal* 36 (1926): 68; Paul Goldstein, *Copyright's Highway: From Gutenberg to the Celestial Jukebox* (New York: Hill and Wang, 1994); and Julian Warner, "Information Society or Cash Nexus? A Study of the United States as a Copyright Haven," *Journal of the American Society for Information Science* 50 (1999): 461.

37. Paul Goldstein, *Copyright's Highway: From Gutenberg to the Celestial Jukebox*, p. 181.

38. Dickens devoted much of his public tours of the United States in 1841–42 and 1867 to this subject; Anthony Trollope, in 1868, wrote "The argument . . . is that American readers are the gainers—that as they can get for nothing the use of certain property, they would be cutting their own throats were they to pass a law debarring themselves from the power of such appropriation. . . . In this argument all idea of honesty is thrown to the winds. . . . [T]his argument, as far as I have been able to judge, comes not from the people, but from the book-selling leviathans, and from those politicians whom the leviathans are able to attach to their interests."

7. Revising Copyright Law for the Information Age

Jessica Litman

When we examine the question whether copyright needs redesign to stretch it around digital technology, we can look at the issues from a number of different vantage points. First, there is the viewpoint of current copyright stakeholders: today's market leaders in copyright-affected industries. Their businesses are grounded on current copyright practice; their income streams rely on current copyright rules. Most of them would prefer that the new copyright rules for new copyright-affecting technologies be designed to enable current stakeholders to retain their dominance in the marketplace.[1]

One way to do that is to make the new rules as much like the old rules as possible. Current copyright holders and the industries they do business with are already set up to operate under those rules: they have form agreements and licensing agencies and customary royalties in place. There are other advantages in using old rules: If we treat the hypertext version of the *New York Times* as if it were a print newspaper, then we have about 200 years worth of rules to tell us how to handle it. We can avoid the problems that accompany writing new rules, or teaching them to the people (copyright lawyers, judges, newspaper publishers) who need to learn them.

Using old rules, however, has the obvious disadvantage that the rules will not necessarily fit the current situation very well. Where the new sorts of works behave differently from the old sorts of works, we need to figure out some sort of fix. Here's a simple example: Newsstands turn out to be an effective way of marketing newspapers and magazines in part because it is difficult as a practical matter to make and distribute additional copies of newspapers and magazines that one buys from the newsstand. If one "buys" a newspaper by downloading it from the World Wide Web, on the other hand, it is pretty easy to make as many copies as one wants. The old rules, customs, and practices, therefore, will not work very well unless we can come up with a way to prevent most of those copies from getting made. Relying on old rules encourages us to solve the problem that the World Wide Web is not like a newsstand by disabling some of its non-newsstand-like qualities. We could enact rules requiring the proprietors of Web pages to set them up to behave much more like newsstands; we could demand that they insert code in each of their documents that would prevent downloading or would degrade any downloaded copies; we could require modem manufacturers to install chips that disabled the transfer of digital data unless some credit card were charged first.

But why would we want to do that? Adopting rules that disable new technology is unlikely to work in the long term, and unlikely to be a good policy choice if it does work. We have tried before to enact laws that erect barriers to emerging technology in order, for policy reasons, to protect existing technology. The Federal Communications Commission did precisely that when it regulated cable television to the point of strangulation in order to preserve free broadcast TV. That particular exercise didn't work for very long.[2] Others have been more successful. Direct broadcast satellite television subscriptions still lag far behind cable television subscriptions in the United States, and no small part of the reason is that our current legal infrastructure makes it much more difficult for direct satellite broadcasters than for cable operators or conventional broadcasters.[3]

If our goal in reforming current law were to make things more difficult for emerging technology, in order to protect current market leaders against potential competition from purveyors of new media, then cleaving to old rules would be a satisfactory, if temporary, solution. Adhering to old rules might distort the marketplace for new technology for at least the short term (since that, after all, would be one of its purposes), which might influence how that technology developed in the longer term, which, in turn, might influence whether and how the affected industries would compete in the markets for those technologies in the future. It would probably delay the moment at which the current generation of dominant players in information and entertainment markets were succeeded by a new generation of dominant players in different information and entertainment markets.

If instead of looking at the situation from the vantage point of current market leaders, we imagined the viewpoint of a hypothetical benevolent despot with the goal of promoting new technology, we might reach an entirely different answer to the question. Such a being might look at history and recognize that copyright shelters and exemptions have, historically, encouraged rapid investment and growth in new media of expression. Player pianos took a large bite out of the markets for conventional pianos and sheet music after courts ruled that making and selling piano rolls infringed no copyrights; phonograph records supplanted both piano rolls and sheet music with the aid of the compulsory license for mechanical reproductions; the jukebox industry was created to exploit the 1909 Act's copyright exemption accorded to the "reproduction or rendition of a musical composition by or upon coin-operated machines." Radio broadcasting invaded everyone's living rooms before it was clear whether unauthorized broadcasts were copyright infringement; television took over our lives while it still seemed unlikely that most television programs could be protected by copyright. Videotape rental stores sprang up across the country shielded from copyright liability by the first sale doctrine. Cable television gained its initial foothold with the aid of a copyright exemption, and displaced broadcast television while sheltered by the cable compulsory license.[4]

Why would a copyright exemption promote development? Conventional wisdom tells us that, without the incentives provided by copyright, entrepreneurs will refuse to invest in new media. History tells us that they do invest without paying attention to conventional wisdom. A variety of new media flourished and became remunerative when people invested in producing and distributing them first, and sorted out how they were going to protect their intellectual property rights only after they had found their markets. Apparently, many entrepreneurs conclude that if something is valuable, a way will be found to charge for it, so they concentrate on getting market share first, and worry about profits—and the rules for making them—later. The sort of marketplace that grows up in the shelter of a copyright exemption can be vibrant, competitive, and sometimes brutal. Some prospectors will seek to develop market share on a hunch; others from conviction. Still others may aim only to generate a modestly valuable asset that will inspire some bigger fish out there to eat them. In any event, new products may be imagined, created, tested, and introduced, and new media may be explored. Fierce competition is not very comfortable, but it can promote the progress of science nonetheless.

In addition, by freeing content providers from well-established rules and customary practices, a copyright shelter allows new players to enter the game. The new players have no vested interest—yet—so they are willing to take more risks in the hope of procuring one. They end up exploring different ways of charging for value. Radio and television broadcast signals are given to their recipients for free; broadcasters have figured out that they can collect money based on the number and demographics of their audiences. Many valuable software programs obtained their awesome market share by being passed on to consumers at no extra cost (like Microsoft Windows®), or deliberately given away as freeware (like AOL® or Netscape®). Other software programs may well have achieved their dominant market position in part by being illicitly copied by unlicensed users. Indeed, industry observers agree that at least half of all of the copies of software out there are unauthorized, yet the software market is booming; it is the pride of the U.S. Commerce Department. Perhaps all of the unauthorized copies are part of the reason.

Our hypothetical benevolent despot, then, might propose a temporary period during which the Internet could be a copyright-free zone. Nobody seems to be making that sort of proposal these days, so perhaps I am mistaken about what a wise ruler would view as good policy. Or perhaps all the benevolent despots in the neighborhood are off duty, on vacation, or just simply hiding. Perhaps they've sought alternate employment.

A number of other viewpoints are possible. I'd like to focus on a third: The classic formulation of copyright as a bargain between the public and copyright holders.[5] In the efforts to enact the Digital Millennium Copyright Act, stakeholders focused almost exclusively on the copyright holders' side of that bargain. Copyright owners, however, have never been entitled to control all uses of their works. Instead, Congress has accorded copyright owners some exclusive rights, and reserved other rights to the general public. Commonly, copyright theorists assess the copyright bargain by asking whether it provides sufficient incentives to prospective copyright owners.[6] Yet, economists tell us that, at the margin, there is always an author who will be persuaded by a slight additional incentive to create another work, or who will be deterred from creating a particular work by a diminution in the copyright bundle of rights. If we rely on the simple economic model, we are led to the conclusion that every enhancement of the rights in the copyright bundle is necessary to encourage the creation of *some* work of authorship.

Asking "What should copyright holders receive from this bargain? What do they need? What do they want? What do they deserve?" then, may be less than helpful. We might instead look at the other side of the equation, and ask, "What is it the public should get from the copyright bargain? What does the public need, want, or deserve?" The public should expect the creation of more works, of course, but what is it that we want the public to be able to do with those works?

The constitutional language from which Congress's copyright enactments flow describes copyright's purpose as "[t]o promote the Progress of Science and useful Arts." We can begin with the assertion that the public is entitled to expect *access* to the works that copyright inspires. That assertion turns out to be controversial. Public access is surely not necessary to the progress of science. Scientists can build on each others' achievements in relative secrecy. Literature may flourish when authors have the words of other authors to fertilize their own imaginations, but literature may thrive as well when each author needs to devise her own way of wording. If we measure the progress of science by the profits of scientists, secrecy may greatly enhance the achievements we find.

Still, if valuable works of authorship were optimally to be kept secret, there would be no need for incentives in the copyright mold of exclusive rights. Authors could rely on self-help to maintain exclusive control of their works. Copyright makes sense as an incentive if its purpose is to encourage the dissemination of works, in order to promote public access to them. It trades a property-like set of rights precisely to encourage the holders of protectable works to forgo access restrictions in aid of self-help. For much of this country's history, public dissemination was, except in very limited circumstances, a condition of copyright protection.[7] While no longer a condition, it is still fair to describe it as a goal of copyright protection.[8]

But why is it that we want to encourage dissemination? What is it we want the public to be able to do with these works that we are bribing authors to create and make publicly available? We want the public to be able to read them, view them, and listen to them. We want members of the public to be able to learn from them: to extract facts and ideas from them, to make them their own, and to be able to build on them. That answer leads us to this question: how can we define the compensable units in which we reckon copyright protection to provide incentives (and, since the question of how much incentive turns out to be circular, let's not worry about that for now) for creation and dissemination, while preserving the public's opportunities to read, view, listen to, learn from, and build on copyrighted works?

In 1790, Congress struck this balance by limiting the compensable events within the copyright owner's bundle of rights to printing, reprinting, publishing, and vending copyrighted works.[9] (That translates, in current lingo, into an exclusive right to make, distribute, and sell "copies."[10]) Public performances, translations, adaptations, and displays were all beyond the copyright owner's control. Courts' constructions of the statute supplied further limitations on the copyright owner's rights. The statutory right to vend was limited by the first-sale doctrine.[11] The statutory right to print and reprint did not apply to translations and adaptations,[12] did not prevent others from using the ideas, methods, or systems expressed in the protected works,[13] and, in any event, yielded to a privilege to make fair use of copyrighted works.[14]

Congress, over the years, expanded the duration and scope of copyright to encompass a wider ambit of reproduction, as well as translation and adaptation, public for-profit performance, and then public performance and display. It balanced the new rights with new privileges: Jukebox operators, for example, enjoyed an exemption from liability for public performance for more than fifty years, and were the beneficiaries of a compulsory license for another decade after that.[15] Other compulsory licenses went to record companies, cable television systems, satellite carriers, and noncommercial television.[16] Broadcasters received exemptions permitting them to make "ephemeral recordings" of material to facilitate its broadcast; manufacturers of useful articles embodying copyrighted works received a flat exemption from the reproduction and distribution rights to permit them to advertise their wares. Libraries received the benefit of extensive privileges to duplicate copyrighted works in particular situations. Schools got an express privilege to perform copyrighted works publicly in class; music stores got an express privilege to perform music publicly in their stores; and small restaurants got an express privilege to perform broadcasts publicly in their restaurants.[17] Congress did not incorporate specific exemptions for the general population in most of these enactments because nobody showed up to ask for them.[18] At no time, however, until the enactment of the access-control anti-circumvention provisions of the DMCA, did Congress or the courts cede to copyright owners control over looking at, listening to, learning from, or *using* copyrighted works.

The right "to reproduce the copyrighted work"[19] is commonly termed the fundamental copyright right. The control over the making of copies is, after all, why this species of intellectual property is called a *copy*right. So it is tempting, and easy, to view the proliferation of copying technology as threatening copyright at its core. However we revise the copyright law, many argue, we need to ensure that the copyright owner's control over the making of every single copy of the work remains secure. This is especially true, the argument continues, where the copies are digitally created and therefore potentially perfect substitutes for the original.[20]

Copyright holders have long sought to back up their legal control of reproduction with functional control. In the 1970s, copyright owners sought without success to prohibit the sale of videocassette recorders.[21] In the 1980s, copyright owners succeeded in securing a legal prohibition on rental of records or computer software to forestall, it was said, the unauthorized copying that such rental was likely to inspire.[22] In the 1990s, copyright owners and users groups compromised on the adoption of the Audio Home Recording Act,[23] which, for the first time, required that recording devices be technologically equipped to prevent serial copying. The Digital Millennium Copyright Act incorporated language prohibiting *any* devices or services designed to circumvent technological protection. Supporters of the anti-circumvention provisions insisted that technological protection was the only feasible way to prevent widespread, anonymous digital copying.[24] The popular justification for giving copyright owners the legal right to control access to their works is that unauthorized access can lead to a ruinous proliferation of unauthorized copies. The underlying premise of the anti-circumvention approach appears to be the notion that the right to make copies is central to the integrity of the copyright system, and must be protected by any available means.

131

The right to make copies, though, is not fundamental to copyright in any sense other than the historical one. When the old copyright laws fixed on reproduction as the compensable (or actionable) unit, it was not because there is something fundamentally invasive of an author's rights about making a copy of something. Rather, it was because, at the time, copies were easy to find and easy to count, so they were a useful benchmark for deciding when a copyright owner's rights had been unlawfully invaded. Unauthorized reproductions could be prohibited without curtailing the public's opportunities to purchase, read, view, hear, or use copyrighted works. They are less useful measures today. Unauthorized copies have become difficult to find and difficult to count. In addition, now that copyright owners' opportunities to exploit their works are as often as not unconnected with the number of reproductions, finding and counting illicit copies is a poor approximation of the copyright owners' injury.

The reasons that copyright owners might have for wanting to treat reproduction as a fundamental copyright right are obvious. By happenstance (at least from the vantage point of 1790, or 1870, or even 1909 or 1976), control over reproduction could potentially allow copyright owners control over every use of digital technology in connection with their protected works. This is not what the Congresses in 1790, 1870, 1909, and 1976 meant to accomplish when they awarded copyright owners exclusive reproduction rights. The photocopy machine was not invented until the baby boom. Printing presses used to be expensive. Multiple reproduction was, until very recently, a chiefly commercial act. Pegging authors' compensation to reproduction, therefore, allowed past Congresses to set up a system that encouraged authors to create and disclose new works while ensuring the public's opportunities to read, view, or listen to them, learn from them, share them, improve on them, and, ultimately, reuse them. Today, making digital reproductions is an unavoidable incident of reading, viewing, listening to, learning from, sharing, improving, and reusing works embodied in digital media. The centrality of copying to use of digital technology is precisely why reproduction is no longer an appropriate way to measure infringement.

As recently as the 1976 general copyright revision, the then-current state of technology permitted Congress to continue its reliance on the exclusive reproduction right by enacting a lot of arcane, hypertechnical rules and exceptions, at the behest of all of the stakeholders who argued that they required special treatment. That did not pose major problems because very few people needed to understand what the rules were, and many if not most of them could afford to hire lawyers. Unauthorized reproduction was illegal, said the rules, unless you were a "library or archives," a "transmitting organization entitled to transmit to the public a performance or display of a work," a "government body or other nonprofit organization," or a "public broadcasting entity"; or unless you were advertising "useful articles that have been offered for sale," "making and distributing phonorecords," or making pictures of a building "ordinarily visible from a public place."[25] Those entitled to exemptions knew who they were and knew what limitations their privileges entailed.

We no longer live in that kind of world. Both the threat and promise of new technology center on the ability it gives many, many people to perform the 21st century equivalents of printing, reprinting, publishing, and vending. Copyright owners all over want the new, improved rules to govern the behavior of all citizens, not just major players in the copyright-affected businesses. And, since anyone who watches citizen behavior carefully to detect copyright violations can easily find enough to fill up her dance card in an afternoon, copyright owners have taken to the argument that citizens must be *compelled* to obey the rules, by installing technology that makes rule breaking impossible for the casual user and difficult for the expert hacker. Otherwise, they've argued, there's no hope of everyone's obeying the law.

Well of course not. How could they? They don't understand it, and how could we blame them? It isn't a particularly easy set of rules to understand, and even when you understand it, it's very hard to argue that the rules make any sense—or made any sense, for that matter, when they were written. What nobody has tried, or even proposed, is that we either scrap the old set of rules, or declare the general citizenry immune from them, and instead devise a set of rules that, first, preserve some incentives for copyright holders (although not necessarily the precise incentives they currently enjoy); second, make some sense from the viewpoint of individuals; third, are easy to learn; and fourth, seem sensible and just to the people we are asking to obey them.

The first task, then, in revising copyright law for the new era, requires a very basic choice about the sort of law we want. We can continue to write copyright laws that only copyright lawyers can decipher, and accept that only commercial and institutional actors will be likely to comply with them, or we can contrive a legal structure that ordinary individuals can learn, understand, and even regard as fair. The first alternative will take of itself: The Clinton Administration appointed a Task Force in 1993 to generate administration policy on networked digital technology. The Task Force's Working Group on Intellectual Property, chaired by Patent Commissioner Bruce Lehman, produced a "white paper" report two years later, recommending that Congress enact laws enhancing copyright protection for works in digital form. That legislative proposal inspired precisely the sort of log-rolling that has achieved detailed and technical legislation in the past,[26] and culminated in the swollen DMCA. The second alternative is more difficult. How do we define a copyright law that is short, simple, and fair?

If our goal is to write rules that individual members of the public will comply with, we need to begin by asking what the universe looks like from their vantage point. Members of the public, after all, are the folks we want to persuade that copyright is just and good and will promote the progress of science. They are unlikely to think highly of the Lehman Working Group's argument that they need to secure permission for each act of viewing or listening to a work captured in digital form. They are unlikely to appreciate the relentless logic involved in concluding that, while copyright law permits the owner of a copy to transfer that copy freely, the privilege does not extend to any transfer by electronic transmission.[27] They are unlikely to be persuaded that the crucial distinction between lawful and unlawful activity should turn on whether something has been reproduced in the memory of some computer somewhere.

If we are determined to apply the copyright law to the activities of everyone, everywhere, then I suggest that the basic reproductive unit no longer serves our needs, and we should jettison it completely.[28] That proposal is radical: If we stop defining copyright in terms of reproduction, we will have to rethink it completely. Indeed, we will need a new name for it, since *copy*right will no longer describe it. What manner of incentive could we devise to replace reproduction as the essential compensable unit?

The public appears to believe that the copyright law incorporates a distinction between commercial and noncommercial behavior. Ask nonlawyers, and many of them will tell you that making money using other people's works is copyright infringement, while noncommercial uses are all okay (or, at least, okay unless they do terrible things to the commercial market for the work).[29] Now, that has never, ever been the rule but, as rules go, it isn't a bad start. It isn't very far from the way, in practice, the rules have actually worked out. Noncommercial users rarely get sued and, when they do, tend to have powerful fair use arguments on their side. Moreover, if it is a rule that more people than not would actually obey because it struck them as just, we would be a long way toward coming up with a copyright law that would actually work. So why not start by recasting copyright as an exclusive right of commercial exploitation? Making money (or trying to) from someone else's work without permission would be infringement, as would large-scale interference with the copyright holders' opportunities to do so. That means that we would get rid of our current bundle-of-rights way of thinking about copyright infringement. We would stop asking whether somebody's actions resulted in the creation of a "material object . . . in which a work is fixed by any method now known or later developed,"[30] and ask instead what effect those actions had on the copyright holder's opportunities for commercial exploitation.[31]

Such a standard is easy to articulate and hard to disagree with in principle. The difficulty lies in predicting how it would work out in practice. Routine free use of educational materials by educational institutions seems like a good example of the sort of noncommercial use that should be classed as "large-scale interference" with copyright holders' commercial opportunities.[32] On the other hand, the fact that a particular individual's viewing or copying of a digital work might itself supplant the sale of a license to view or copy if such licenses were legally required should count neither as making money nor as large-scale interference with commercial opportunities. Under this standard, individual trading of MP3 files would not be actionable, but Napster's activities would be, despite the fact that Napster collects no money for its service or software. Other users, though, would need at least initially to be evaluated individually. So general a rule would necessarily rely on case-by-case adjudication for embroidery. One significant drawback of this sort of standard, then, is that it would replace the detailed bright lines in the current statute with uncertainty.[33] But the bright lines Congress gave us embody at least as much uncertainty, although it is uncertainty of a different sort. The detailed bright lines have evolved, through accident of technological change, into all-inclusive categories of infringers with tiny pockmarks of express exemptions and privileges, and undefined and largely unacknowledged free zones of people-who-are-technically-infringing-but-will-never-get-sued, like your next-door neighbor who duplicates his wife's authorized copy of Windows 98® rather than buying his own. The brightness of the current lines is illusory.

Giving copyright holders the sole right to exploit commercially or authorize the commercial exploitation of their works is a more constrained grant than the current capacious statutory language. It removes vexing (if rarely litigated) everyday infringements, like your neighbor's bootleg copy of Windows 98®, from the picture entirely. Is surgery that radical necessary? Probably not. It would, however, have some significant advantages.

First, to the extent that current constructions of the reproduction right have shown a rapacious tendency, their proponents commonly defend them on the ground that a single isolated unauthorized digital copy can devastate the market for copyrighted works by enabling an endless string of identical illegal copies. Sometimes they explain that a single harmless copy would never give rise to a lawsuit. If that's so, copyright owners lose nothing of value by trading in their reproduction rights for exclusive control over commercial exploitation. If the danger of an unauthorized copy is that it might ripen into a significant burden on the commercial market, then defining that harm as an actionable wrong will address the danger without being over inclusive.

Moreover, the common law interpretative process we would necessarily rely on to explicate a general standard unencumbered by all of the detailed exceptions in the current statute is better set up to articulate privileges and limitations of general application than our copyright legislative process has proved to be. While judicial lawmaking may not succeed very well, very often, at arriving at sensible solutions, the process constrains it to try to draw lines that make sense. The public is more likely to accept lines drawn by drafters who are attempting to make sense. And the public's involvement, as jurors, in drawing these lines just might allow us to incorporate emerging social copyright norms into the rules we apply.

Finally, once we abolished the detailed, specific exemptions in the current law, the industries that have been able to rely on them would need to seek shelter within the same general limitations on which the rest of us depend. It is common for large copyright-intensive businesses to insist that they are *both* copyright owners and copyright users, and that they are therefore interested in a balanced copyright law.[34] They typically fail to mention that unlike the vast majority of copyright users, and unlike new start-up copyright-affected businesses, they were able to negotiate the enactment of detailed copyright privileges. In most cases, those privileges both gave them what they believed at the time they would need, and also, if they were clever or lucky, were drafted with enough specificity to prove unhelpful to new, competing media that might crawl out of the woodwork in the future. Eliminating current stakeholders' structural advantages from the copyright law would do much to restore a more durable balance.

In addition to separating copyright owners from a useful tool for overreaching, abandoning the reproduction right in favor of a right of commercial exploitation would have the benefit of conforming the law more closely to popular expectations. That would ease enforcement and make mass education about the benefits of intellectual property law more appealing.

I don't suggest for a minute that limiting copyright's exclusive rights to a general right of dissemination for commercial gain will solve all of the problems I have raised for the public's side of the copyright bargain. Most obviously, copyright holders will rely, as they have in the past, on mechanisms outside of the copyright law to enhance their control over their works. The technological controls reified by the Digital Millennium Copyright Act are one such mechanism.[35] Adhesion contracts purporting to restrict users' rights as part of a license are another.[36] Indeed, one of the most important items on the content industry's continuing agenda seems to be the reinforcement of efforts to find contract law work-arounds for privileges that current copyright law accords to users.[37] Even if the copyright grant is narrowed in scope, the public will need some of *its* rights made explicit.

For example, the public has had, under traditional copyright law, and should have, a right to read. Until recently, this wasn't even questionable. Copyright owners' rights did not extend to reading, listening, or viewing any more than they extended to private performances. The Lehman Working Group, though, seized on the exclusive reproduction right as a catch-all right that captures every appearance of any digital work in the memory of a computer. The white paper insisted that it applied to private individuals as well as commercial actors.[38] The recording industry's recent litigation strategy reflects that view. Invocation of the fair use privilege to exempt private, temporary copying from the reach of the current statute is not much help, because one needs a hideously expensive trial to prove that one's actions come within the fair use shelter. More importantly, content owners are increasingly enclosing their works within technological copy protection, and have thus far succeeded in arguing that fair use can never be a defense to suits for circumvention.[39] Recasting copyright as a right of commercial exploitation will do much to solve that problem, since consumptive or incidental use would almost never come within the scope of the redefined right. Still, principles are important, and it is easy to argue that facilitating individual consumptive uses significantly interferes with the copyright owner's opportunities to charge individuals for each incident of use. The public needs and should have a right to engage in copying or other uses incidental to a licensed or legally privileged use. So, let's make the right explicit. If temporary copies are an unavoidable incident of reading, we should extend a privilege to make temporary copies to all.

Further, the public has always had, and should have, a right to cite. Referring to a copyrighted work without authorization has been and should be legal. Referring to an infringing work is similarly legitimate. This was well settled until the world encountered hypertext linking. The fear that hypertext links enabled people to find and copy unauthorized copies inspired lawsuits claiming that linking to infringing works was itself piracy. Drawing a map showing where an infringing object may be found or dropping a footnote that cites it invades no province the copyright owner is entitled to protect even if the object is blatantly pirated from a copyrighted work. Posting a hypertext link should be no different. If the only way to offer effective protection for works of authorship is to prevent people from talking about infringing them, then we're finished before we even start.

Moreover, until the enactment of the DMCA, the public had, and the public should have, an affirmative right to gain access to, extract, use, and reuse the ideas, facts, information, and other public domain material embodied in protected works. That affirmative right should include a limited privilege to circumvent any technological access controls for that purpose, and a privilege to reproduce, adapt, transmit, perform, or display so much of the protected expression as is required in order to gain access to the unprotected elements.[40] Again, both long copyright tradition and case law[41] recognize this right, but the new prohibitions on circumvention of technological access protection threaten to defeat it. Copyright owners have no legitimate claim to fence off the public domain material that they have incorporated in their copyrighted works from the public from whom they borrowed it, so why not make the *public's* rights to the public domain explicit?

Finally, the remarkable plasticity of digital media has introduced a new sort of obstacle to public dissemination: Works can be altered, undetectably, and there is no way for an author to insure that the work being distributed over her name is the version she wrote. My proposal to reconfigure copyright as a right of commercial exploitation would certainly not solve this problem; indeed, it would exacerbate it. Authors of works adapted, altered, misattributed, or distorted in noncommercial contexts would have only limited recourse under a commercial exploitation right.[42] The fear of rampant alteration has inspired some representatives of authors and publishers to insist that the law give copyright holders more control over their digital documents, over access to those documents, and over any reproduction or distribution of them. Only then, they argue, will their ability to prevent alterations give them the security they need to distribute their works in digital form. That solution is excessive; as framed in current proposals, it would give copyright holders the means to prohibit access to or use of the contents of their works for any reason whatsoever. As sympathetic as we may find creators' interest in preserving their works from distortion, that interest is not so weighty that it impels us to sacrifice long-standing principles ensuring public access. Fortunately, there is a more measured alternative.

Most countries who have acceded to the most important international copyright treaty, the Berne Convention for the Protection of Literary and Artistic Works, protect authors' interests in assuring the integrity of the works they create. American lawmakers have always found the notion hard to swallow. Although the United

States, as a signatory to Berne, has undertaken the obligation to protect authors' interests in assuring the continuing integrity of their works,[43] it has followed up only in token ways.[44] Some copyright owners view integrity rights as a dangerous opportunity for individual authors to interfere with the exploitation of works by the copyright owners and licensees. Some copyright experts view integrity rights as yet another way that authors exert unwarranted control over the uses of their works.

The United States, however, could address the distinct problems posed by digital media while avoiding those concerns. We could adopt a narrowly tailored safeguard that framed the integrity right to meet the particular threats posed by digital technology. Authors have a legitimate concern, and that concern is often shared by the public. Finding the authentic version of whatever document you are seeking can in many cases be vitally important. Moreover, while traditional Berne integrity rights include the ability to prohibit mutilations and distortions, digital media gives us the opportunity to devise a gentler solution: any adaptation, licensed or not, commercial or not, should be accompanied by a truthful disclaimer and a citation (or hypertext link) to an unaltered and readily accessible copy of the original. That suffices to safeguard the work's integrity, and protects our cultural heritage, but it gives copyright owners no leverage to restrict access to public domain materials by adding value and claiming copyright protection for the mixture.

The most compelling advantage of encouraging copyright industries to work out the details of the copyright law among themselves, before passing the finished product on to a compliant Congress for enactment, has been that it produced copyright laws that the relevant players could live with, because they wrote them. If we intend the law to apply to individual end users' everyday interaction with copyrighted material, however, we will need to take a different approach. Direct negotiation among industry representatives and a few hundred million end-users would be unwieldy (even by copyright legislation standards). Imposing the choices of the current stakeholders on a few hundred million individuals is unlikely to result in rules that the new majority of relevant players find workable. They will not, after all, have written them.

If the overwhelming majority of actors regulated by the copyright law are ordinary end-users, it makes no sense to insist that each of them retain copyright counsel in order to fit herself within niches created to suit businesses and institutions, nor is it wise to draw the lines where the representatives of today's current stakeholders insist they would prefer to draw them. Extending the prescriptions and proscriptions of the current copyright law to govern the everyday acts of noncommercial, noninstitutional users is a fundamental change. To do so without affecting a drastic shift in the copyright balance will require a comparably fundamental change in the copyright statutory scheme. If we are to devise a copyright law that meets the public's needs, we might most profitably abandon copyright law's traditional reliance on reproduction, and refashion our measure of unlawful use to better incorporate the public's understanding of the copyright bargain.

Notes

From Jessica Litman, *Digital Copyright*, pp. 166–191 (Amherst, NY: Prometheus Books, 2001). Reprinted by permission of the publisher.

1. Note, here, that we are talking not only about author-stakeholders, or publisher-stakeholders, but also about collecting-agency-stakeholders. A report issued in 1994 suggested that an electronic transmission of a musical recording should be treated as a distribution of a copy of that recording rather than as a performance of the recording. That recommendation proved to be the single most controversial proposal among conventional copyright-affected stakeholders. On one side of the dispute were the record companies and the Harry Fox Agency, which collects composers' royalties for the sale of recordings. On the other side were ASCAP, BMI, and SESAC, which collect composers' royalties for the public performance of music. The composer would have gotten the royalties either way, but the collecting entity's cut would have gone to a different stakeholder. See *Public Hearing at Andrew Mellon Auditorium before the Information Infrastructure Task Force Working Group on Intellectual Property Rights*, September 23, 1994, pp. 19–22 (testimony of Stu Gardner, composer); pp. 25–28 (testimony of Michael Pollack, Sony Music Entertainment); pp. 28–31 (testimony of Marilyn Bergman, ASCAP); pp. 31–33 (testimony of Hillary Rosen, Recording Industry Association of America); pp. 33–38 (testimony of Frances Preston, BMI); pp. 38–43 (testimony of Edward Murphy, National Music Publishers' Association).

2. See Jonathan Weinberg, "Broadcasting and the Administrative Process in Japan and the United States," *Buffalo Law Review* 39 (1991): 615, 694–700.

3. See Jessica Litman, "Copyright Legislation and Technological Change," *Oregon Law Review* 78 (1989): 275, 342–46; Hearing Regarding Copyright Licensing Regimes Covering Retransmission of Broadcast Signals before the Subcommittee on Courts and Intellectual Property of the House Judiciary Committee, 105th Cong., 1st sess., Oct. 17, 1997.

4. See Litman, *Digital Copyright*, pp. 106–107.

5. See, for example, *Sony Corp. of America v. Universal City Studios*, 464 U.S. 417, 429 & n.10 (1984) (quoting H.R. Rep. No. 2222, 60th Cong., 2d sess. [1909]).

141

6. See, for example, Rochelle Cooper Dreyfuss, "The Creative Employee and the Copyright Act of 1976," *University of Chicago Law Review* 54 (1987): 590; Jane C. Ginsburg, "Creation and Commercial Value: Copyright Protection of Works of Information," *Columbia Law Review* 90 (1990): 1865, 1907–16; Wendy J. Gordon, "Fair Use as Market Failure: A Structural and Economic Analysis of the Betamax Case and Its Predecessors," *Columbia Law Review* 82 (1982): 1600; Linda J. Lacey, "Of Bread and Roses and Copyrights," *Duke Law Journal* (1984): 1532.

7. The 1976 Copyright Act extended federal statutory copyright to unpublished works. Before that, copyright protection was available for published works and for works, such as lectures or paintings that were typically publicly exploited without being reproduced in copies. See generally William F. Patry, *Copyright Law and Practice* 1 (1994): 414–21.

8. See L. Ray Patterson, "Copyright and the 'Exclusive Right' of Authors," *Journal of Intellectual Property Law* 1 (1993): 1, 37.

9. Act of May 31, 1990, cg. 15, § 1, 1 Stat. 124.

10. See 17 U.S.C. § 106(1), (3) (1994).

11. *Bobbs Merrill v. Strauss*, 210 US 339 (1908); *Harrison v. Maynard, Merril & Co*, 61 F. 689 (2d Cir. 1894). The first-sale doctrine allows the owner of any lawful copy of a work to dispose of that copy as she pleases.

12. *Stowe v. Thomas*, 23 F. Cas. 201 (C.C.E.D. Pa 1853) (No. 13,514); *Kennedy v. McTammany*, 33 F. 584 (C.C.D. Mass. 1888).

13. *Baker v. Selden*, 101 U.S. 99 (1879).

14. See *Folsom v. Marsh*, 9 F. Cas. 342 (C.C.D. Mass 1841) (No. 4,901).

15. See 2 Patry, supra note 8, at 971–87.

16. See 17 U.S.C. §§ 111, 115, 118, 119 (1994).

17. See ibid. §§ 108, 110 (1), 110(5), 110(7), 112, 113(c).

18. There is one, sort of. Section 1008 includes a provision, enacted as part of the Audio Home Recording Act of 1992, that bars infringement suits "based on the noncommercial use by a consumer" of an audio recording device for making "musical recordings." 17 U.S.C. § 1008 (1994). The provision carefully omits any statement that such recordings are not infringement, and was demanded by the consumer electronics industry as a condition for supporting the Audio Home Recording Act.

19. 17 U.S.C. § 106(1).

20. See Jane C. Ginsburg, "Essay: From Having Copies to Experiencing Works: The Development of an Access Right in U.S. Copyright Law," in *U.S. Intellectual Property: Law and Policy*, ed. Hugh Hansen (London: Sweet & Maxwell, 2000).

21. See *Sony Corporation of America v. Universal City Studios*, 464 U.S. 417 (1984); Hearing on Home Recording of Copyrighted Works before the Subcommittee on Courts, Civil Liberties and the Administration of Justice of the House Judiciary Committee, 97th Cong., 2d sess., 1982.

22. Record Rental Amendment of 1984, Pub. L. No. 98-450, 98th Cong., 2d sess., 98 Stat. 1727 (1984); Computer Software Rental Amendments of 1990, Pub. L. No. 101-650, 101st Cong., 2d sess, 104 Stat. 5089, 5134–37 (1990) (codified at 17 U.S.C. § 109 (1994)). See generally Patry 2, supra note 8, at 842–62.

23. Audio Home Recording Act of 1992, Pub. L. No. 102-563, 102d Cong., 2d sess., 106 Stat. 4237 (1992). See Audio Home Recording Act of 1991: Hearing on H.R. 3204 before the Subcommittee on Intellectual Property and Judicial Administration of the House Committee on the Judiciary, 102d Cong., 2d sess., 1993.

24. See, for example, Marybeth Peters, Register of Copyrights, Testimony on NII Copyright Protection Act of 1995: Hearing on H.R. 2441 before the Subcommittee on Courts and Intellectual Property of the House Committee on the Judiciary, 104th Cong., 1st sess., Nov. 15, 1995.

> The Copyright Office supports the concept of outlawing devices or services that defeat copyright protection systems. One of the most serious challenges to effective enforcement of copyright in the digital environment is the ease, speed and accuracy of copying at multiple, anonymous locations. In order to meet this challenge, copyright owners must rely on technology to protect their works against widespread infringement. But every technological device that can be devised for this purpose can in turn be defeated by someone else's ingenuity. Meaningful protection for copyrighted works must therefore proceed on two fronts: the property rights themselves, supplemented by legal assurances that those rights can be technologically safeguarded.

25. See 17 U.S.C. §§ 108, 112(a), 112(b), 113(c), 115, 118, 120.

26. Compare S. 1121, 104th Cong., 1st sess., 1995, with S. 2037, 105th Cong., 2d sess., 1998.

27. The white paper's explanation of why this should be so seems particularly unpersuasive:

> Some argue that the first sale doctrine should also apply to transmissions, as long as the transmitter destroys or deletes from his computer the original copy from which the reproduction in the receiving computer was made. The proponents of this view argue that at the completion of the activity, only one copy would exist between the original owner who transmitted the copy and the person who received it—the same number of copies at the beginning. However, this zero sum gaming analysis misses the point. The question is not whether there exist the same number of copies at the completion of the transmission or not. The question is whether the transaction when viewed as a whole violates one or more of the exclusive rights, and there is no applicable exception from liability. In this case, without any doubt, a reproduction of the work takes place in the receiving computer. To apply the first sale doctrine in such a case would vitiate the reproduction right.

Information Infrastructure Task Force, Intellectual Property and the National Information Infrastructure: The Report of the Working Group on Intellectual Property Rights, pp. 93–94 (1995) (hereinafter white paper).

28. The discussion in this chapter completely omits the immense practical difficulties in getting such a proposal enacted into law, over the presumed antagonism of current copyright stakeholders, and in apparent derogation of our obligations under international copyright treaties. Other copyright lawyers who have gone along with my argument thus far are invited to leave the bus at this station.

29. See, for example, Office of Technology Assessment, U.S. Congress, Intellectual Property Rights in an Age of Electronics and Information 121-23, 121–22, 209 (1986); see generally The Policy Planning Group, Yankelovich, Skelly & White, Inc., Public Perceptions of the "intellectual Property Rights" Issue (1985) (OTA Contractor Report). That ethos seems to be behind the public's ambivalent attitude toward Napster: sharing music files is cool, but the sheer scale of Napster has persuaded many that its operation must be illegitimate. See, for example, Catherine Greenman, "Taking Sides in the Napster War," *New York Times*, Aug. 31, 2000, p. D1.

30. 17 U.S.C. § 101 (1994).

31. As an illustration, consider the case of Robert LaMacchia. Mr. LaMacchia was unsuccessfully prosecuted under the wire fraud statute for providing a computer bulletin board where users uploaded and downloaded unauthorized copies of commercially published software. See *U.S. v. LaMacchia,* 871 F. Supp. 535 (D. Mass. 1994). LaMacchia had no commercial motive and gained no commercial advantage by this activity, but his bulletin board made it possible for some number of people who might otherwise have purchased authorized copies of software to obtain unauthorized copies for free. Congress has amended the copyright law to ensure that people like Robert LaMacchia can be successfully prosecuted for criminal copyright infringement from now on. See No Electronic Theft (NET) Act, Pub. L. No. 105–147, 111 Stat. 2678 (1997). Under the standard I propose, that activity would be infringement only if copyright holders demonstrated to the trier of fact that LaMacchia's BBS worked a large-scale interference with their marketing opportunities. Merely proving that if such activities were to become widespread (because of the similar activities of lots of individuals like LaMacchia) they would have potentially devastating marketing effects, on the other hand, would not satisfy the standard.

32. For a contrary view, see Jane C. Ginsburg, "Putting Cars on the 'Information Superhighway:' Authors, Exploiters and Copyrights in Cyberspace," *Columbia Law Review* 95 (1995): 1466, 1478–79. Professor Ginsburg argues that because the private copying market has supplanted traditional distribution, even temporary individual copying in cyberspace will impair the copyright owner's rights, although she concedes that fully enforcing those rights may be impractical. Ibid. That copyright holders have recently begun to exploit the market for licenses to make individual copies, however, tells us little about the scope of their entitlement to demand such licenses under current law, and even less about whether a revised law should extend to such claims. See *Michigan Document Services v. Princeton University Press,* 74 F.3d 1512, 1523 (6th Cir. 1996) ("It is circular to argue that a use is unfair, and a fee therefore required, on the basis that the publisher is therefore deprived of a fee."), *vacated en banc,* 74 F.3d 1528 (6th Cir. 1996).

33. There is a substantial literature on the relative merits of rules and standards. See, for example, Jonathan Weinberg, "Broadcasting and Speech," *California Law Review* 81 (1993): 1110.

34. See, for example, William Barwell, Times Mirror Company, Testimony, Public Hearing at University of California Los Angeles before the Information Infrastructure Task Force Working Group on Intellectual Property, September 16, 1994, p. 22.

35. See Pamela Samuelson, Intellectual Property and the Digital Economy: Why the Anti-Circumvention Regulations Need to Be Revised, *Berkeley Technology Law Journal* 14 (1999): 519.

36. See, for example, Mark A. Lemley, "Intellectual Property and Shrinkwrap Licenses"; Steven Metalitz, "The National Information Infrastructure"; Pamela Samuelson, "Legally Speaking: Software Compatibility and the Law," *Communications of the ACM* 38 (August 1995): 15, 20. The National Conference of Commissioners on Uniform State Laws has proposed that every state adopt a complicated uniform law to assist sellers of digital information products by permitting them to bind purchasers to the terms of form licenses that have, up until now, been deemed by many courts to be unenforceable. The Uniform Computer Information Transactions Act would make it possible for content owners to restrict consumers' uses of both copyright-protected and uncopyrightable material contained in digital works by denominating transactions related to those works as "licenses." Supporters of UCITA explain that

it would make users' rights under copyright irrelevant by permitting sellers to require a waiver of those rights as a condition of access. See generally "Symposium: Intellectual Property and Contract Law in the Information Age: The Impact of Article 2B of the Uniform Commercial Code on the Future of Transactions in Information and Electronic Commerce," *Berkeley Technology Law Journal* 13 (1998): 809; and *California Law Review* 87 (1999): 1.

37. See white paper, supra note 28, pp. 49–59.

38. See ibid., pp. 64–66.

39. See *Universal Studios v. Reimerdes*, 111 F. Supp. 2d 294, 324 (S.D.N.Y. 2000); *Universal Studios v. Reimerdes*, 82 F. Supp. 2d 211 (S.D.N.Y. 2000).

40. See, for example, Julie E. Cohen, "Copyright and the Jurisprudence of Self-Help," *Berkeley Technology Law Journal* 13 (1998): 1089.

41. *Baker v. Selden*, 101 U.S. 99 (1879); *Sega Enterprises, Ltd. v. Accolade, Inc.*, 977 F.2d 1510 (9th Cir. 1993); *Atari Games, Inc. v. Nintendo of America*, 975 F. 2d 832 (Fed. Cir. 1992).

42. Such noncommercial alteration would be actionable only if it worked a large-scale interference with the author's ability to exploit the work commercially. Authors of works that are not intended for commercial distribution and that are commercially distributed without authorization would, of course, be able to recover, but authors whose works are adapted, misattributed, or altered for personal, private, or limited noncommercial consumption would not.

43. "Integrity right" is a term of art for an author's right to object to or prevent mutilation or gross distortions of protected works. See generally Edward J. Damich, "The Right of Personality: A Common-Law Basis for the Protection of the Moral Rights of Authors," *Georgia Law Review* 23 (1988): 1, 15–23. The Berne Convention, a treaty the United States ratified in 1989, requires its members to protect authors' moral rights, including integrity rights. The United States has relied chiefly on the Lanham Trademark Act, 15 U.S.C. §§ 1051–1127 (1994), to fulfill those obligations. The integrity right I propose is probably more consonant with the Lanham Act's approach to trademark issues than the Copyright Act's approach to authorship rights in any event. For a different spin on integrity rights and the Internet, see Mark A. Lemley, "Rights of Attribution and Integrity in Online Communications," *Journal of Online Law*, art. 2 (1995).

44. See Visual Artists Rights Act, codified at 17 U.S.C. § 106A.

8. How Copyright Became Controversial

Drew Clark

How did copyright become controversial? In a phrase, the Digital Millennium Copyright Act (DMCA). Although many of the legal controversies that have swirled since its October 1998 passage trace their roots to other elements of copyright law, the DMCA created a new feature in copyright law that has crystallized why so many academics, librarians, computer users, and technology entrepreneurs object to what they regard as the overreaching nature of copyright law. That signal feature is the ban on the cracking of encryption codes used by content owners to restrict access to digital works on which they hold copyrights.

Now encoded in Section 1201 of the Copyright Act, the statute reads: "No person shall circumvent a technological measure that effectively controls access to a work protected under this title" (17 U.S.C. 1201(a)(1)(A)). The definitions of those terms are broad enough to bar almost all unauthorized decryption of content. Subsequent language in the section also prohibits the manufacture, release, or sale of products, services, and devices that can crack encryption designed to thwart either access to or copying of material unauthorized by the copyright holder.

In other words, for the first time in history, it isn't the copyright violation that is the crime. It is the creation of the technological tools to violate copyright that has become the crime.

The law germinated from a 1995 white paper drafted by Bruce Lehman, the first patent office chief and intellectual property guru in the Clinton administration. Heavily supported by copyright holders, the key rationale behind the white paper was that content owners would be unwilling to put their content in digital form were it not for new laws against those who defeat the digital locks they place on their products. The anti-circumvention concept gained momentum in 1996 when it was endorsed in a World Intellectual Property Organization Copyright Treaty. It was subsequently adopted as

DMCA's Title I, the WIPO Copyright and Performance and Phonograms Treaties Implementation Act.

Critics of current copyright law point to many expansions in its power over the past decade. Among the more recent measures are the Digital Performance Right in Sound Recording Act of 1995 (creating a new copyright in digital music performances), the No Electronic Theft Act of 1997 (eliminating noncommercial use as a defense against copyright infringement), the Sonny Bono Copyright Term Extension Act of 1998 (adding 20 years to the already-lengthy terms of all copyrights), portions of the DMCA mandating new royalties for digital music performances, and the Digital Theft Deterrence and Copyright Damages Improvement Act of 1999 (stiffening penalties for infringement). There are a few measures that arguably limit the power of copyright holders, including the Fairness in Music Licensing Act of 1998 (granting a limited exemption from music licensing for food service and drinking establishments) and elements of the DMCA that limited Internet service provider liability for copyright infringement if they comply with procedures to take down allegedly infringing material from Web sites they control.

Some of those changes in law are directly at issue in current copyright controversies, such as the debate over extending copyright terms—a challenge to Congress's authority over copyright law that has been accepted by the Supreme Court—and what rates should be paid by Internet radio stations for the right to stream digital music over the Web. Other issues, like what to do about the free digital music Web site Napster and its many successor clones, delve into more fundamental questions: how file-sharing technologies can be held liable for contributing to the copyright infringement of their users, and whether users of a technology have a "fair use" defense against charges of infringement.

Yet it is the DMCA's anti-circumvention prohibition—which has been upheld by the 2 nd Circuit Court of Appeals—that is likely to have more sweeping effects on the future of copyright law because it is seen as undergirding the technological protection measures increasingly taken by content owners. This provision is also an illuminating lens through which to view the copyright debate.

I will examine four major positions about how extensive copyright law should be and evaluate the justification for each position. I will argue that the DMCA's anti-circumvention provision itself demonstrates the technology-specific nature of copyright law and suggests that it is difficult and perhaps impossible to draw the technological boundaries needed to sustain a coherent defense of copyright law, once one has accepted the premise of copyright law. It may well be that the weaknesses of the concept of copyright in a digital world make it hard to sustain a principled defense for the enshrinement of state power represented by copyright law.

I will also discuss the challenges to Section 1201 in greater detail. I will then outline four major positions about copyright law, each with substantial support in the public debate. Finally, I will offer reasons for my conclusions that by injecting anti-circumvention into the concept of copyright law, the DMCA exposes inherent weaknesses in what copyright law should do.

The Controversial DMCA

Although the DMCA's section 1201 has been at issue in an extremely limited number of court cases thus far, both supporters and critics agree that its implications for the future are enormous because of the desire by copyright holders to deploy more sophisticated copy protection devices. The movie, book, and commercial software industries already routinely use such digital locks in an effort to keep unauthorized users from accessing and copying portions of works for which they have not paid.

An example of such technology is the Content Scrambling System (CSS) for digital video discs (DVDs) developed by a group of technology companies working in collaboration with the motion picture industry through the Copy Protection Technical Working Group (CPTWG). The technology, which is governed by the DVD-Copy Control Association controlled by both Hollywood and the consumer electronics manufacturers, scrambles the content on the DVDs in a manner that makes them unviewable unless they are played on a DVD-licensed player. Those players, in turn, deactivate all copying functions.

But after Norwegian teenager Jon Johansen cracked the encryption code and published it on the Internet as DeCSS, Web sites including the hacker magazine *2600* posted the software and provided links to other sites that had posted it as well. In *Universal Studios v. Reimerdes*, the major Hollywood studios sued *2600* Web site owners Eric Reimerdes, Eric Corley, and Roman Kazan, none of whom were themselves accused of using the software code to engage in video piracy or commit other copyright violations. Purely on grounds of violating the DMCA, the company won in both district court and before the 2nd Circuit Court of Appeals. The Electronic Frontier Foundation, a civil liberties group representing the defendants and taking the lead on litigation opposing the DMCA, has sought reconsideration of the decision by the full court of appeals.

A second case involved Princeton University computer science professor Edward Felten, who found holes in the Secure Digital Music Initiative, a copyright protection scheme supported by the Recording Industry Association of America. Attorneys for RIAA and Verance, one of the companies involved in designing elements of the music encryption, threatened Felten with a lawsuit alleging DMCA violations if he presented his research at an academic conference in April 2001. Felten backed down, but the media outcry against the RIAA led it to say that it never intended to block Felten from speaking, and he did so at an August 2001 computer conference. EFF sought an injunction against the law, but a federal district judge in New Jersey threw out the case on the grounds that there was no case or controversy at issue.

A third case was the criminal prosecution of Dmitry Sklyarov, a Russian programmer arrested and charged in July 2001 after he attended a prominent hacker conference in Las Vegas. In the first criminal application of the law, the U.S. Attorney's Office in San Francisco alleged that Sklyarov and Elcomsoft, his Russian employer, had reverse-engineered Adobe's e-book reader, permitting users to decrypt electronic books and read them "in the clear." Adobe's product is an example of the emerging field of digital rights management technologies. It relies on encryption to forbid such reading, because without the scrambling, computer users could e-mail e-books to their friends or share them with strangers over a peer-to-peer network like Napster, where the material is transferred from one personal computer to another over the Internet. But the Elcomsoft work-around also permitted a user to read an e-book on both his desktop and his laptop, an application that some regard as a fair use defense under copyright law. Prosecutors initiated their charges after being informed of Elcomsoft's activities in a meeting with Adobe executives. Again after public outcry—and meetings with EFF officials—Adobe said it did not support his prosecution. In December 2001, the U.S. Attorney's office deferred the charges against Sklyarov—essentially dropping them—although the office insists it is continuing to build a case against Elcomsoft for future trial.

Perhaps more important are the new threats of DMCA actions on the horizon. Because the recording industry fears declining sales of compact discs (CDs) because of the widespread availability of digital music files on peer-to-peer networks like Aimster, Grokster, Kazaa, and Morpheus—each of which they have sued—some studios have begun introducing CDs that will not play on computers at all. A digital flaw inserted onto the CDs in the manufacturing process renders them inaudible except on conventional, dedicated CD players. Done in an effort to stop consumers from copying and sharing digital files "ripped" into MP3 tracks, the effort again runs afoul of consumers' expectations that they be able to make personal and backup copies of their CDs, including the ability to "mix" and rearrange tracks before "burning" them onto their own CDs, or put them on a portable MP3 player. Technology providers have said that they can provide the tools to enable consumers to play such copy-protected CDs on their computers but have held back from doing so because of the DMCA's strict language.

Rep. Rick Boucher (D-Va.) one of Capitol Hill's most knowledgeable experts on copyright law, said he believes that the Sklyarov indictment and the record companies' efforts to put out copy-protected CDs show that the DMCA needs to be amended to permit fair use. He has said he will propose legislation to allow circumvention so long as it is done for a permissible use under the fair use doctrine.

Codified in the Copyright Act at 17 U.S.C. 107, fair use provides judges with four factors that they must consider in determining whether a copyright infringement has occurred: (1) the purpose and character of the use, including whether it is commercial or for nonprofit educational purposes; (2) the nature of the copyrighted work itself; (3) whether the section used constitutes a substantial portion of the work as a whole; and (4) the effect of the use upon the potential market for, and value of, the copyrighted work. In a letter to RIAA president Hilary Rosen, Boucher also said he believed the Audio Home Recording Act of 1992 limited the recording industry's ability to make copy-protected CDs. But at the very least, he said in second letter to the RIAA, the record labels need "to make sure that the copy-protected CDs carry appropriate labels informing consumers and retailers of the specific reduced functionality or quality degradation of the product that they are purchasing."

The question about circumvention to permit fair use raises one of the core questions about the DMCA: what happens to individuals' traditional conception of fair use when companies use digital rights management (DRM) technologies to lock down copyrighted material? And should copyright owners be able to rely on the law to limit the use of their copyrighted material when their technologies fail? The examples above show that the sweeping nature of the DMCA could easily lead courts to privilege copyrights over other rights, including the right to free speech in the development of software code.

And yet the questions above are given especially sharp focus by the introduction of legislation that goes considerably beyond this. Hollywood studios have persuaded Senate Commerce Committee Chairman Ernest "Fritz" Hollings (D-S.C.) to introduce legislation that would actually bar the creation of all computer software and hardware that does not include government-sanctioned DRM technology. Dubbed the Consumer Broadband and Digital Television Promotion Act and presented as a measure designed to spur their adoption, S. 2048 was introduced in March 2002.

S. 2048 is an extreme example of legislative deference to perceived interests of some copyright holders at the expense of nearly everyone else. It gives the information technology industry and Hollywood one year to create "security system standards that will provide effective security for copyrighted works." If they agree, the Federal Communications Commission will implement them; if they do not, the Commission is obliged to attempt to create its own DRM standards. Device manufacturers and software creators who fail to include the mandated standard would be subject to the same criminal penalties as are violators of the DMCA.

In other words, beyond simply criminalizing the circumvention of private DRM technologies voluntarily deployed by copyright holders, the Hollings legislation would itself mandate the DRM technology to be used, force compliance upon the entire technology industry, and then penalize those who failed to use them as if they had cracked them.

Four Camps of Thinking

The foregoing discussion sets the stage for considering what I view as the four major positions about the proper scope for copyright in a digital world. Whereas each of the following views commands some significant portion of the public debate, none currently represents a consensus view. This very fluidity—with divergent views driven by the interests of the industries and professions that they represent—underscores the controversial nature of copyright law and suggests that this is an opportune moment for rethinking exactly what it is that copyright is designed to protect and why.

The four groups are (1) supporters of government-mandated DRM technologies, (2) supporters of the DMCA's anti-circumvention language, (3) those who emphasize the importance of copyright's fair use doctrine and criticize the DMCA for undermining it, and (4) critics of the current state of copyright law, including all uses of the DMCA, who highlight its clash with free speech rights. For short, I'll call these mandatory DRM, DMCA, fair use, and free speech, and show how these positions play into the debates over the use of content.

Mandatory DRM

Walt Disney Company and News Corporation executives have been among the loudest advocates of the principles embodied in Senator Hollings' S. 2048, and they have gradually dragged along the other five major studios that are members of the Motion Picture Association of America. In testimony before a February 2002 Senate Commerce Committee hearing on Hollings' draft legislation, Disney chief executive officer Michael Eisner and News Corporation chief operating officer Peter Chernin argued that because Internet piracy of digital movies is so widespread, the technology industry is being forced to create the tools to stop their movies from being transmitted digitally.

As mentioned above, Hollywood collaborated with technology industry representatives on the creation of the DVD encryption scheme, an effort begun in 1996 in a technical working group. Also emerging from that effort has been a proposal by a consortium of five equipment manufacturers—Intel Corporation, Matsushita Electric Industry Company, Toshiba Corporations, Sony Corporation, and Hitachi Ltd.— to provide technologies that impede unauthorized access to and copying of cable and satellite broadcasts of digital content. Sony Corporation's Sony Pictures Entertainment and AOL Time Warner's Warner Brothers have signed on to the consortium's technology—dubbed "5C" because it was first proffered by five consumer electronics manufactures, although it is now accepted by many others. The others held off because of a desire to include protections for over-the-air broadcasts of digital television.

Almost all observers acknowledge that unauthorized copying on cable and satellite systems can be limited by voluntary agreements because of a chain of licensing agreements that require distributors, equipment manufacturers, and consumers themselves to abide by such limitations. But such agreements are unable to provide such content protection when television programs and movies are broadcast over the air and "in the clear,"—that is, without encryption. (To broadcast digital content in an encrypted format would mean that hundreds of millions of analog television sets would be unable to view them.) And television and movie producers perceive danger in making such unencrypted digital broadcasts available because digital copies are easily reproduced and do not degrade. For them, the only alternative is simply not to broadcast digitally.

That problem could be solved by means of a broadcast flag to signal the electronic device receiving the digital broadcast that content may not be redistributed in another form, such as over the Internet. Technology industry officials in a broadcast unit of the CPTWG group said that they were set to finalize the technical standards for such a flag by the end of March 2002. Officials at Intel, which has taken the lead in opposing the Hollings legislation because of its interjection of the government in engineering processes, recently agreed with AOL Time Warner that "some narrowly focused government regulation will be necessary," presumably from the Federal Communications Commission.

But solving this broadcast flag program was only the first of three demands that Motion Picture Association of America president Jack Valenti set in his February testimony before the Senate Commerce Committee. The second calls for plugging what he called the "analog hole," or the analog output device on the back of television equipment. Even when video content is delivered in an encrypted digital format, it must be converted into an unprotected analog format to be viewed on existing analog televisions, and viewers may then convert it back to a digital form through which it could be transmitted to a Napster-like file-sharing service. Technology officials say that implementing a proposal to digitally "watermark" copyrighted content—so that it will be garbled whenever copied to another device—would not be as straightforward as the motion picture industry believes.

And they are nearly apoplectic over the third demand, which appears to drive the sweeping nature of S. 2048: that the technology industry do something to develop unspecified technical solutions that would counter the ability of someone to use computers, software, or electronic equipment to make an authorized copy available through a file-sharing service. Many share the view that Princeton professor Edward Felten expressed in written testimony to the Commerce Committee: "A standard for copy protection is as premature as a standard for teleportation." Intel CEO Craig Barrett said that he is aware of no technology that could do what the Motion Picture Association of America wants done, short of monitoring every electronic communication and comparing the bit streams to those of all known or registered copyrighted content.

DMCA

The debate over the Hollings bill has united the technology, consumer electronics, and Internet rights communities against Hollywood. Among those leading the charge against the bill are the Business Software Alliance, the Computer Systems Policy Project, and the Information Technology Industry Council, all of which represent the biggest players in the software and hardware industries.

Many of the same companies, particularly leading lights in the Business Software Alliance such as Microsoft and Adobe, played a key role in lending support to the DMCA. They now argue against Hollings' bill on a number of grounds: that it presumes bad faith on the part of the technology industry, that it gets government involved in the technology standards-setting process, that it would mandate a single DRM technology instead of permitting competing ones to flourish, and that by doing so it would inevitably freeze technological development.

But they also argue that privately created standards must be enforced with bars on circumvention, or "locks for digital doors." Without such a legal infrastructure, they contend, their efforts to secure content via encryption would come to naught as soon as the first crack is made available on the Internet. Not having the DMCA would grant too much flexibility to software pirates in a world where a single digital copy obtained via circumvention could be reproduced countless times.

Sophisticated defenders of the DMCA position also make another point as well. In addition to greatly facilitating unauthorized copying, the emergence of an Internet that is "always on" enables new sorts of access to copyrighted content. Instead of a world in which optical disc factories print CD-ROMs, we are moving to a world where software services are "consumed" on high-speed Internet connections not by means of reproduction but by having the proper access control to the service. In this view of the world, a thief is not a pirate who has copied software but a hacker who publicizes the password to the service.

"Without the anti-circumvention provisions, the business models of the future would not happen," said Tom Rubin, a Microsoft attorney specializing in the DMCA. "You would be cutting off entire new business models and lines of business, all of which ultimately help the public and the consumer."

Among these services are DVDs, pay-per-view movies on subscription-based cable and satellite services, digital music webcasting, and libraries of digital music pre-installed on the hard disks of computers sold though retailers, Rubin and DMCA proponents argue. But DMCA critics counter that copyright holders argued before the DMCA's passage that there would be greater content if there were more protection—which is also being pressed by proponents of the Hollings bill—before the DMCA's passage, and yet digital music and digital video services remain stalled.

Fair Use

Advocates of the fair use doctrine emphasize how much the DMCA upsets traditional habits and patterns of copyright use from the perspective of the user. Among those who hold this view are manufacturers who benefit from the sale of consumer electronics products, Internet service providers who saw demand for bandwidth skyrocket during the heyday of Napster from—July 2000 until the 9th Circuit Court of Appeals ruled that it was engaging in contributory and vicarious copyright infringement in February 2001—librarians who want greater access to copyrighted material, and consumers who believe that the balance in copyright law has swung too far away from consumers.

One strong new representation of this view is a group dubbed DigitalConsumer.org, founded by Joe Kraus, a former co-founder of ExciteAtHome, the Internet portal and broadband company that has since filed for bankruptcy. The group, which includes many technology industry and venture capital luminaries, is attempting to put content owners on the defensive by asserting a six-point "bill of rights" with regard to consumers' use of digital materials:

1. Users have the right to "time-shift" content that they have legally acquired.

   This gives them the right to record video or audio for later viewing or listening. For example, they can use a videocassette recorder to record a television show and play it back later.

2. Users have the right to "space-shift" content that they have legally acquired.

   This gives them the right to use their content in different places (as long as each use is personal and noncommercial). For example, the user can copy a CD to a portable music player in order to listen to the music while jogging.

3. Users have the right to make backup copies of their content.

   This gives them the right to make archival copies to be used in the event that original copies are destroyed.

4. Users have the right to use legally acquired content on the platform of their choice.

   This gives them the right to listen to music on their Rio, to watch television on their iMac, and to view DVDs on their Linux computer.

5. Users have the right to translate legally acquired content into comparable formats.

   This gives them the right to modify content in order to make it more usable. For example, a blind person can modify an electronic book so that the content can be read aloud.

6. Users have the right to use technology in order to achieve the rights previously mentioned.

   This last right guarantees users' ability to exercise their other rights. Certain recent copyright laws have paradoxical loopholes that claim to grant certain rights but then criminalize all technologies that could allow users to exercise those rights. In contrast, this bill of *rights states that no technological barriers can deprive users of their other fair use rights.*[1]

The first right, regarding time-shifting, is the least controversial and flows directly from the 1984 Supreme Court decision in *Universal v. Sony Betamax*, which upheld the sale of videocassette recorders, including its use by consumers to make copies of copyrighted television and movie programs. Regarding the third right, provisions of copyright law already permit backup copies of software but not digital music files. (Music file backup would be included under one of the changes contemplated by H.R. 2724, the Music Online Competition Act introduced by Rep. Chris Cannon [R-Utah] and Rep. Rick Boucher.) But rights two, four, and five—each dealing with some form of altering copyrighted material to suit other formats or devices—are opposed by many copyright interests. And they are particularly critical of right six, which essentially calls for a fair use exception to the DMCA along the lines proposed by Boucher.

Content holders argue that these positions are based on an excessively broad reading of fair use—as understood by some consumers, perhaps, but not by copyright law. They also point to two studies conducted by the Library of Congress's Copyright Office, which rebutted the notion that the DMCA was responsible for limiting consumers' fair use access to material and rejecting almost all calls for exceptions to the anti-circumvention language.

Noting that fair use is a defense against infringement and not an affirmative right to copy, the more extreme among the copyright maximalists actually argue that fair use extends to quotation and parody, not to home and personal copies. They also argue that these broad definitions of fair use sanction those who would justify the use of Napster-like services on such grounds.

Free Speech

Most fair use defenders including Representative Boucher, Digital-Consumer.org, and many consumer electronics companies, blanch at defending the old Napster. (In March 2002, the company was still in the process of preparing to launch its new licensed service.) But free speech advocates—as exemplified by the EFF and many copyright law professors and computer scientists—will rise to the occasion and argue that peer-to-peer services should not be shut down whether or not infringing activity is conducted by individual users of such services.

Perhaps of even greater concern for this group, including librarians, are the DMCA's restrictions on what they see as legitimate scientific research and other activities chilled by the DMCA. Just as cryptographers sought to publish research about and deploy strong encryption free from government export restriction, they oppose private efforts to use the DMCA to quash investigations that could lead to breaking the encryption algorithms used by copyright holders. And they can point to a precedent in the 1999 9th Circuit Court of Appeals decision in *Bernstein v. U.S. Department of State*, upholding a mathematician's view that source code was protected as speech under the First Amendment.

A few of these advocates—such as EFF board member John Perry Barlow and Columbia University law professor Eben Moglen—would like to see the elimination of copyright law in its entirety. But there remains lively debate over what, if anything, should replace it.

Georgetown University law professor Julie Cohen, for example, has argued that fair use is an intrinsic part of copyright law, and that private DRM technologies must not override it. Chapman University law professor Tom Bell takes the opposite tack, suggesting that—absent the DMCA—nothing should preclude content companies from doing what they will to restrict copying of their intangible creations. Instead, the focus should be on "escaping copyright law" and relying exclusively on private contractual remedies against copying. And Stanford University law professor Lawrence Lessig directs much of his criticism about copyright law to the length of its terms. (Lessig is attorney for Eric Eldred, the e-book publisher challenging the Copyright Term Extension Act's 20-year bequest to current and future copyright holders, and will argue the case before the Supreme Court next term.) He argues that if the law limited copyright holders to five years upon registration—renewable for up to 95 years—the public domain would benefit from a huge influx of materials that are currently being locked out of it to no apparent benefit.

The Rise of Mandatory DRM

By linking the concept of anti-circumvention to copyright infringement, the DMCA starkly raises new questions about the nature of copyright law. Originally designed to prevent *copying*, it now also constrains *access*, including access to materials that one has purchased, like a DVD or a computer. Although examining the justification for doing this as a form of contract law is beyond the scope of this essay, I do suggest that this fundamental change in copyright law forces a reevaluation of its grounding.

In the sections above I recounted many of the arguments that technology industry officials, including strong advocates of the DMCA, use to argue against S. 2048, including the presumption of bad faith, putting government in the standards-setting business, mandating a single DRM technology, and freezing technological development. To these must also be added the concerns of those in the fair use and free speech camps: Even if a technological standard or standards were to be agreed upon by Hollywood and the technology industry, would that justify a government imposition of it? Wouldn't such a measure do untold harm to those who wish to design products (including "open source" software) that permit consumers to conduct unfettered copying—whether for fair use purposes, for reproducing uncopyrighted materials, or for infringing purposes not sanctioned by the manufacturers?

When the battle between Hollywood and Silicon Valley was heating up in August 2001, two top officials in key trade associations squared off at a dinner conversation at the Progress and Freedom Foundation conference in Aspen, Colorado.

"High-definition recent [movie] releases absolutely must have a secure distribution path to the consumer," said Fritz Attaway, executive vice president for government relations at the Motion Picture Association of America. "Unfortunately, some segments of the information technology industry have not reached this conclusion. The information technology industry rebels at that very thought of producing a trusted device"—or a computer with its copying functions disabled—he said. "I think that is a shame because it is going to drive high-quality content to cable, satellite and other secure distribution systems and away from the Internet."

Several tech officials snapped right back at Attaway's contention. "We take a back seat to no one in protecting intellectual property," said Rhett Dawson, president of the Information Technology Industry Council. "We are committed to protecting your intellectual property, but we are not committed to protecting your business model."

In other words, tech industry officials are not willing to short-circuit competition and permit the motion picture or recording industries to assert that their shares of the market for distribution of entertainment goods are a right. They will have to earn those shares by offering competitive services that consumers will support.

But many of the same objections against the Hollings bill apply equally against the DMCA. Although the DMCA is unquestionably less burdensome in some respects, many of the same arguments about S. 2048 seeking to write business models into the law apply equally against the DMCA. Thinking about all the benefits that could flow from tougher copyright laws is an easy exercise for copyright holders not counting the costs to users, to economic welfare, and to free speech rights for their rent-seeking behavior.

By criminalizing technologies that could be used to circumvent copy-protection devices, the DCMA's anti-circumvention provision adds significant new burdens to the already bloated corpus of copyright law. What was once a minor constraint on the capabilities of content users to reproduce copyrighted material is increasingly likely to become an intolerable straightjacket on the way in which individuals may enjoy and experience intangible creations.

But content owners would be loath to return to the pre-DMCA world. Instead, it seems our society will increasingly be forced to choose which vision of the future it would prefer: restrictions on digital devices in exchange for securing copyrights or technological freedom at the price of greater piracy. In either case, copyright law has lost its familiar grounding. In its short period of operation, the DMCA has already changed many fundamental perceptions about copyright law and turned many users of technology against copyright law itself. The DMCA and proposed new laws like the Consumer Broadband and Digital Television Promotion Act are the leading edge of these new digital restrictions. But if copyright is to have a future at all in the digital world, its defenders must articulate a better rationale upon which to build copyright policy in the future.

Note

1. www.digitalconsumer.org/bill.html.

9. A Lukewarm Defense of the Digital Millennium Copyright Act

Orin S. Kerr

When I was invited to come to the Cato Institute to speak in the F. A. Hayek Auditorium on the Digital Millennium Copyright Act, my thoughts naturally turned to this question: What would Friedrich Hayek think of the DMCA? How would the Nobel Prize-winning Austrian economist, author of *The Road to Serfdom*, *The Constitution of Liberty*, and many other works, react to the DMCA?

I concluded that Hayek would have appreciated the underpinnings of the DMCA. Although Hayek was fairly skeptical of intellectual property as a whole,[1] I believe the DMCA fits within his vision of the proper role of government. This is interesting because it suggests that a Cato Institute audience should find the DMCA pretty appealing. The DMCA may be the law that law professors love to hate,[2] but the Cato crowd should find a lot to like in it.

In my remarks, I will use this insight to present what I call a "lukewarm" defense of the DMCA.[3] It's a lukewarm defense because I will not argue that the DMCA is a great law, or even necessarily a good law. Rather, my argument is that Congress was not acting entirely irrationally when it enacted the DMCA. There's a method to the madness here, and that method is rooted in a Hayekian vision of private ordering and free contract that the DMCA is designed to promote. Only time will tell whether this vision makes sense in the Internet age. Twenty years from now we may look back on the DMCA and conclude that it was a dismal failure. But on the other hand, we may not. We may look back and view the DMCA as a respectable model for how to enforce intellectual property rights and contractual rights in cyberspace. I would like to explain how that might turn out to be the case.

Let's start with Hayek. Friedrich Hayek is known for his appreciation of the merits of private ordering. The basic idea is a simple one. The government cannot possibly know and respond to the

163

preferences of every individual in society. Rather than try to plan the economy to guarantee the right distribution of goods and services, the government should create generally applicable rules that allow individuals to pursue their own preferences. In the end, the theory goes, individuals can make the best choices for themselves without the benefit of active state intervention. Private decisions and private choice will tend to maximize public welfare.

This should ring a bell among lawyers because it's the basic approach of the common-law doctrines of contract, property, and tort that lawyers learn in their first year of law school. According to this scheme, everybody starts off with a certain amount of stuff, plus their skills and talents. This is called "property," a bundle of rights defined by the state. People can then trade the stuff they have for the stuff they want in order to maximize their own happiness. If individuals feel they are better off by making a trade, they will; if they feel they are not, they won't. These trades are called "contracts," and the rules of contract law are designed to facilitate exchanges that leave both sides better off. The theory is that if people are allowed to bargain freely for what they want, they can maximize their happiness. In the end, we will do better through private ordering than we would do if the government tried to reach an optimal distribution of property directly.

For this system to work, of course, the promises we make in our exchanges must be enforceable. If I say, "I'll do X for you today if you do Y for me tomorrow," and I then do X but you then refuse to do Y, I won't benefit from the transaction. If I have no way of making reasonably certain that you'll fulfill your end of the bargain, I'm not going to be very interested in making exchanges with you in the future I will want to get what I've been promised. I won't necessarily care what makes the contract enforceable. Perhaps we live in a culture in which social norms exert strong pressures on individuals to honor their promises. Perhaps people feel a moral obligation to honor their promises. Or perhaps the threat of a lawsuit is needed. Either way, the system of private ordering works only if contracting parties have a way of making reasonably certain that they will get what they have been promised.

Enter copyright law. The gist of copyright law is that it gives authors certain rights in their creations. Authors get a type of property right in their creations that lets them sell their rights, giving them an incentive to create more.[4] The basic idea is to create a scheme of private ordering using the authors' rights in their works as a starting point. Consider the following example. Let's say I want to make a living as a writer, and that I print up my stories and sell them for $5 a story. I'll have a copyright in my story, and that makes it illegal for someone else to copy my story and sell it for $2 instead of $5. If people want my story, the easiest way will be to buy it from me. They can get my stories in other ways, such as by buying a copy from a friend or checking out a copy from the public library. But for the most part, if they want my story they have to pay my price, $5. And by buying a copy of my story, they agree to a contract that gives them some rights but not others. Some of the contractual terms will be explicit (such as the price), but others exist by default in the copyright laws.[5] Under this scheme, buyers can read the story whenever they want, and they can copy limited parts for specific reasons,[6] but they cannot copy the entire story and sell the copies to others. Those rights are author rights, and as the author and copyright owner, I will not grant them to a buyer for only $5.

In a world without the Internet, this contract is likely to be enforceable, at least in most cases. The reasons are practical ones. Most importantly, copying takes time and effort. A person who purchases my story for $5 has no right to copy my story and distribute it, and the fact that this takes time and effort can help dissuade that person from violating the contract and doing it anyway. If someone nonetheless decides to do it on a wide scale, there's a good chance I'll be able to find them and with the help of the courts persuade them to stop. People will often be able to breach their contracts with me without being held responsible, but by and large I will be able to enforce my contracts. If my stories are good enough, I have a chance at making a living as a writer.

Now let's add the Internet to the mix. Imagine that instead of selling paper copies of my short stories, I set up a website and let people download copies of my stories from the Internet. This is cheaper for me, so I let people download my stories for $4 instead of $5. But now I encounter a difficulty. The Internet lets people make an unlimited number of perfect copies with only a mouse click. A reader might pay $4, download a story, and say, "This story is so great, I want everyone to have a copy." He'll post copies on the Internet. And within hours, within days, within weeks, hundreds

165

or even thousands of copies of the great story that I've written are available for free on the Internet. This is a breach of the contract between myself and the reader: he didn't have rights to distribute my story. The deal was that he could take one copy for $4 but not distribute copies beyond that. Such a breach of contract is easy to do on the Internet, and it's easy to do anonymously. The technology makes it simple. And if people can get free copies from the Internet, they're not going to want to spend $4 to download an authorized copy from my website, or $5 to buy a paper copy. They'll want the free version. The audience for my stories will expand because my story will be free, but it makes it harder for me to make a living as a writer.

So how do I deal with this technological problem? Like most technological problems, there is a technological solution. One answer is access and copy control devices—technological means of stopping people from doing what they would otherwise be able to do. An electronic lock, if you will. Let's go back to my website. I used to give readers my story for $4, but that didn't work because the contract became unenforceable. For my next story, I will use technological controls that block readers from accessing or copying the story except under specific conditions. Maybe I'll offer the new version of my story from my website for $3 but make it impossible for readers to copy the story. My offer, in effect, is a limited right in exchange for a lower price. This time the terms of the contract are more explicit: a reader gets the rights that the technology allows— namely, the rights to access but not to copy. Anyone who wants my story under these conditions will pay their $3; if they don't want my story, they won't pay it. Thanks to the copy control device, the terms of my contract will prove more enforceable: while the Internet as a whole makes it easy to make unlimited copies in breach of the contract, the copy control device makes it difficult.

Does this solve the problem? Not necessarily. As with most technological solutions, there are technological problems that come along with it. In particular, there are limitations on the technological controls. They're not foolproof; you can circumvent them. My contractual offer let you get my story for $3 but not copy it. But what if somebody else comes up with a way of picking the electronic lock I put in place? That lets you breach the contract once again. Even though you have agreed to pay only $3 for a version of my story that cannot be copied, you might say, "Hey, I've got this great tool that allows me to breach the contract. It lets me strip off the copy control and copy the story as many times as I want. I only pay for the rights to one copy, but actually I'm getting much more than I paid for."

This is where the DMCA comes in. Its goal is to stop people from breaching their contracts by interfering with the market for contract-breaching tools. The DMCA refers to such a contract-breaching tool as a "technology, product, service, device, component, or part thereof" that either "is primarily designed or produced for the purpose of circumventing a technological measure that effectively controls access to a work protected under [the Copyright Act],"[7] or else "is primarily designed or produced for the purpose of circumventing protection afforded by a technological measure that effectively protects a right of a copyright owner under this title in a work or a portion thereof."[8] In other words, access control devices and copy control devices. And the DMCA tries to interfere with the market for such technologies primarily by making it illegal to "manufacture, import, offer to the public, provide, or otherwise traffic in"[9] such technologies, subject to exceptions for research, reverse engineering, and the like.[10] The idea is that you can make copyright's regime of private ordering work by making contracts enforceable, and you can help make contracts enforceable by deterring people from making and distributing contract-breaching devices.

What is interesting about this approach is that it tries to define a category of bad tools that are associated with allegedly harmful activity (here, contract breaching and copyright infringement), and tries to go after the tools that facilitate the activity, rather than just the harmful activity. This is a fairly common strategy in American law, albeit a controversial one. At the state law level, for example, there are laws that make it illegal to possess burglar's tools, or to possess drug paraphernalia. And at the federal level, the federal wiretap law makes it illegal to possess wiretapping and eavesdropping devices.[11] The idea with all of these laws is to block harmful activity by going after the markets for otherwise innocent tools that facilitate the harmful activity. That tends to be a difficult task, because it requires the law to draw a line between innocent tools and other tools that are harmful simply because they are used to facilitate harmful activity. That can be pretty tough. Such tools usually have legitimate uses in at least some circumstances. But as I said, the basic strategy is a fairly common one in American law.

So what does this tell us about the merits of the DMCA? I think it tells us that the merits of the DMCA boil down to two distinct sets of issues. The first set considers the merits of private ordering. Does private ordering work? More specifically, does free contract work on the Internet with regard to the protection of copyrighted works? Is the regime of private ordering that the DMCA tries to enforce one that is worth enforcing? The second set of questions considers the merits of the DMCA's particular approach to enforcing private ordering. Is it really possible to draw a line between bad contract-breaching tools and good software programs? Is the line so blurry that the law's attempt to deal with the former will have chilling effects on the development of the latter? The first set of questions asks whether the DMCA's goals are worth pursuing. The second set asks whether the DMCA pursues those goals in an effective way.

Those are all legitimate questions. But I find it interesting that the first set of questions has received much more attention than the second set. A good chunk of the debate about the DMCA seems to be a thinly-disguised debate about the merits of private ordering and free contract.[12] Many people do not like the terms that the copyright owners offer in their contracts. They would prefer different terms. They want more rights, and they want to pay less for them (or else they want the rights for free). They want the government to intervene and set the terms of the contract so that the contracts are more favorable, have more balance, guarantee fair use rights, and the like. From this standpoint, the DMCA is bad because it helps enforce a bad system, a system of private ordering that lets the record companies and other copyright owners set the terms of contracts over copyrighted materials. In this world, the argument runs, a little contract breaching is a good thing. If it's impossible to enforce contracts on the Internet, then bravo for the Internet: let's keep it that way and not interfere with it.

But let's say you're a supporter of the Cato Institute. You like private ordering, and you like free contract. You buy the argument that the state should not step in and make contracts "fair," but instead should let private parties contract and agree upon terms themselves. From this perspective, at least some of the critiques of the DMCA should fall flat. They will sound a bit like "from each according to his ability to pay for copyrighted materials, to each according to his appetite for it." You'll see no reason why the market can't solve these problems. If copyright owners offer a contract that their potential customers don't like, then no one will buy the works and the copyright owners won't earn any money; this will force copyright owners to offer terms that members of the public are willing to accept. If you accept this view, you're likely to want to wait and see how the DMCA works out in practice. Maybe the DMCA will work, maybe it won't. We don't know yet because the law is less than five years old. But at the very least, you should respect what the DMCA is trying to do. It's trying to enforce a technological solution (access control devices) to a technological problem (the Internet's facilitating of breach of contract and copyright infringement).

Time will tell whether the DMCA is a success or a failure. I confess that I don't know which it will be. But in the meantime we should recognize that the Act reflects an intellectually coherent effort to protect copyrights and enforce contracts in an Internet age. As I said at the beginning of these remarks, Congress was not acting entirely irrationally when it enacted the DMCA. There's a method to the madness. That method is a private ordering scheme that has worked before and just might work again.

Notes

1. See, for example, Friedrich A. Hayek, *The Fatal Conceit: The Errors of Socialism* (Chicago: University of Chicago Press, 1988).

2. For representative articles critical of the DMCA, see Glynn S. Lunney, Jr., "The Death of Copyright: Digital Technology, Private Copying, and the Digital Millennium Copyright Act," *Virginia Law Review* 87 (2001): 813; Julie Cohen, "Lochner in Cyberspace, The New Economic Orthodoxy of 'Rights Management,'" *Michigan Law Review* 97 (1988): 462.

3. My remarks will be limited to the anti-circumvention provisions of the DMCA found in p. 2, 17 U.S.C. § 1201.

4. See *Sony Corp. v. University City Studios*, 464 U.S. 417, 432 (1984).

5. I recognize it is more common to view copyright laws as laws that define property or monopoly rights, rather than contract rights. But I think it will help us to think of copyright laws as setting an initial property right and then default contractual terms that can be contracted around by private parties. This may be an unusually loose sense of the word "contract," but I think a contractual perspective sheds the most light on the purpose and function of copyright and the DMCA.

6. See 17 U.S.C. § 107.

7. 17 U.S.C. § 1201(a)(2).

8. Ibid., at § 1201(b)(1)

9. Ibid. The DMCA also makes it illegal to directly circumvent an access control device but not a copy control device.

10. See 17 U.S.C. § 1201(e)–(g).

11. See 18 U.S.C. § 2512.

12. Compare David Friedman, "In Defense of Private Orderings: Comments on Julie Cohen's 'Copyright and the Jurisprudence of Self-Help,'" *Berkeley Technology Law Journal* 13 (1998): 1151.

10. The DMCA: Providing Locks for Digital Doors

Emery Simon

The anti-circumvention provision of the Digital Millennium Copyright Act seeks to protect copyrighted works such as software, books, movies, and music by providing that "No person shall manufacture, import, offer to the public, provide, or otherwise traffic in any technology, product, service, device, component, or part thereof, that is primarily designed or produced for the purpose of circumventing a technological measure that effectively controls access to a work."

One of the puzzling aspects of the way the debate over the anti-circumvention provisions of the DMCA has played out is that both proponents and opponents of the DMCA have portrayed the issue as a battle of good versus evil. The DMCA is either considered to be evil and vilified—or it is put on a pedestal as a wonderful kind of panacea.

The vilification of the Act is wide-ranging, tugging on every legal and emotional heartstring. Opponents cast about with ease, alternatively, and sometimes in the same breath, characterizing the DMCA with statements such as "it's unconstitutional"; "it will limit free speech"; "it will limit my freedom"; "it will criminalize basic research, the lifeblood of the software industry"; "it will put scholars at risk of going to jail"; "it will be the end of creativity"; "it will be the death of our educational system";—and so on.

But this really is not a battle of good versus evil. That the fight over the DMCA has been framed that way reflects the fact that the dialogue is taking place at mismatched levels. Participants are talking past one another.

At one level we have a really interesting, complicated, academic, and extremely difficult puzzle about what is good law and what is good policy as we move into an era of dramatically different ways of using and distributing information. The other level to consider is the marketplace reality. The marketplace reality is that business-men are rational profit maximizers. Most of the copyrighted works that we talk about today are not created by a destitute person sitting in an attic and writing poetry; they're really about commercially viable and valuable property in the form of copyrighted products.

The notion that it is somehow in the interest of companies—whose very function is distributing books, movies, or software for a profit—to create obstacles to their consumer base that will frustrate their customers and make them angry enough not to buy their product is on its face a nonsensical proposition. Contrary to the claims of the DMCA's opponents, it is simply not in the self-interest of compa-nies to so restrict the distribution of software and other copyrighted products to their customers that those customers no longer want the product.

The software industry has struggled mightily with various aspects of copy protection and access control for almost 20 years. The indus-try has gone through cycles of applying strong protection to prevent pirates from stealing and distributing its products—and it has suf-fered consumer backlashes when those controls went too far. This is an ebb and flow—an unavoidable market process—that is com-mon in the business world.

But the reality we face—as do other digital content industries—is that there are bad people out there who steal. You want to stop the thieves but at the same time avoid hurting customers and driving them away. You don't want to create disincentives for your custom-ers to use your product. You merely want to stop the piracy that threatens to make your business unworkable—piracy that ultimately harms your customers.

There is a balance that needs to be struck here. But in striking that balance all software companies face a challenge: they need to avoid incorporating copy-protection technologies that are so incon-venient or cumbersome that they go beyond the goal of merely thwarting piracy. Ease of use and customer-friendly protections against piracy are vital to successful acceptance and diffusion of new software technologies, and are thus of prime importance to the marketplace and to our bottom line.

In a sense, the debate over the anti-circumvention provisions in the DMCA and the appropriate punishment for malicious piracy reminds me of the great struggles, romanticized in classic Hollywood westerns, of the struggle between cattlemen and sheepmen, and bringing law, and sometimes fences, to the prairies. In these movies cowboys are American icons, good and noble people. They came first to the prairie and loved the wide open spaces and freedom. Their cattle roamed over vast areas, grazing where the grass was fresh and plentiful. Then the sheepmen and ranchers came along, more settled and more dependent on fixed areas, and they wanted to fence in the prairie and bring law to the Wild West. Sheepmen, usually a white hat bunch, in this context were often the source of conflict, cast as bad people, because their business model, raising sheep, required putting up fences on the open rangeland. All those sheep and cattle, competing for the Wild West. In reality though, there were simply two different economic models. Eventually evolution, change, and adjustment won the day. Peace prevailed.

Those developments are comparable to the situation we have today with respect to the DMCA. It really is a paradigm shift in the marketplace, and we're sorting out what makes sense moving forward with respect to the protection of intellectual property, like software. Just as reasonable fences on the prairie led to successful husbandry and agricultural wealth, reasonable copy protection "fences" are crucial to the viability of digital content in the marketplace.

It is too early to tell whether the DMCA is a good law or a bad law in the same sense that it's too early to tell whether or not the Internet as a distribution model will truly succeed or fail. I think it will ultimately succeed. But the reality is that all industries are in the process of adjusting their business models, adjusting their distribution models, and trying to figure out how to respond to a dramatic change in how people acquire and use copyrighted works.

The software industry is probably a little bit ahead of the other copyright-based industries because we have always been a digital industry and our products have always been subject to perfect copying by pirates. Our industry obviously distributes software online and has had to cope with piracy from the outset. Although other industries are only now experiencing the paradigm shift of finding their products translated into perfect digital form, they too will adjust their distribution models sooner rather than later as broadband Internet access becomes ubiquitous. Publishing is shifting from a paper book to a digital book; music shifted about 15 years ago from vinyl to tape to digital compact discs; and movies are now in the process of changing from analog tape to digital disks.

A lot of the controversy that we're seeing in the digital era arises from the struggle of rights-holders, who perceive a serious and legitimate threat of theft, to try to engage in self-help, to try to use the technology of copy protection to secure their works. And the DMCA is a means of helping to protect their ability to use technology as a self-help mechanism.

Technology can be used for good purposes or it can be used for bad ends. As an example, the explosion in peer-to-peer file sharing over networks like Napster and MusicCity is a great example of this axiom. Peer-to-peer is one of the most important and dynamic developments in the software industry. Not enough has been written about it from that perspective. Peer-to-peer is about collaborative work. It's about expanding the number of people with whom you can work. Those are good things that promise to revolutionize the workplace, and communications itself.

But when a technology like peer-to-peer file sharing is exploited for purposes of unauthorized and uncompensated exchange of copyrighted works, that is a bad use of the technology.

The DMCA is there to deal with the latter issue: its purpose is to try to thwart harmful violations of copyright, not to impede noninfringing uses of important technological developments like peer-to-peer file sharing. The often heard claim that the DMCA is a substantially miscast, unbalanced, overreaching kind of statute, one that punishes scholarship and research by preventing the breaking of copy-protection code, I think is a facile answer to complex questions and, frankly, a lazy approach.

Consider the widely cited case of the Russian company Elcomsoft, and its programmer, Dmitry Sklyarov, who stands accused of distributing software that would allow protected files to be read in electronic book format. Let us step back from the admittedly unfortunate circumstances that surrounded his arrest. You have a very able and successful young programmer, who has a young son, who happens to be attending a conference of hackers in Las Vegas. Just as he is walking out, he is arrested. That looked pretty ugly.

But let's take a step back: What did this guy do? He basically sold a product that was advertised for the sole purpose of making copies of works without authorization. It was sold for profit at $99 per copy. We may talk about Dmitry's actions as "space-shifting" digital content in order to view it elsewhere, such as enabling transfer from a computer to a handheld e-book or a PDA (personal digital assistant) without deleting it from the original device. But when you're shifting that space with respect to someone else's protected product, you've made an illegitimate copy. It is a violation of the copyright law. Putting a stop to Dmitry's action is about exercising the right to prevent others from making unauthorized copies of your work. This is not a difficult notion to fathom. Elcomsoft was engaged in distributing a technology specifically for the purpose of enabling others to engage in copyright infringement. It is worth noting that Mr. Sklyarov was recently quoted in the *Moscow Times* saying, "As a person who writes programs that are then illegally copied and sold, I feel that if anyone can use them without paying, I will not be able to earn my living."

Under the DMCA, actual infringement need not be demonstrated. The mere fact that one is aiding and abetting infringement—a well-established concept in criminal law—or distributing tools to aid and abet is enough to constitute a violation. That is all the DMCA codifies, and it is actually quite limited, and not a threat to legitimate research, free speech, or the Constitution. The DMCA essentially says that if you are a person who sells products that are primarily designed or advertised for the purpose of defeating locks on my doors, or in this case the locks on my copyrighted works, you have committed a criminal act. It is a criminal act when you're doing it for a physical lock on a door; and there is no reason the standard should be any different with respect to digital technologies that feature locks.

Should those who engage in deliberate copy infringement go to jail? Is circumvention of digital copyright a crime for which people should be incarcerated? The bottom line is that copyright violations are serious criminal acts. Pirates are thieves. But the notion that somehow a person's acts should be without consequence because he happens to be an encryption researcher and capable of furthering science is too simplistic. If the product is sold illegitimately, designed specifically for the purpose of circumventing copy protections, for $99 a pop on the Internet, from a U.S.-based Web page, consequences should follow. This is not a hard thing to get your mind around. Elcomsoft is a for-profit operation, specifically designed to defeat a technology that the copyright owner has put in place to protect digitized works.

The Internet changes things dramatically for copyright owners because it creates an enormous opportunity at the same time that it creates new risks of exposure to piracy. The opportunity the Internet provides is the ability to reach a much broader marketplace. And marketplaces are price sensitive; the cheaper your product, the more you can distribute. However, on the Internet, zero-priced products represent both an enormous promise and an enormous threat. Zero-priced products that represent the ultimate threat, of course, are goods that are stolen and redistributed to the mass marketplace without authorization. The challenge for the software industry, as well as other industries whose very lifeblood is the creation of copyrighted works, is how to balance the opportunity the Internet presents against the risk of theft that it also presents.

Did the Congress calibrate that balance correctly in 1998, when the DMCA was passed? I think so. Are we calibrating that balance correctly in 2001, as various copyright infringement cases that involve the DMCA unfold in America's courts? It's probably too early to tell. Indeed, the DMCA may not be a panacea. But the Act does represent a sensible effort to achieve a balance, one that is likely to work. To vilify this statute as unconstitutional, anti-individual liberty, and the death knell of free speech strikes me as closeminded, as a misinterpretation of the Act's function in the digital age.

11. The New Legal Panic over Copyright

Mike Godwin

The first thing I want to say is: I too appreciate Friedrich Hayek. Of course, what Hayek I have read, I read in the public library. And I'm feeling guilty about it, because I didn't pay anything.

It was a government-funded library, and, worse, I was a kid and hadn't even paid taxes yet.

Now that I've gotten that out of the way, let me explain why I wanted to speak last on this panel. At the beginning of the hour I was desperately arranging to speak last because I needed more time to outline my remarks. I had planned to write up my notes last night, but, unfortunately, as I sat down to work I discovered that I had accidentally trashed the system folder on one of the important volumes of my Macintosh Powerbook. And so I ended up spending several hours reconstructing my software on the laptop that I had taken home.

Now, if you like technology, as I do, a system folder crash of this sort is not an insuperable problem. If you want to reinstall software to recover from a computer disaster at home, and if you have the installers at home, you can reinstall. As long as you have the serial numbers recorded at home, you can type them in at the appropriate places when you reinstall, so the reinstallation will work. I wasn't quite that well prepared, but fortunately I had alternatives at hand: I powered up another laptop I already had at home, and connected the two laptops together over the tiny wireless local network I run in my apartment. I transferred software and other installation files over the network from one machine to the other, and in doing so I may be said to have violated an assortment of software licensing agreements that (to invoke the language of the Digital Millennium Copyright Act) "control my access" to the technology, to the copyrighted work. Technically, perhaps, I had violated the DMCA. Please let's not let the news of my transgression leak out.

My struggle to reconstruct the software on my laptop got me thinking—and what it reminded me of was a situation that existed in the 1980s, in the first full decade of the software industry in the United States. In the 1980s software providers and vendors were pricing their software at various price points, believing quite rationally that there was some percentage of individuals who would engage in unlicensed copying of the software and there would even be infringement. To thwart those so-called software "pirates" they built copy-protection schemes into their software that worked by configuring the software diskettes in a way that (it was hoped) would prevent us from using our computers and disk drives to make copies of the diskettes. Try to make copies of these software diskettes the same way you made copies of your data diskettes, and either the copies couldn't be made, or the copied software wouldn't work.

The problem with computers, the scary aspect of computers for copyright holders, is of course that they reproduce digital works with 100 percent fidelity. So, absent copy protection, copies of software generally will work as well as the originals do. And as Emery Simon of the Business Software Alliance has pointed out, this was a trend in the software industry. There has long been a cycle of building copy protection into software and then taking it away a little bit, and then maybe reinstating it in a new form, and trying to find some balance between control of copying and customer convenience.

One of the things that I thought was interesting in the 1980s—because I was a big computer user, even then—was that we had a dynamic of forces that rationalized the copy-protection trends of the time. That dynamic consisted of tools that you could buy that allowed you to remove the copy protection from Lotus 123 or Microsoft Word or AutoCAD, so that you could reinstall the software on another system. Other tools simply enabled you to copy the copy-protected software diskette and were marketed, perhaps disingenuously, as "archival" tools. I don't think there is any serious dispute that people used them to pirate. But they were marketed openly in the software and computer magazines, and people did use them for archival purposes, to make it more convenient to restore a damaged volume and so on, and to do the kind of thing that I found myself doing last night, in the dim hours after "Buffy the Vampire Slayer" was over.

Notable here is the fact that the movement of the industry in that environment was away from copy protection, partly because consumers complained and partly because consumers actively had supported this aftermarket for tools that defeated (that is to say, circumvented) copy protection. There was a kind of arms race between the major software vendors and the copy-protection-defeating utility vendors as copy-protection schemes became more complex. There was a high degree of evolution of copy protection before it finally collapsed of its own weight. And the general trend, at the end of the 1980s and the beginning of the 1990s, was for software to be relatively unencumbered by copy protection, if not outright unprotected.

Now, as we know, Microsoft since the 1980s has utterly collapsed in the absence of strong copy protection. The company has gone down the economic drain, and they have our sympathy. You know, I pass Mr. Gates on the street with his cup every now and then and I put a dime in, or sometimes a quarter.

Seriously, though—I think the experience that the software industry had in the 1980s tells us that at least some of the fears about digital copying defeating or destroying the markets for digital copyrighted works were overblown. Nevertheless, we have a world of content producers that is worried about the presumption that individuals will steal the music on compact discs or the text in e-books, and never again buy intellectual content. Of course, few of us know anybody who actually reads e-books, much less is motivated to steal them.

But the theory is that they will steal the text of e-books and that these and other pirates will somehow destroy the revenue model for the various sectors of the content industry. If that scenario really were the likeliest one, I think we would have seen it in the 1980s—we would have seen Lotus and Microsoft go down the drain, with their much higher priced products that in the 1980s were much smaller and more easily copied.

I'm not going to defend unauthorized copying, especially when people could afford legitimate copies, and especially when people were engaging in piracy. As a member of the bar, I can't promote lawbreaking. In fact, I'm against lawbreaking, which I hope settles that question. What I am troubled by is that the balances that we have built into our copyright law seem to have been sidestepped by the DMCA and by newer measures that are being proposed.

The DMCA prohibits circumvention regardless of whether the underlying circumvention of copy control, or access control, is in service of infringement. I think this result is sufficiently absurd that it allows me to take the risk of saying that we already know the DMCA is badly crafted.

Here's an instructive hypothetical: Look at Stephen King, whom I like to use as an example not only because he is a great market success but also because he owns a Macintosh. All Macintosh users know each other or of each other—it's like a secret handshake.

In 2000, King conducted a couple of experiments in online fiction publishing. The first one was a novella, called *Riding the Bullet*, which was issued in Windows-based copy-protected formats. That event started my legal mind working: I imagined that Stephen King, who has expressed some contempt for Windows machines in the past, couldn't actually read his own story on his Macintosh laptop. Now, of course, he probably knows what he wrote. Still, he might want to check the formatting or check the copy editing or something.

But it occurred to me that if I showed up at Stephen King's house in Maine, and got past the guard dogs, and knocked on his door and offered him a tool that allowed him to strip the protection away from this Windows proprietary format and get the text out and read it directly on his Mac laptop, I would have committed an offense under the DMCA. The Act prohibits one from distributing tools that circumvent access control or copy protection—even for the author's benefit.

Now, you might think, Isn't there a defense under the Act if there is no underlying copyright infringement? The answer is no—that is not a defense. In other words, even though I could reasonably argue that, if anyone has the right to circumvent copy protection and look at Stephen King's copyrighted work, Stephen King does—it doesn't matter. It is not a defense.

That is an absurd result, and the reason for it is that the DMCA uncouples the enforcement of anti-circumvention provisions from the balances that are built into the substantive copyright law. Julie Cohen of the Georgetown Law Center has addressed this issue when describing "leaky rights." That is, even when the term of copyright protection for a work is in force, we expect a certain amount of noninfringing copying, and a certain amount of de minimis copying. Another way of looking at this issue is to say that we normally invoke penalties in the copyright context for serious, damaging infringers, and not against noninfringers, and not against de minimis infringers. That has been the history of our copyright law until relatively recently.

But the DMCA has changed all that. Now our law says that it doesn't matter whether you are an infringer or not, it does not matter whether you are a bad actor or not. It says that if you engaged in development or distribution of circumvention technology, you are going to be criminally or civilly liable. This development has unmoored the copyright enforcement framework from its original policy infrastructure, from its original policy foundation.

Which brings me back to recent remarks about the DMCA and its critics made by Orin Kerr. Kerr, now a law professor but formerly a prosecutor at the Department of Justice, divided the world into those who like the DMCA and those who don't. According to him, those who like the DMCA are the providers and the copyright holders and those who don't are the "contract breachers"—people who want to breach the social contract with regard to copyright.

But a few other types of people were left out of Kerr's binary characterization. They may be librarians. They may be people like me, who occasionally need to defeat access control or copyright protection in order to restore their damaged hard drives. They may be people who are engaging in fair use. It is troubling that the policy balances in the substantive copyright law are not reflected in the DMCA's anti-circumvention provisions.

Having said that, I think the natural conclusion is that you can imagine a version of the DMCA that looks more humane. Such a version would outlaw circumvention when one is infringing, or when one actively promotes infringement—in other words, when one is a deliberate contributory infringer. In that context, no one seriously objects to the prospect that people who are actively and knowingly promoting lawbreaking will be punished.

I don't think such reform of the DMCA will be on the table any time soon, but some of the constitutional challenges that are often dismissed by the content owners as radical and ill-founded actually have the potential to lead to legislative revisiting of the provisions of the Act.

Unfortunately, on the agenda now are measures that make the DMCA—even in its current, flawed form—seem humane, nuanced, and limited. I am referring particularly to the "security standards" bill proposed by Sen. Ernest Hollings (D-S.C.) and circulated in draft form. It would require that every consumer electronics manufacturer, every computer maker, and every Internet company build digital rights management and digital rights control into all future versions of their technologies, in the name of preventing piracy.

To get an idea of the difference in scope between that and the DMCA, consider this: The DMCA forbids a certain narrow class of activities having to do with a relatively narrow class of technologies called circumvention tools. In contrast, the Hollings bill promotes a legislative technology requirement that affects *everybody* and will require building digital rights management into *everybody's* new technologies, and in fact will make it an offense if you don't. This has immense potential effects for all sectors of the economy.

Underlying that approach is, once again, a very rational attitude on the part of the content companies. Specifically, in a world where individuals are empowered to engage in large-scale copyright infringement more easily than in past decades, the problem is that those individuals are mostly judgment-proof. It does not matter that you can go after the Rutgers sophomore who is spreading your music around; he hasn't got any money to pay a judgment, and putting him in jail won't undo the damage. And if you are a music company, you don't necessarily feel entirely comfortable about putting a music consumer in jail anyway—you want to have good relations with music consumers.

Still, in economic terms, one way to understand what a measure like the Hollings bill represents is to say that it represents an effort by the content companies to impose the costs of enforcing their interests on other parties. In the criminal provisions, it takes the externalities of enforcement and gives them to the FBI and to other police agencies. In the civil arena, it takes the externalities of enforcement and imposes them on other companies, in terms of technology requirements on every other sector of the digital economy.

Somehow that doesn't seem entirely fair. And I find myself wondering how rapidly Professor Hayek would be spinning in his grave at the prospect of one industry sector's using government to unload its burdens onto every other sector. In fact, I think he would be spinning right out of his grave.

Although, I don't want to emphasize it too much, I do think there are constitutional problems with the DMCA. I'll close by saying this:

182

If it is true, as Emery Simon of the Business Software Alliance has asserted, that those of us who believe that aspects of the DMCA are anti-Constitution, anti-liberty, and anti-free speech are "close-minded," well, I can live with that. Because I don't want to be so open-minded that my brain falls out.

Note

This article was adapted from remarks I gave at a November 2001 Cato Institute panel on copyright issues. Our panel focused in particular on the Digital Millennium Copyright Act and its "anti-circumvention provisions." To the extent possible, I've tried to maintain the conversational mode in which the remarks were given. The panel was held before a remarkably attentive and engaged audience at the Cato Institute's F. A. Hayek Auditorium. As the fourth of four speakers, I couldn't help noticing that the first three panelists each made an effort to invoke Hayek in support of their respective positions. This of course obligated me to find a way to invoke Hayek too.

12. Life after the DMCA and Napster

Mitch Glazier

By now, many people have spent many years of their lives working on the enactment of and litigation stemming from the Digital Millennium Copyright Act.

Having worked on the bill on the staff of the House Judiciary Committee, I find it interesting now to look back and compare what people thought at the time the Act was being debated and to see the evolution of the music industry since its enactment. Our industry was both lucky and unlucky to be the developer of the first major type of intellectual property available in the digital environment.

It has been an interesting process to watch the evolution of how the music companies have embraced, over several years' time, new business models, to try to figure out exactly what the consumers will want, how their content will be protected, how to work with technology companies, *and* how to make sure that technology and content will work in an interdependent way. And I have to say that I am amazed at the fervent commitment of music companies to develop legitimate businesses on the Internet.

One thing I think everyone learned during the policy debate was how interdependent technology delivery systems and content are in this new world. We also ran into a lot of difficult copyright law questions. What does a "reproduction" mean now? What does a "distribution" mean now? How in the world are we going to negotiate with not just technology companies but other content owners, with music publishers who own the musical work in the sound recording and with performance rights organizations who represent songwriters who are entitled to a royalty from the performance?

Given all of the new marketing and business deals and legal changes, we are now at a crucial point. Services like digital rights management systems, evolving legitimate peer-to-peer file-sharing systems, on-demand digital music subscription services, interactive and noninteractive radio, and regular downloads that retailers sell are all coming together in various combinations.

There is now only one huge question: Nobody knows what the consumer will want, what will succeed, or how all of this will work. Nobody knows yet, and can't know until the services are launched, for example, whether or not the copy protection systems that people think will work fairly effectively with respect to mainstream music consumers (we acknowledge that a certain level of piracy is always to be expected) will also provide those same customers an easy and convenient listening experience.

There have been many companies that have tried to establish legitimate commercial marketplaces on the Web over the past five years. And while some of them have had phenomenal advertising campaigns—sock puppets and other great things—they didn't last. Many learned that the consumer base in the Net world is an extremely fickle population. So when you launch online content, you have to ensure that it's something that is easy, convenient, and desirable, of course, from the musical standpoint, that it sounds great. It has to be something that is representative of the creators that we represent.

So we started out with the easy part. We started out, after negotiating with the music publishers, with a royalty rate for downloads (the same as the rate for a track on a compact disc in a record store) to licensed retailers who offered downloads on their sites. The consumer price for downloads started at around $2 per song and eventually came down to around 99 cents. The availability of downloads on a per-song basis got mixed reviews. Some consumers thought it was fair, but there was not a huge marketplace. Retailers did not find that it significantly affected either online or physical market sales. Some shut down. Some continue to offer music downloads. Downloads kept on the consumers' hard drive for later access—especially given the slow modem speeds at the time a lot of these services were first licensed—ended up being a market that didn't grow much, but one for which there is still hope in the future.

Webcasting is another advance. A statutory license first negotiated in 1995 and updated in 1998, established a system to allow noninteractive radio services to get online. Many of them are very successful. Some legal questions still remain, such as whether or not simulcasting over-the-air broadcasts online, would or would not be included in the license, and the courts have just come out with the answers to some of those questions.

So licenses for downloads and for webcasting were the earliest forms of legitimate online licensing, because the legal and marketing worlds were a little clearer on those types of services.

Interactive radio required licensing agreements that had to be negotiated. Now those agreements are starting to work and new services are beginning to come on board. ClickRadio, Listen.com's Rhapsody, Music Choice's Backstage Pass—there are a plethora of them. These are interactive radio services that that involve the listener. Some have a bar or button and ask you if you like or don't like the song that's playing. In effect, you are able to create your own radio station based on your own tastes.

The final frontier in the evolution to date is the advent of on-demand digital music subscription services. Everything that we learned about what didn't work in regular downloads, in noninteractive radio, or in interactive radio services seems to boil down to the consumer's desire to get the song or the artist that they want when they want. Whether it's streamed or downloaded or partially downloaded, consumers want their music available to them in a manner that is convenient and simple.

There was a great test market for this kind of service; unfortunately it happened to be illegal. Napster blew open the world of peer-to-peer services. It created a software program that provided an easy-to-use, efficient way for consumers to get whatever music they wanted whenever they wanted it.

The problem was that no licensing agreements were sought, and no musicians were compensated. So a lawsuit was brought. In the lawsuit the court began to figure out some of the rules of the road for how both the Digital Millennium Copyright Act and regular copyright principles would apply to these types of services. We now have some guidelines in light of the lawsuit, which is still proceeding.

There has since been a deal between the Recording Industry Association of America and the music publishers that will determine how people will treat on-demand streaming services. There are still some questions about permanent downloads. But now that some of the marketing and legal questions have been resolved, we see the launching of several new competing subscription services, including full audio, which will be available on 25 clear channel radio stations in five U.S. markets; Music, Music, Music; MusicNet; Pressplay; StreamWaves; Web Audio Net; Rioport; and Listen.com. More services are on the way. These on-demand services, which will launch and compete with each other—in addition to proposed services from CenterSpan/Scour and about two dozen others that are in negotiation right now—will represent the next wave in both legal and marketing questions as to how this evolution will continue to come about.

We know that there is one clear constant, and that is the consumer. Only the consumer will be able to determine whether these services will survive and whether it is worth putting in the investment from both the distribution and the content side to make it happen. Successful deployment of all this content requires respect for intellectual property. No one is going to allow their content to go unlicensed or accept less than market value for what is produced and made available on the Internet. Content providers must feel comfortable that there is a secure system for protecting their shareholders' investments and their artists' creations when they are offered on the Internet.

But we are getting to a point technologically, both from a business model point of view and from a legal point of view, where the road ahead is becoming clearer. Other content industries—motion pictures, software, books—will be able to benefit from the transformation that we in the music business have gone through over the past five years. It has been incredibly difficult, but I think we have learned a lot. Companies that we now work with every day have learned a lot. And at the end of the day, consumers will have a lot of great competing services out there, trying to offer them the best content for the lowest price. And may the best one win.

13. Copyright Zealotry in a Digital World: Can Freedom of Speech Survive?

Robin D. Gross

In Article I, Section 8, Clause 8, the U.S. Constitution sets out the purpose of copyright law, "to promote Progress of Science and useful Arts." The United States Supreme Court has made clear that the immediate effect of our copyright law is to secure a fair return for an author's creative labor. But its ultimate aim in providing this incentive is to stimulate artistic activity for the general public good. The original purpose of copyright under U.S. law was to provide an economic incentive for artists to create, thus ultimately benefiting the public. The Framers designed copyright not as a primary right but as a means to disseminate information in a time when the only way for information to spread was by attaching it to a medium like paper. Copyright law is designed to allocate a particular bundle of rights to the authors of works, but it reserves the remainder of rights to the public.

A basic premise of the U.S. intellectual property system is that the rights granted to creators as an incentive to produce creative works must be carefully balanced with the rights retained by the public. Hence, publishers and authors are not the only rights holders in the equation—members of the public are rights holders too under the copyright bargain. In exchange for the exclusive monopoly privilege granted to authors, the public is promised a rich and abundant public domain for all to use and share.

Fair use privileges are an important part of the public's side in the copyright bargain. The fair use doctrine acts as an intentional limitation on the author's right to control copying of a work. Fair use allows an individual to copy a work, in certain socially important circumstances—even when the copyright holder does not wish to allow such copying to occur. The Supreme Court has been clear that not all copying should be banned. Copying for purposes such as education, commentary, criticism, and personal use is generally permitted by copyright law, despite any lack of "authorization" from the author.

Meanwhile, Hollywood and the recording industry are busily developing technological methods of controlling the use of intellectual property, systems often referred to as "digital rights management" (DRM) technologies. But these systems present a powerful threat to freedom of expression. Because they only permit uses expressly authorized in advance, these schemes prevent many lawful uses of a copyrighted work. It is a mistake to think that the only uses of a work that are lawful are those that are authorized by the publisher; and a DRM technology may not be capable of distinguishing between legal and illegal uses. The U.S. Supreme Court has been quite clear, if not redundant, in holding that authorization is not required in order to make a fair use of a copyrighted work.[1]

The Court has also stated that fair use provides the necessary breathing space so that copyright does not conflict with the public's First Amendment guarantees.[2] Promises by Hollywood and the recording industry that their DRM schemes can accommodate fair use by permitting certain personal use copying of works simply does not qualify as fair use. Fair use, by definition, is lawful, but *unauthorized*, use of a work.[3]

This distinction—between license and liberty—is crucial. These DRM control systems entirely replace copyright as the means of mediating the public's access to and use of creative expression.

The industry complains that the advent of digital technology leaves it helpless in the face of unchecked piracy, but this claim is not completely true. In fact, technology grants publishers more, not less, control over their works. These DRM schemes promise to give copyright holders total control over their intellectual property— more efficiently and completely than law has ever been willing to grant authors. These schemes promise authors the power to control each access and use, the power to disable all fair uses, and the ability to maintain control over a work long after it should have passed into the public domain.

By essentially privatizing copyright law, these DRM schemes maintain none of the balance that the public law of copyright enshrines. Ironically, society is embarking on a dangerous path of narrowing the public's access to creative expression at exactly the time that technological advances protect publishers' rights more effectively than ever before.

Both sides of the copyright bargain deserve respect. Copyright imposes responsibilities as well as rights upon both authors and the public. It is simply not fair for one side to take all the benefit and accept none of the responsibility of the copyright bargain. This applies equally to authors and the public. The public must ensure that authors are economically rewarded for their creative gifts, and authors must ensure that the public is able to retain its rights and abilities to use and access creative expression.

DRM schemes are designed to respect only one side of the copyright bargain, so that Hollywood and the recording industry take all the privileges from the government-created monopoly but none of the responsibilities like ensuring fair use and contributing to the public domain.

"Architecture is policy."[4] Since control and regulation are primarily imposed by computer code in the digital environment, the way these systems are designed architecturally dictates the way society may use creative expression in a digital world.

While copyright law has granted authors the right to control public performances of a work, private performances have always been a right granted to the public under its side of the copyright bargain. But these DRM schemes attempt to usurp control over private performances of a work, giving control over the private performance to the publisher at the expense of the individual's right. Hollywood and the record companies, for example, want to control what you can do with the DVD (digital video disc) you bought, or the music you lawfully downloaded in the privacy of your own home on the equipment that you own. This new control over private performances creates a tremendous chilling effect on free expression since works may only be experienced in ways pre-approved by the publisher.

History has taught that every time a new technology was introduced, whether it was piano rolls, radio, videocassette recorders, or MP3 players, the industry's reaction has been litigation, claiming that because the technology is new and better, it poses too great a danger to their ability to profit to be allowed in the hands of the public. Yet in each case, the courts have prevented the industry from outlawing the technology and the industry has found a way to profit from the new opportunities brought on by the new technology.

The latest wave of lawsuits may indicate a change in direction from this policy choice, a direction where third parties can be found liable for the illegal actions of those who use the tools they build. In *A&M Records v. Napster*[5] software creators were held liable for the infringing acts of others and ordered to rewrite their software to prevent any unlawful trading of music. The 2d Circuit Court of Appeals recently upheld an injunction against a journalist for publishing information in violation of the anti-dissemination provisions of the Digital Millennium Copyright Act, forbidding the magazine from even telling the public via hyperlinks where technical information on code capable of overriding a particular form of copy protection could be found.[6] MP3.com was crushed by the Recording Industry Association of America in copyright lawsuits for providing the public with an online listening service that would have allowed people to take advantage of the personal use rights they have enjoyed with respect to compact discs they have purchased.[7]

In October 2001 Hollywood filed a new lawsuit against technology it cannot control, peer-to-peer file-sharing software called Morpheus, which is distributed by software company MusicCity.[8] This file-sharing program enables individuals to connect directly with each other and share any kind of information without any mediator or other central control or distribution point. So now Hollywood is suing software developers and distributors who provide this software to individuals—software that enables the public to exercise its lawful right to use creative expression. Because peer-to-peer networks cannot distinguish lawful from unlawful transmissions, Hollywood wants to stamp out the entire technology.

Through aggressive litigation, the industry is attempting to overturn an important legal precedent established when Hollywood tried, and failed, to outlaw videocassette recorders because they could be used to make unauthorized copies of copyrighted movies and television programs. In the famous 1984 Betamax case, the Supreme Court held that a communication technology that is capable of substantial noninfringing uses cannot be outlawed.[9] That the court ruled against the studios proved lucky for them, because VHS movie rentals and sales are now the most profitable segment of their industry. Unwilling to learn from its mistakes, Hollywood continues in its battle to ban technology it cannot control.

The Electronic Frontier Foundation has joined the Morpheus legal defense team to challenge attempts to overturn the Betamax legal principle. Through its lawsuit against this file-sharing program, Hollywood and the recording industry are again using the existence of their copyright powers to try to leverage control over a new technology. Under the guise of copyright, the industry is attempting to force software developers to beg Hollywood for permission each time they want to build products that can play or otherwise interact with their content. This would be the equivalent of allowing book publishers to control photocopy machines. If it is allowed to succeed, Hollywood and the recording industry's short-sightedness and obsession with controlling content will grossly stifle innovation and chill freedom of expression for everyone.

Software should be treated no differently than other technologies, whether guns, knives, or cars, that can be used for both lawful and unlawful purposes. We don't outlaw the technology altogether because we know some will use it for unlawful purposes. Few suggest society should hold employees of Smith & Wesson liable, even though we know guns are used to kill people. Yet somehow copyrights are more sacred and need more protection than human life under the industry's theory of broad liability. Individuals, not just software vendors, are being targeted. In January 2002, Norwegian teenager Jon Johansen was indicted by Norwegian authorities on a complaint by the Motion Picture Association of America for trying to build a DVD player for the Linux operating system.

The challenges authors and society currently face stem from the fact that we are moving from a world of information scarcity to one of abundance. Our legal rules were originally designed to work— and indeed have worked well for some for 200 years—in a world of scarcity. But we are now trying to use these old-world rules to navigate through a new world of abundance. In so doing, we risk creating an artificial scarcity for ideas and information where there need be none. Considering that copyright's ultimate objective is to spread knowledge and creativity, it is truly ironic that it may now serve as the primary tool used to stifle the very creativity, innovation, and free exchange of ideas that copyright was designed by the Framers to foster.

> If nature has made any one thing less susceptible than all others of exclusive property, it is the action of the thinking

power called an idea. . . . He who receives an idea from me, receives instruction himself without lessening mine; as he who lights his taper at mine, receives light without darkening me. That ideas should freely spread from one to another over the globe, for the moral and mutual instruction of man, and improvement of his condition, seems to have been peculiarly and benevolently designed by nature, when she made them, like fire, expansible over all space, without lessening their density at any point, and like the air in which we breathe, move, and have our physical being, incapable of confinement or exclusive appropriation. Inventions then cannot, in nature, be a subject of property.

—Thomas Jefferson

Jefferson and the other Framers realized that our Constitution was founded on the principle that great minds beget great minds and that no one rises alone. These principles have allowed this country to learn from the mistakes of our ancestors and avoid the traps of censorship and repressed expression that are the natural results of turning thought into a form of property, to be bought and sold, given and withheld. Shedding this constrictive history has allowed our country to develop a nation of unbridled thinkers who have changed the way we view the world.

However, a nation of unbridled thinkers is not always conducive to the success of corporate monopoly. The word monopoly itself is extreme; it suggests a complete lack of balance. The movie studios would like the public to believe that the only alternative to their uber-protection agenda is the opposite extreme: anarchy, a total loss of regulation that leaves the intellectual property of artists thoroughly unprotected. However, that picture is grossly out of sync with what their perceived enemies are fighting for, which is simply balance: a middle ground that gives artists rights that they deserve, and simultaneously supports and protects fair use rights and a rich public commons.

Creating and maintaining such a delicate balance is difficult, especially as new technology continues to change the way we exchange thoughts, ideas, and information. But the effort will pay off in far more rewarding ways than simply using the law to effectively "shut up" a perceived threat. Outlawing communication technology will create far greater problems for freedom of speech than it will solve for piracy.

Notes

1. See *Sony Corp. of America v. Universal City Studios, Inc.*, 464 U.S. 417, 104 S.Ct. 774 (1984); *Stewart v. Abend*, 495 U.S. 207, 110 S.Ct. 1750 (1990); *Campbell v. Acuff-Rose Music, Inc.*, 510 U.S. 569, 114 S.Ct. 1164 (1994); *Harper & Row Publishers, Inc. v. Nation Enterprises*, 471 U.S. 539, 105 S.Ct. 2218 (1985).

2. *Campbell v. Acuff-Rose Music, Inc.*, 510 U.S. 569, 114 S.Ct. 1164 (1994).

3. "Even unauthorized uses of a copyrighted work are not necessarily infringing. An unlicensed use of the copyright is not an infringement unless it conflicts with one of the specific exclusive rights conferred by the copyright statute." *Twentieth Century Music Corp. v. Aiken*, 422 U.S. 151, 154–155, 95 S.Ct. 2040, 2043, 45 L.Ed.2d 84; *Sony Corp. of America v. Universal City Studios, Inc.*, 464 U.S. 417, 447, 104 S.Ct. 774 (1984).

4. The Electronic Frontier Foundation often uses the slogan, "Architecture is Policy," an updated version of its co-founder Mitchell Kapor's famous slogan, "Architecture is Politics." See Mitchell Kapor, "The Software Design Manifesto," www.kei.com/homepages/mkapor/Software_Design_Manisfesto.html; David Farber, "A Note on the Politics of Privacy and Infrastructure," November 20, 1993, icepobox.com/cis590/reading.045.txt; see also Pamela Samuelson et al., "A Manifesto Concerning the Legal Protection of Computer Programs," *Columbia Law Review* 94 (1994): 2308. See also Lawrence Lessig, *Code and Other Laws of Cyberspace* (New York: Basic Books, 1999) p. 20.

5. 239 F.3d 1004 (9th Cir. 2001).

6. *Universal City Studios et al. v. Corley (2600 Magazine)*, 273 F.3d 429 (2d Cir. 2001).

7. *UMG Recordings, Inc. v. MP3.Com, Inc.*, 92 F. Supp.2d 349 (S.D.N.Y) 2000.

8. *MGM Studios et al. v. Grokster, MusicCity, Consumer Empowerment/FastTrack* CV #01-8541-SVW filed in United States District Court for the Central District of California in Los Angeles on Oct. 2, 2001.

9. *Sony Corp. of America v. Universal City Studios, Inc.*, 464 U.S. 417, 104 S.Ct. 774 (1984).

14. Copyright in the Post-Napster World: Legal or Market Solutions?

Stan Liebowitz

I am an economist. So my view with respect to the digital copyright wars of today boils down to, "I don't care what the courts say, I'll tell you what they *should* have said." That economic perspective is a fairly narrow one, concerned usually with economic efficiency.

The balance to be struck over intellectual property is simple enough to state. People who invest in creating things need to receive sufficient rewards to make it worthwhile for them to make the investment—as long as the investment is one that should have been made in the first place, which is a very hard thing to know. But the key thing is whether or not that linkage between creation and reward can continue to exist in the Internet era. The digital revolution has raised the question of whether law or markets are the best means of incentivizing the creation of intellectual properties, such as movies, music, and books.

The truth of the matter is that copyright owners have often cried "wolf" when a new technology appeared at the door, particularly when they didn't understand the technology or its implications well and merely assumed that it would threaten them. The most famous example is Hollywood's reaction to the videocassette recorder (VCR), a campaign that resulted in the Supreme Court, by but a single vote, allowing the VCR to remain legal. History has demonstrated that Hollywood was fortunate to have lost the case. Even though content owners cried "wolf" for copying technologies in the past, however, I have a feeling they're right about Napster and peer-to-peer networking. Rampant file sharing of digital copies of what had once been relatively safe content really does represent a wolf at the door.

However, even though Napster and its descendants like Audio-Galaxy, MusicCity, and other peer-to-peer systems have considerable potential to harm copyright owners, there is a potential solution out there, known to as digital rights management (DRM). DRM refers to any of a number of copy-protection techniques whereby content owners can encode their products to protect them from unauthorized duplication.

Now, it's certainly not the case that DRM is going to put a stop to all copying. It can't be a solution in that strict sense since any copy-protection schemes can be broken by someone who's determined enough. So zero-piracy can't be the goal. But if DRM is capable of thwarting the bulk of the unauthorized copying that might otherwise occur—the wholesale piracy by the average Joe that Napster embodied in its heyday—that may be good enough. Furthermore, if DRM techniques can allow copyright holders to charge for each use whether large or small, that's actually a plus. Some worry that the ability to lock up content or charge "micropayments" for even the most limited of uses is a violation of fair use rights guaranteed under the copyright bargain. But that worry is overblown, as we'll see.

So we have two kinds of concerns in the digital age. Producers worry about piracy, and users worry over the loss of fair use rights that may occur when producers try to defend themselves against piracy.

Let's start with the fears over piracy itself. First of all, as noted above, there exists considerable misunderstanding among creators regarding the impact of new technology. Copying doesn't always hurt the producers of new technology, even when it is unauthorized. One reason is that, in many instances, it turns out to be possible to increase the price of originals in a manner that can compensate for copying that takes place.

The debate stretches back a long way. My first involvement with the copyright issue was in a paper investigating the impact of photocopying, particularly in libraries, which was a concern in the 1980s just as digital piracy is today. Actually looking at data concerning what people were photocopying, and what was happening to the price of the items that were being photocopied, was interesting. It turned out that the producers of the published materials began to charge higher prices in a way that would compensate for most of the photocopying.

Most of the photocopying was occurring in libraries, and most of the material that was copyrighted was journal articles. In response to the reality of copying, libraries were getting charged two, three, or four times the price that individuals were being charged for subscriptions to academic journals. The disparity in price that evolved between library or institutional subscriptions on the one hand, and individual subscriptions on the other, persists today.

Through this pricing technique, publishers were able to generate sufficient revenues that the net impact of unauthorized copying engendered by the photocopier ended up benefiting the publishers. The marketplace shifted so that journals overtook books as the primary academic resource (books are tedious to copy, after all), a boon to academic journal publishers.

So the claims by publishers that the photocopier was going to kill them were an exaggeration of the threat they faced. Therefore it's quite reasonable that the courts have concluded that photocopying is, to a large extent, legal.

The overreaction that occurred with respect to the VCR was similar. For starters, the "time shifting" of television programs that the VCR allowed was something that was not likely to harm the revenues of the television producers, despite their worries. Interestingly, when the case was being considered, the copying of movies was not the primary concern; it really was the fear of time shifting. But time shifting just meant that the advertisements were seen at a different time, albeit perhaps with some fast-forwarding; it didn't really do any harm to the revenues of the television programmers. And with respect to the piracy question, as has often been noted, movie rentals are now the leading profit maker for the movie industry—movies that are played on the dreaded VCR.

The key mechanism by which producers can actually benefit from piracy is what I refer to as "indirect appropriability," and it has implications for the Napster debate. Recall the previous example of journal publishers who could charge higher prices for originals in a venue in which copying would likely occur—the library.

Before considering its application to the digital realm, it's worth noting how the concept of indirect appropriability could apply to yet another episode over which copyright owners were quite upset: the audio-taping of records onto cassette tapes in the 1970s and 1980s. (Although today everyone buys compact discs [CDs], the audio-taping controversy centered around the taping of vinyl records.) Indirect appropriability likely played a role here as well, perhaps as follows. People often like to make a cassette copy of their music to use in their car's tape player. This might be considered an example of "space shifting," as contrasted with the time shifting that was of so much concern in the VCR debate.

But this kind of copying is not necessarily bad for the copyright holder. Assume that everyone who bought a record made one cassette and played it in their car. In that case, the record would be of more value to the owner than would be the case if it were impossible to make a copy of it on cassette. Consumers would attach a greater value to the record because they do place a positive, although perhaps implicit, monetary value on the ability to make a cassette. That means the record companies might simply raise the price of the original vinyl record to capture much of that value to the user of making a copy. Everyone gets to do the copying they want, and the producer catches the revenue through the mechanism of indirect appropriability, and quite possibly, everyone is better off.

Despite that market mechanism for recapture of value by the industry, interestingly enough Alan Greenspan testified before Congress on behalf of the record producers, explaining how the cassettes were going to destroy the record industry. But of course that destruction never occurred.

In many instances of copying, some variant of indirect appropriability is possible. But in order for indirect appropriability to work, one must to be able to identify who it is that is doing the copying or where it is that the copying is going on, in order to charge the higher price. If everyone is making a copy, that's fine; you just charge a higher price to everyone. That was the story with records. With photocopying, it was charging more to libraries that allowed copyright holders to capture much of the value of making copies.

The problem with respect to the copying that Napster engendered, or with that allowed by any of the newer peer-to-peer network options like MusicCity, is that some of the original CDs get turned into copies that are themselves made over and over again into copies, and no one can identify which of the originals are going to be pirated and exchanged and which ones aren't. So even though the copyright owners cried "wolf" about Betamax and they were wrong, and they cried "wolf" about photocopying and they were wrong, and they cried "wolf" about audio cassettes and they were wrong, they probably are right about peer-to-peer networks. The theory of indirect appropriability indicates they will be.

It is important to note that, if you go through the actual evidence in the Napster case, the recording industry utterly failed to provide any reasonable evidence that Napster had in fact done them any harm. The evidence the industry put forward never made the case for the piracy-induced harm that they intended to make.

The record industry had, for example, raised the issue of CD sales at record stores near universities versus sales elsewhere, which I think is a reasonable experiment to make if one wants to find out if harm is occurring. The story they were telling was that students at universities were more likely to use Napster, and so CD sales at stores near universities ought to be compared with sales at stores that are not near universities, to see whether or not there is any difference between the two.

The record companies claimed that sales at stores near universities did not grow as rapidly as sales at other stores. That might have been some good evidence that Napster use was cutting into sales. However, it turns out that even before Napster's existence sales at stores near the universities were not growing as fast as they were at other stores. An explanation for this of course might have been that students—who use the Internet more than the general population—might have been *purchasing* music online through outlets like Amazon.com, which predated Napster. One would need to look at online sales data to determine it. But in any case, the evidence didn't bear out the record company claims.

One reason I suspect Napster didn't do measurable harm so early in the game is that it wasn't really replacing the sales of CDs. Most people couldn't, and still can't, take music downloaded onto a computer and play it on their stereo system. Most people do not have CD writers, or burners as they are often called. They could listen to downloaded songs on their computers, but if they wanted to listen to them on their stereos, they still had to buy the CD. When everybody gets a CD writer—and more and more of them are being sold—presumably that's when the harm will really show up. Although the record companies didn't make a viable case in my judgment, I do think that file-sharing over peer-to-peer networks can do harm to them as more people go online. As the number of people using broadband Internet connections grows, it may magnify their problems.

Without the possibility of indirect appropriability, it is very likely that in fact there will be harm to the copyright owners. Some take that fact and argue that the peer-to-peer networks should be shut down after all. But I'm not sure how such a thing could be accomplished. Napster is at least theoretically controllable because it has a central server, and if record companies had cooperated with Napster early on, they might have mitigated some of the harm they face by developing reasonable pricing and service options.

But the pure peer-to-peer networks that have taken Napster's place have no central server, and afford the record companies no perceivable partnership and control options. Even if Napster were to remain shut down, the genie is out of the bottle. But there is hope yet, embodied in digital rights management.

Now, I don't claim to be a computer scientist. I know that DRM technologies intended to protect intellectual property will be cracked, because protected software has always been cracked. For the copy protection to do its job, however, the key is that it be cracked in such a small number of cases that most people still buy legitimate copies. Cracking has to be the exception rather than the rule, a scenario that stands an even better chance if the products are priced right: indeed, one of the rationalizations by defenders of Napster has been that the prices of CDs are too high. But if encrypted downloads are priced appropriately, piracy may be less of a problem.

Pirates won't go away, of course. Persistent subgroups of them collect pirated software, like games, sometimes for no particular purpose; they may not even use the software but simply amass collections of it to trade with others. This behavior has always been largely relegated to a subgroup, occupying a small place in the economy. And as long as the pirating stays isolated, the copyright owners will be okay.

The imperative for copyright holders is to use technology to prevent massive unauthorized duplication of their material, as exemplified by widespread downloading of music by the general public. DRM claims to be able to do something like that.

One of the requirements for the technology to succeed is likely to be the charging of "micropayments" for limited access to, or use of, copyrighted material. But the charging for each use is precisely what disturbs many critics of DRM. They argue that the ability to make limited copies without paying is a legitimate part of the copyright bargain, and that to require payments for every little use is a violation of those "fair use" rights.

It may be true that having to pay for every little use of copyrighted material would represent a substantial change. However, from an economic perspective, that turns out to be a great thing, if one's concern is that the socially optimal amount of intellectual property be produced.

It is an established principle in economics that charging users different prices, depending on how much they are using a product, results in the production of the economically optimal amount of a given product. Economists call this phenomenon perfect price discrimination, which means that everybody gets charged a different price, one related to the maximum they are willing to pay. For small uses of a product, the amount consumers are willing to pay is likely to be small, and DRM technologies will have to accommodate that reality.

So it would appear that variable pricing under various regimes of digital rights management can actually go a long way toward the goal of achieving efficient levels of production of intellectual properties in the new era of digital music, movies, and books. Indeed, without those techniques, it would seem that optimal incentives for creation and distribution of intellectual property would be very hard to achieve. So DRM should be viewed as a good thing, not a bad thing.

Some might persist in arguing that pay-per-use DRM can lock up content inappropriately. What about when one simply wants to quote from a paragraph in an online article, for example?

I don't understand why that's a problem. There is something called the "ink pen." It's sort of old-fashioned; it's analog. But if there is a paragraph that I want to take out of someone's paper and put it in mine and don't want to pay to cut-and-paste it digitally as DRM may demand of me, it can still be done the old-fashioned way, as it was done even before photocopiers. You sit there and you write out the material you want to quote, letter by letter—and I know it's difficult and I know it's time consuming, but people did just that for many, many centuries. You still end up with the paragraph you want to quote, and it qualifies as a fair use of the material. The fact that it was digitally protected so that you couldn't make a copy of it electronically in cut-and-paste fashion doesn't restrict fair use of the material in any meaningful way. That's how fair use works; it isn't necessarily incumbent on producers to make it *easy* to borrow from their material, especially when doing so can open the door to digital piracy.

Note that there will be demands for cutting and pasting cheaply, and the very existence of such fair use rights in itself is a check on any efforts to charge too much for minor uses, so the need to actually "copy by hand" is likely to be minimal. Indeed, it is more likely that limited uses will remain free, much like movie trailers or the sample book pages provided on Amazon.

Obviously, the realities of the ease of digital copying will mean that we may not always be able to copy material in exactly the way we might prefer, because producers will seek to protect their property. But if fair use really does mean limited use, which is what the copyright bargain is supposed to protect, market-based DRM ought to be quite viable and capable of satisfying all parties. I don't think DRM creates a fair use problem in the digital age. On the contrary, digital rights management, if it can work the way its proponents suggest, will be an increasingly economically advantageous solution to what in fact remains a very difficult problem in a digital age—that of maximizing the output of intellectual products that are otherwise susceptible to piracy of such magnitude that it could hinder such output.

15. Protecting Intellectual Property in the Digital Age

Frank G. Hausmann

In this chapter I'll make the following points.

- Peer-to-peer (P2P) communication between Internet users, as opposed to users and Web sites, is both the origin and the future of the Internet. Contrary to the impressions generated by the Napster controversy, P2P systems are not inherently infringing or nonsecure, as is evidenced by the increasing use of P2P systems within enterprises to facilitate the sharing of secured content. "Mediated" P2P systems offer substantial cost savings with respect to the storage and bandwidth requirements necessary to support games, music, and video, thus enabling the continued growth of digital content distribution services. Overall, mediated and secure P2P systems can deliver a mix of audio and video content at one-third the cost of traditional client-server downloads and one-tenth the cost of streaming.

- Existing digital rights management technologies provide sufficient security to address the legitimate concerns of copyright owners.

- A legislated, affirmative fair use "safe harbor" would be the most positive action Congress could take to facilitate the growth and consumer acceptance of legitimate digital content distribution services. A "middle way" must be established between the conflicting agendas of copyright anarchists and copyright maximalists in order to provide marketplace stability.

- Ongoing antitrust oversight of the digital media market is expected. Vigorous competition and diverse consumer choice are key assurances of a vibrant and successful online content industry.

- The nondiscriminatory licensing provisions of legislation such as the proposed Music Online Competition Act would, as drafted, be of dubious assistance to companies like CenterSpan that seek to expand digital distribution.
- Legislative proposals to mandate inclusion of government-selected content security technologies in a broad array of electronic devices should be rejected in favor of marketplace solutions.
- New or expanded compulsory licenses for interactive media may be appropriate for "streaming" distribution that is analogous to commercial broadcasting, but not for "downloading" that enables the provisioning of permanent copies and truly revolutionizes the distribution and sale of digital content.
- The first-sale doctrine is not meaningful or applicable in the digital environment.
- Consumers may require enhanced legal protections to assure that when they participate in online media services, including those that use P2P delivery systems, their legitimate privacy expectations are respected. They should not be subjected to unwanted marketing and spamming from third-party commercial entities.

Content Protection in the Peer-to-Peer Environment

Today's technology, and tomorrow's, will enable vast numbers of individuals to have access to high-quality digital media, and entertainment on demand 24/7 from nearly any location through a variety of wired and wireless digital devices. The challenge that confronts content owners, digital distribution entities, and policy-makers is to determine whether the current state of copyright law empowers or detracts from our ability to fulfill that potential. The question that faces us is whether statutory change is required—and, if change is to be made, how to balance the maintenance of incentives that "promote the Progress of Science and the useful Arts," the goal set forth in Article I of the Constitution, against the technological progress that can undermine creators' "exclusive Right to their respective Writings and Discoveries" envisioned by that founding document.

The subject of entertainment delivery over the Internet is certainly not an issue of life and death, or of war and peace. But it is an important subject and no apology need be given for according it serious attention. What we are talking about is nothing less than the technological means by which the abundant fruits of our culture of free thought and expression will be disseminated among Americans, and to the world. We are focused as well on the need for a legal structure that strikes the proper balance between the legitimate needs and expectations of content creators and owners, digital distribution entities, and consumers, and that sets terms that assure vigorous competition in the digital media marketplace.

The decisions that will be made by both the public and private sectors will also have important ramifications for our economy, consequences that go far beyond the size and profitability of the music, movie, gaming, and Internet industries. That is because the availability of broadband-intensive digital content directly affects the economic demand for an "always on" digital telecommunications architecture capable of scaling to greater capacity and functionality. This in turn affects investment, jobs, and U.S. technological leadership in the 21st century. In remarks before the National Summit on Broadband Deployment, Federal Communications Commission Chairman Michael Powell noted "deployment will have very positive benefits for the nation and the world." He then commented upon the linkage between content and broadband, as well as the possible misapprehensions of copyright owners:

> There exists a chicken and egg problem with respect to broadband content and distribution. Much of what is holding broadband content back is caused by copyright holders trying to protect their goods in a digitized environment (in other words, a perfect reproduction world). Stimulating content creation might involve a reexamination of the copyright laws. Arguably, VCRs would not be widely available today if Universal Studios had won its infringement case against Sony in 1984. [Sony] won in the Supreme Court by a vote of 5-4.

Chairman Powell reminds us that the Supreme Court, by that single vote, let distribution of the videocassette recorder (VCR) proceed because it was found to have substantial noninfringing uses, and among them was time shifting for personal viewing. A single justice's vote allowed us to have VCRs that record, rather than merely play back. It seems ludicrous now that we might not have that capability, yet the movie industry sincerely believed that the

"R" in VCR would lead to massive infringement and economic ruin. Today, its studios reap greater income from video sales and rentals than they do from first-run box office revenues. But is the past prologue? Does that lead to the conclusion that the broadcasters who filed suit against ReplayTV are mistaken in their dire predictions of the consequences of a digital video recorder that automatically deletes commercials and allows an individual to share a digital recording over the Internet? Not necessarily. There is a vast qualitative difference between an analog and a digital recording, as well as a far broader range of consequences stemming from the multifunctional capabilities of digital electronics and the distributive power of the Internet. But it does raise the possibility that the infringement fears of copyright owners are obscuring their recognition of the very significant new revenues that can flow from new media services businesses, even if some infringement "leakage" occurs. Microsoft, after all, became the most highly valued stock in the world, and its CEO the richest man in the world, despite the widespread piracy of its software. Perhaps the quest for perfect piracy protection should yield to the acceptance of digital rights controls that are an adequate foundation for legitimate new services.

That approach makes sense because the marketplace has certainly not advanced in the way Congress envisioned when it enacted the Digital Millennium Copyright Act in October 1998. Nor does it seem to be heading in a direction that bodes all that well for copyright owners. We are only just beginning to see limited rollout of major record label subscription music services, much less packages that have all major label content and a price and usage value proposition sure to garner large numbers of subscribers. Although the licensing agreement announced in October 2001 between the major record labels and music publishers was a step in the right direction, it only covers on-demand streaming and limited downloads. It also incorporates a "mutual understanding" of relevant copyright law that will increase applicable royalty costs beyond what many others believe copyright law would require even while the applicable royalty rates, which will be owed retroactively, remain undetermined.

Although millions of dollars have already been expended in litigating against and effectively shutting down Napster and other infringing services, the research firm Webnoize has reported that users of the many FastTrack P2P network services traded 1.8 billion media files during October 2001, an astounding 480 percent increase over just four months. (FastTrack has been a dominant P2P successor to Napster.) Moreover, Webnoize reported that the system in November 2001 would surpass the 1.6 million simultaneous users that Napster enjoyed at its peak. Those 1.8 billion files traded in October did not produce a single penny in direct revenue to copyright owners, music publishers, songwriters, or musicians, and that is an untenable situation. The recording and movie industries have filed suit against the FastTrack services, but FastTrack claims that the court decision in the Napster case is not controlling because, unlike Napster, it merely distributes software and does not maintain a central indexed file directory. Whatever this new lawsuit's outcome, after many months of delay and many more millions in legal fees, does anyone doubt that more pirate content-sharing networks will arise and find users as long as there is a lack of diverse, competitive, and legitimate online content services?

Meanwhile, another recent Webnoize survey found that students are buying and listening to significantly fewer compact discs (CDs) than a year ago, instead using Internet radio and pirated CDs. Some have questioned whether the movement of record labels toward copy-protected CDs that will not play on personal computers is an effective way to prevent piracy yet keep this critical audience, when, for many if not most students, the personal computer is their primary stereo system.

Clearly, we can and must do better for all the stakeholders in creative works. If the content-as-product business confronts new and inevitable challenges, that is all the more reason to accelerate the introduction of the content-as-service business. Both legal and technological protections have their place in safeguarding the rights of content owners, but ultimately the best defense is a good offense. And that offense must be the rollout of digital distribution services that provide consumers with access to the audio, video, and gaming content they choose, to be used in the manner that suits their preferences, at a cost that is not simply attractive but compelling.

CenterSpan's peer-to-peer (P2P) system is based upon the utilization of a variety of digital rights management (DRM) technologies that allow content owners to set and enforce rules of usage for copyrighted materials. Scour, for which consumer trials have been launched, is now the first secure and legal P2P "digital distribution channel" supporting the delivery of audio and video entertainment. Tens of thousands of users are participating in the free trial. We are using the trial to fine-tune and showcase C-star, our proprietary content delivery network that underlies Scour and provides its security. Our ultimate goal is to roll out a tiered-price subscription service when key business criteria are satisfied, including the resolution of content licensing issues with the music and film industries. Our plan calls for the offering of different service options depending on the type, quantity, and "use rules" of content that subscribers wish to access. Eventually, Scour could also support e-books, photos, and graphics. Our proprietary market research, as well as extensive conversations with all segments of the digital entertainment world, convince us that there will be substantial consumer demand for such a service, provided that it offers the right combination of ease of use, content, and price.

P2P: Origin and Future of the Internet

P2P networks and applications are both the origin and the future of the Internet. The Internet's fundamental support of a widely dispersed and virtually limitless number of participants, coupled with the transmission of digital information through packet switching that breaks up messages and content and sends it between users via multiple routes, was chosen to assure the maintenance of communication regardless of attacks on any single component of the system. The result is the most robust, resilient, and useful communications system in history.

Internet media business models that rely solely on content distribution from central servers, and do not support further dispersal by individual users, will not be successful in the marketplace. P2P systems can best take advantage of the "viral marketing" that occurs when fans enthusiastically promote and share their secure digital entertainment files with others. Where video and gaming content is concerned, the significant storage and bandwidth requirements are best and most efficiently met through the dispersal of content to end users within a P2P environment. In effect, P2P systems enable consumers to choose to make a portion of their hard drive storage and bandwidth available for the benefit of other users.

The cost savings for P2P are very compelling, especially since legitimate services may be facing off against free pirate services for some time to come. For example, CenterSpan's C-Star mediated P2P platform is the basis for a content delivery network (CDN) that provides secure and reliable distribution services that are far more cost-effective than the most efficient server-based streaming or client-server systems. Assuming the delivery of audio content to two million subscribers, the annual cost of operating a P2P CDN would be $6 million—versus $19 million for traditional client-server downloads and $207 million for traditional streaming. The potential cost savings for video are also large; P2P CDN delivers video content at one-third the cost of client-server systems and one-sixth the cost of streaming.

Taking into account the annual audio-video content mix of a hypothetical service provider and consumer consumption patterns, we conservatively estimate the overall average annual delivery costs of a P2P CDN to be approximately one-third that of central server networks and one-tenth that of central server streaming networks. The vast majority of these cost savings result from reduced bandwidth costs. These impressive savings are achieved while providing content owners with the same level of security, and subscribers with the same speed and reliability, as centralized networks. Files on a C-star CDN system are encrypted, signed with a digital signature, and encased in a DRM wrapper before being introduced into the system. The content is centrally controlled, indexed, and tracked through the network. User machines must be authenticated before content can be downloaded or streamed. These revolutionary networks scale easily and naturally because peers provide additional network redundancy while keeping a tight lid on bandwidth costs. The mediated P2P approach is the only economically viable means of delivering digital content to a large audience.

It is unfortunate that Napster created the public impression that P2P networks only support illegal distribution of inherently nonsecure content. Given the tremendous potential of legitimate, DRM-enhanced P2P systems, nothing could be further from the truth. In remarks delivered on November 6th, 2001, before the O'Reilly Peer to Peer Conference here in Washington, Recording Industry Association of America head Hilary Rosen noted: "The problem with peer to peer is not the technology but how it is used. The multiple exciting applications of P to P . . . show the limitless potential of the technology in multiple ways. The ability to achieve cost savings on storage

211

and bandwidth, the web tools, the meeting applications, the communications applications, the customer service applications are all extremely exciting."

On February 13, 2001, when the Ninth Circuit Court of Appeals issued its decision that Napster's original design and operation were in substantial violation of our copyright laws, I applauded that ruling and stated, "The rights of copyright holders must be protected in the new digital distribution paradigm." The protection of copyrights through licensing and the utilization of advanced DRM technologies is completely compatible with the distributional and cost advantages of P2P systems.

Policy Choices: The Middle Way between Copyright Maximalism and Piracy

Since enactment of the DMCA, Congress has engaged in a dual enterprise. Its first objective has been to ascertain the current state of digital entertainment technology and applicable law. Its second task has been to determine whether additional legislative intervention is required to protect the goals of copyright law and the rights of copyright holders while promoting the further development of digital distribution of music, movies, and other genre of entertainment and culture. Once again, Congress must balance traditional legal values with new technology that, depending on its use or misuse, may promote or undermine the progress of science and the useful arts.

The sentiments expressed in the February 14, 2001, Senate floor remarks of Sens. Orrin Hatch (R-Utah) and Patrick Leahy (D-Vt.) in response to the Ninth Circuit's Napster decision were largely on the mark. Sen. Hatch called for "an open and competitive environment in the production and distribution of content on the Internet," as well as for "a marketplace resolution to . . . digital music controversies." Sen. Leahy observed that "the availability of new music and other creative works. . .depends on clearly understood and adequately enforced copyright protection. . . . [C]opyrights may not be ignored when new online services are deployed. The Internet can and must serve the needs not only of Internet users and innovators of new technologies, but also of artists, songwriters, performers and copyright holders." What is needed is a supportive legal framework that sets forth nondiscriminatory and clearly understood principles for all market participants.

Some legislative intervention would be desirable to establish a "middle way" that steers between the copyright anarchists, who celebrate and promote massive infringement, and the copyright maximalists, who appear to seek the effective elimination of traditional fair use concepts through overbearing technologies that control and seek to monetize every aspect of the utilization of copyrighted digital media. This middle way should be firmly grounded in clarifying and protecting the rights of consumers, because the digital media distribution business is a consumer service business and failing to meet the legitimate expectations of consumers will inevitably lead to the failure of digital media ventures. The notion of a new and affirmative basis for assuring the goals of "fair use" was set forth in a pioneering 2000 report by a National Research Council committee called *The Digital Dilemma: Intellectual Property in the Information Age*. After concluding that "fair use and other exceptions to copyright law should continue to play a role in the digital environment," and that "the fair use doctrine may also prove useful as a flexible mechanism for adapting copyright to the digital environment," it issued this policy advice:

> *Recommendation: The committee suggests exploring whether or not the notion of copy is an appropriate foundation for copyright law, and whether a new foundation can be constructed for copyright, based on the goal set forth in the Constitution ("promote the progress of science and the useful arts") and a tactic by which it is achieved, namely, providing incentive to authors and publishers. In this framework, the question would not be whether a copy had been made, but whether a use of a work was consistent with the goal and tactic (i.e., did it contribute to the desired "progress" and was it destructive, when taken alone or aggregated with other similar copies, of an author's incentive?). This concept is similar to fair use but broader in scope, as it requires considering the range of factors by which to measure the impact of the activity on authors, publishers, and others.*

Other Key Public Policy and Technical Questions

Clarifying Fair Use

Federal legislation should carve out a fair use "safe harbor" both to preserve this key protection of informed discussion, criticism, and debate and to affirmatively delineate consumer rights. In testimony submitted to the Senate Judiciary Committee in April 2001, our company suggested that the marketplace was the best place to determine the reuse limitations supported by DRM technologies and was most likely to set the optimal balance between the desires of consumers, the needs of scholars and commentators, and the legitimate concerns of content owners.

However, we have reluctantly concluded that the best means to stabilize the digital media marketplace, reduce disruptive and horrendously expensive litigation, and encourage consumers to utilize legitimate services would be the enactment of federal legislation stating, as clearly as possible, what reasonable and legitimate uses consumers may make of lawfully acquired digital media. Such legislation must recognize and be in harmony with the statutory rights of copyright holders. But it must also go beyond the existing concept of fair use, which is, after all, but a defense against allegations of copyright infringement. This legislation should be as explicit as possible in laying out how consumers can legally use their copyrighted digital materials. Since it may be impossible to envision all the types of use that may be abetted by future technologies, the legislation should provide clear principles to guide the courts. It will by no means be easy to write, much less enact, such a bill, but it could be the single most important and useful thing that Congress could do to spur the development of legitimate online media services.

Digital Security in the Marketplace

Current DRM technologies do provide sufficient protection to satisfy the legitimate concerns of copyright holders, and support for a variety of DRM solutions is achievable.

Compulsory Licenses

It is worthwhile for Congress to consider the establishment of new or expanded compulsory licenses to facilitate the digital distribution of interactive media content over the Internet. In this regard, it may be useful to distinguish between those forms of "digital distribution" that are analogous to broadcasting and those that are more akin to ownership of a CD or DVD. Respectively, these are "streaming" and "downloading," and, as noted, digital content may be distributed either way. Streaming is analogous to radio and broadcast television, whereas downloading represents the next-generation distribution channel of digital copies. This distribution mechanism facilitates the sale or use of permanent or quasi-permanent content, subject to the consumer's fair use transfer to other devices, be they in the home or car, or to a handheld portable device. Compulsory licensing may be more appropriate for streaming media that allow for listening or viewing but do not provide for the retention of a permanent copy.

First-Sale Doctrine

The "first-sale" doctrine, which allows individuals to sell the physical copies of books or recordings they own, is not meaningful or applicable in the digital environment. The doctrine makes sense for analog media, such as used books or records. But there is simply no way to adequately assure that an individual selling a "used" digital file has not retained a perfect digital copy for continued use. The Copyright Office reached the same conclusion (in an August 2001 report mandated under the DMCA) based upon the fact that digital retransmission requires the creation of a new copy, an act outside the scope of the traditional first-sale privileges to distribute. Whatever loss may occur from the absence of a first-sale right in the digital environment should be more than offset by the lowered costs and vastly broader selection of content made possible by Internet distribution.

Pending Legislation

Music Online Competition Act (MOCA)—Rep. Rick Boucher made an impassioned case for the Music Online Competition Act, which he and Representative Cannon introduced in August 2001. It is an ambitious proposal, as well as a highly controversial one, intended to provide some assistance and certainty to digital distribution companies. But it is not clear it would have that effect.

MOCA has generated intense opposition from a coalition that includes the recording, movie, computer games, and publishing industries, as well as major league sports organizations. It has also triggered a "Dear Colleague" letter signed by six prominent members of Congress who maintain that it amounts to premature and ill-advised regulation of the digital media marketplace.

On the other hand, the bill has garnered support from digital media and consumer electronics companies, video distributors, and libraries.

MOCA contains language designed to ensure nondiscriminatory licensing of copyrighted content to independent entities, triggered when a copyright owner licenses to an "affiliated entity" in which it holds at least a five percent equity stake. This provision is intended to assure that the record labels that stand behind the MusicNet and Pressplay ventures would have to license to other online music distribution entities on no less favorable terms and conditions.

Despite its intentions, it is not at all clear how or whether this provision, if it were the law today, would benefit rivals. My company, for example, would request licenses with material differences from those granted to MusicNet and Pressplay, which are services that are in turn materially different from one another. BMG, EMI, and AOL Time Warner are the backers of MusicNet, with its technological infrastructure provided by RealNetworks. Sony and Universal back Pressplay. MusicNet is a development platform offered to online businesses that adds functionality, e-commerce, and billing systems, whereas Pressplay is a finished product to which consumers subscribe directly. Some critics have questioned whether either service will capture consumers' hearts and wallets since, at least initially, song files will only be leased but not owned, and transfers to portable listening devices will not be permitted. Both are central server based systems rather than P2P systems.

In other words, CenterSpan would seek to license content from all the major labels for a service that would likely differ in every material aspect—technology and type of service, range of sound recordings offered, frequency of consumer use, number of subscribers served, and duration of retained content—from these rival, label-backed services. Under the language of the bill, although we would be entitled to be licensed, the labels would be entitled to establish different contractual terms and conditions as long as they were limited to and accurately reflected any material differences in the scope of the requested licenses. I suspect that the differences between the labels and us as to what the license prices and conditions should be would be substantially similar to those that separate us today. What MOCA would give us, and what doesn't exist now, is a legislated ability to seek intervention by the attorney general if we thought the labels were being unreasonable. That request would almost certainly bring our negotiations to a halt, with no assurance that the Justice Department would intervene, much less any guidance as to what standards should apply to its review, or any assurance that its decisions would receive concurrence from the courts.

Even if we could be assured of aggressive Justice Department action that would receive judicial affirmation, the bill would allow content owners to rather easily sidestep these licensing requirements. As they are only triggered by licensing to an "affiliated entity," a content owner could simply divest its equity interest in such an entity. It would then be free to license to any fully independent company, on whatever terms and conditions it negotiated, without any requirement that it similarly license to others. Or, perhaps more likely, large content owners that are associated with an Internet service provider or other online business within a common corporation could license internally, again without any requirement to do so with third parties. Finally, even if content owners chose to retain their equity stake in affiliated entities, they could negotiate high royalty fees, relying on those fees rather than return on equity for their profits, an option that does not exist for independent distribution entities.

In short, MOCA's promise of nondiscriminatory licensing may well be illusory in practice, and the licensing terms and conditions it will produce are impossible to predict and use to make business plans. This key provision, as proposed, appears to add little to the present situation, in which the Justice Department and Congress are both making serious inquiry into the antitrust compliance of various content distribution practices and entities. That inquiry is not unexpected, having been preceded by similar inquiries into online ventures such as the Orbitz airline-booking site, which is jointly owned by many of the major airlines. The European Commission has also undertaken a similar investigation of the record labels' online distribution activities. Antitrust oversight of this developing sector demonstrates the strong government interest in assuring a vibrant and competitive digital media marketplace.

Some have suggested that MOCA should be strengthened to establish traditional compulsory licenses. Again, our company could support new or expanded compulsory licenses for streams but not downloads. Yet even this would do little or nothing for competition in the near term. Given the huge potential variation in offerings and services from Internet content distributors, the complexity of delineating and pricing applicable licenses would be daunting. And the process could well drag on for years. We need only look at the single compulsory license for noninteractive webcasting that was established by the DMCA. Three years after enactment, the copyright arbitration panel (known as CARP) is still deliberating on a proper royalty rate, and once it releases its recommendation it must be reviewed and endorsed by the Library of Congress. Ironically, once the rate is set it may provide not certainty but a death notice to many remaining webcasting services because they will owe those royalties retroactively to October 1998, and few may have set aside sufficient reserves to pay the bill.

Second, although MOCA's proposal to create a statutory exception for multiple ephemeral copies used to facilitate the transmission of a performance is sensible, it should be broadened to include a far wider range of transmission services than just those that comply with the very restrictive conditions required to qualify for the noninteractive compulsory license established by the DMCA.

Senate Commerce Committee Chairman Ernest Hollings (D-S.C.) has been readying a bill to require a broad range of digital devices to include government-mandated anti-piracy protections (Security Systems Standards and Certification Act). Two large media conglomerates, unhappy with the limited successes so far regarding video copy controls and encryption technologies, are reportedly promoting the bill. So here we have companies that normally advise government to let the market make such decisions suggesting government intervention because they disagree with the market's consensus regarding the requisite level of technological security.

We certainly cannot prejudge this draft legislation. Senator Hollings' office has emphasized that he is committed to a fair and open process. Nonetheless, the draft reveals a bill that could substantially curtail fair use, when instead consideration should be given to legislation that affirmatively grants fair use rights to spur consumer acceptance of DRM-protected media subscription services. The relationship between the bill and copyright laws that address the same subject, such as the DMCA and the Audio Home Recording Act of 1992, is unclear. The range of digital devices that would be required to incorporate government-mandated security standards appears to be vast, and could include not just personal computers, personal digital assistants, and digital media players but also TV sets, radios, and even digital wristwatches and microwave ovens.

The proposed bill raises other concerns as well. But the overwhelming argument against it is that, when dealing with rapidly evolving technology and a marketplace that has yet to develop, much less gel, it is inappropriate for government to mandate technologies that are best left to the market decisions of content providers, electronics manufacturers and retailers, and consumers. There is also the danger that this approach could lock us in to faulty and inadequate encryption and watermarking technologies. Existing DRM technologies provide not just adequate but robust protection for content owners. We would be going down the wrong road to substitute a slow, legalistic, and inflexible regulatory system for the much faster and far more flexible regime of consensus standards set among private actors in a competitive marketplace.

Privacy

Preservation of consumer privacy remains important for the growth of online media. If consumers believe that the use of online technologies and services is at odds with their reasonable expectations of personal privacy, the growth of Internet commerce will suffer. One's listening and viewing habits may not raise the same level of concern as medical and financial data, but it is notable that, years ago, Congress saw fit to make it illegal for video rental stores to reveal the records of individual consumers.

P2P systems raise unique privacy questions and challenges. A consumer who subscribes to any P2P entertainment service agrees to make a portion of his computer's hard drive available to serve other subscribers. Not all P2P applications may be secure. Consumers do not want third parties to gain unauthorized access to those collections and to use the information obtained about personal tastes for marketing and promotional purposes. Even where such activities violate the P2P provider's terms of service, as they would CenterSpan's, they may be difficult for the P2P service to detect and deter if it does not utilize adequate protective technologies.

Most privacy policies prohibit the sharing of personally identifiable customer information with third parties, except for information required to facilitate payment transactions. Our company will not allow our customers to be subjected to unwanted solicitation and spamming from unauthorized third parties. We encourage Congress to consider whether existing legal protections are adequate to assure

219

that the legitimate privacy expectations of online media customers, including P2P system users, are fully respected.

Conclusion

We look forward to working with all those who strive to assure that the legal and policy structure for digital media in the 21st century is fully relevant, and that it strikes the proper balance between the rights and interests of all stakeholders in this exciting and rapidly evolving sector.

16. How Can They Patent That?

Peter Wayner

Hey you, downloading audio or video clips from the Net—yeah, you! Drop that animated GIF. Put down that QuickTime movie. Forget about those MP3 files. Didn't you know that buying copies of those things over the Internet is patented? If someone doesn't pay royalties, someone's going to be liable.

Patent fear is gripping the Net these days, as media coverage highlights new patents covering the flow of multimedia, music, money, and whatnot over the Internet. In the past, news stories about patents were tales filled with strange chemicals, weird industrial processes, arcane contraptions with odd levers, or microscopic things. To get a patent in the old days, you couldn't be just any schmoe—you needed horn-rim glasses and a white lab coat. But the latest batch of patents that focus on the Internet aren't anywhere near as impressive. In fact, they look as if any schmoe did "invent" them—by taking some everyday occurrence and adding to it the phrase "with a computer network."

Consider U.S. Patent 5848161, which describes the flash of genius that hit two Canadians and an American: They "invented" the practice of locking up the data traveling over the Internet between the customer and the store—that is, they use encryption functions to hide credit card account numbers from prying eyes.

Or consider patents 5191573 and 5675734, created by Arthur Hair when he lived in Pittsburgh. He claims to have invented the concept of "selling electronically . . . through telecommunications lines, the desired digital video or digital audio signals"—in short, pay-per-view over the Internet.

It's not really fair for me to single out these three patents, because there are many more like them. Plus, it's hard to summarize the scope of a complex legal document in a short paragraph. (And no doubt some readers will want to point to similar patents I've been granted over the years: They're not exactly a cure for polio, either—they don't even make the short cut of my résumé.)

The problem is that the patent system wasn't meant to be just an opportunity to pad the resume of a person or corporation. Patents are meant to reward inventors of products by giving them the sole right to control who uses their invention. This is usually enforced by another invention popular in America, the lawsuit.

Most people don't really begrudge the inventor of something truly new, novel, and useful the right to force royalties from everyone using the invention. This sort of quid pro quo is what the Founding Fathers imagined when they deemed that inventors would get exclusive rights for a limited time (the current period is 20 years) in compensation for disclosing the invention to the public; after that time, the invention is free to everyone. This is a pretty good deal for the public if the invention is something like a vaccine for a major disease.

But no one is happy when a bright person grabs a patent on something that doesn't seem particularly new or novel—especially when he or she demands royalties. This is just what some of the "inventors" of the Internet patents are doing, to the consternation of many. They're sending out letters demanding payment of royalties and backing the demand with the threat of a lawsuit. Half the people who get the letter are wondering, "Is that really patentable?"—and the other half are kicking themselves for not filing the patent first.

The good news is that most of the truly silly patents will fall by the wayside, and the patent system still works for protecting serious and important ideas, providing ample reward for the folks who do something like cure AIDS. The bad news is that the U.S. Patent and Trademark Office isn't particularly helpful, and the process only works when fueled by plenty of cash.

To understand how we ended up where we are today, you must understand the patent process—and how clever inventors and their patent lawyers are preying on its weaknesses. The system begins the instant an inventor says, "Eureka!" and starts to scribble down a description of the invention. This description is known as the "claims," and it is a structured list enumerating all of the important parts of the invention. The inventor tries to make this description as broad as possible in order to claim the maximum intellectual-property turf.

The patent office has the job of examining the claims and canceling all but the good claims. About this, the law is pretty explicit. For a claim to be good, it must be new, it can't be "obvious," and the inventor must really be the first one to invent it.

Clearly, one person's definition of "obvious" is not the same as another's, so this term generates many fights. But an inventor has many different types of appeals available, and the inventor's lawyer can make life difficult for the patent examiners, who are often judged by how many applications they process each year. The potential patent holder argues and argues and argues with the patent office until the arguments over "obviousness" fall by the wayside. This explains why so many people are thinking, "That's so obvious."

These arguments between the inventor and the patent office aren't entirely worthless because they often narrow the scope of the claims dramatically. In many cases, the patents aren't really as all-encompassing as they might seem because the negotiations have limited the breadth of the claims.

For instance, patent 5675734—one of Hair's patents for online pay-per-view—doesn't really apply to all sales of audio or video over the Internet. One claim requires that the signal be copied into a "sales random access memory chip which temporarily stores a replica of the coded desired digital video or digital audio signals purchased by the second party." If your Web site doesn't have a "sales random access memory chip" or some equivalent, then the patent doesn't apply to you. Patent 5675734's claims also specify that money is involved. That is, a person must provide "a credit card number . . . so the second party is charged money." If no money is exchanged, then the patent probably doesn't apply.

Sometimes the limitations can be worked around. Amazon's famous "one-click" patent (5,960,411) hasn't really stopped e-commerce. If anything, many people feel more comfortable with two or three confirming clicks.

The give-and-take between the patent office and the inventor's lawyers often narrows the focus to something that seems nonobvious. But establishing who was the first person to think of an idea is a trickier problem. In theory, a patent application should contain a good summary of all "prior art"—that is, a summary of all of the similar ideas that were previously invented. The new patent only covers the new ideas that weren't previously invented, and the scope of previous invention is defined by this search for prior art.

In practice, no one can do a perfect job with this process because no one can possibly search all of the world's prior knowledge. So virtually everyone does a half-baked job—they poke around for a bit and then give up. More diligent people will look around a bit longer to find examples; the fly-by-night inventors will spend much less time. Some diligent people even punt with the cynical assumption that anything they discover will only hurt their patent. No one has time to search the world as thoroughly as it should be searched.

The patent office tries to check the search and conduct its own, but it has a limited budget for searching and is not allowed to talk about the applications. That means the examiner can't call up IBM and say, "Didja ever think of selling videos over the Internet?"

In practice, the job of searching for prior art falls upon the shoulders of the other companies being sued for violating the patent. They often have the most incentive to find it, and they're usually much more resourceful than either the inventor or the Patent Office. (New online resources like IBM's Intellectual Property Network are helping make this process a bit more accessible.)

It usually isn't hard to come up with some credible prior art. I wrote a book in 1995 called *Digital Cash* that described several systems that were pretty close to 5848161 (the encryption for credit cards idea). The application for 5848161 was filed on May 16, 1996, so my book preceded it. That should be a potent weapon for anyone threatened by this patent. But there are also complications: I might not describe exactly the same system as patent 5848161, so the book might not disqualify all aspects of the patent. Plus there are thousands of loopholes and grounds for argument in the system. Nonetheless, the material in the book can't be claimed as an invention by someone after the book is published.

Andrew Milne, an engineer for N2K Entertainment is evaluating what patents 5191573 and 5675734 mean to his company's plans for selling music over the Internet. He's already been doing research looking for past products and services that might qualify as prior art, and he's uncovered a wide range. One *Wall Street Journal* article from 1981 that he cites describes a system for downloading digital music from a Western Union satellite. There are so many other examples, he says, that it's hard to know where to begin. Still, he is not sure how his company will proceed—the final decision lies with the lawyers who will analyze the results of his survey.

Scott Sander, the president of Sightsound.com, the owner of the Hair patents, said in an interview that he's interested in what Milne turns up but he isn't too worried. He said that his company has been negotiating with many major content, software, and computer companies since 1993. Many of these conducted their own search for prior art and gave up. "Do I assume that people will try vigorously to avoid giving us a seat at the table?" he asked. "Absolutely. But that's what patents are for—to give little guys like us a seat at the table."

Many patents fall by the wayside because of good searching by people being threatened by a lawsuit. That might not be the best way to run a system—it forces people who are ultimately innocent to defend themselves against charges of infringement—but it's the way the system has evolved. Searching is just too complicated and expensive.

More efficient mechanisms are emerging. Amazon itself was savvy enough to embrace a Web site called BountyQuest that offered cash rewards for prior art fostered by the book publisher, Tim O'Reilly. The site offered $10,000 to anyone who offered some example of an article on, or a manifestation of, the one-click idea that knocked out the Amazon patent.

Many offered ideas from popular culture like a Doonesbury cartoon showing a character pointing at objects and ordering them. One dug up a patent granted in Europe for one-click shopping with an interactive television. No one earned the $10,000, however, because none of these ideas intersected with the ideas in the Amazon patent. The notoriety was much greater than the reality. In the end, O'Reilly decided to split the award among three people who came close enough to "strike at the heart of Amazon's claims."

Sometimes these mechanisms can help everyone. At first glance, Bezos's decision to embrace BountyQuest seems like an act of putting out a contract on himself or his business. In reality, it may be a cheap way of finding out the true value of an asset. Consultants and lawyers often cost much more than $10,000. After no one found anything that destroyed the patent, Amazon could claim that they really had something serious. Of course, the entire investigation made it easier for everyone to understand the boundaries of the patent itself—something that it would be nice to have for every patent.

Better searching is a problem for everyone. Greg Aharonian, a San Francisco patent agent specializing in high-tech patent searching, publishes an e-mail newsletter about patent issues that often takes incendiary positions. He feels that the government, or some in private industry, should fund a better database that maintains some order with regard to computer-related patents.

"You talk to, say, the biotech or the chemical people—they don't really complain as much about the quality of the patents in terms of stupid stuff being patented," he said in an interview. "The reason is that they have access to two very good databases: Chem Abstracts and Medline. These are databases that have additional content. They have staffs that add value. If you have a new idea and it's in one of the databases, then you're not going to get a patent."

Still, he also pointed out that ideas in computer science are particularly prone to shape-shifting, and it's difficult to keep all of the terminology straight. "Do you consider a Cobol module type of software technology that's 30 years old an 'object'?" he asks. "I've heard some people make the argument that Cobol's been 'object-oriented' since day one. Would I consider an old Cobol program a reference on an object-oriented patent in the '90s? It's hard to tell." (Computer scientists use many metaphors to organize their thoughts about data and the ideal of a "data object" became popular in the 1980's. The concept shared much, though, with earlier metaphors.)

There are deeper philosophical problems that also haunt the system. The law has always forbidden patenting "laws of nature," and that prohibition could cover anything from the principles of mathematics to ways of doing business. But many people are getting patents in these areas by formulating their claims as machines for doing the same thing. In other words, no one would be granted an overall patent for exchanging coins for candy bars, but it would be perfectly acceptable to get a patent on a new kind of vending machine.

The rise of the digital computer and the Internet has blurred distinctions even more, because computers and automation are now part of all businesses. That's why no one ever thought of getting a patent on selling records for cash, but someone wants to patent a mechanism for selling audio files over the Internet.

Part of this problem might be remedied if the Patent Office were able to say that to take a past practice and conduct it electronically or online is now "obvious." That is, shipping audio signals by digital signals is pretty much equivalent to shipping them by vinyl disk—an inventor would need to come up with a more significant improvement than that.

That will probably happen over time when one of these cases is litigated. If a court makes such a ruling, all of the older patents will lose some of their value because they won't be as enforceable.

Many big computer companies are developing their own defense against the vagaries of endless patent litigation: They simply cross-license their patent portfolios with each other. It's not unusual to discover that two mammoth competitors like Xerox and Canon have cross-licensed their large blocks of patents with each other. This saves them endless fighting, while it keeps out the little competitors.

Anthony Clapes, IBM's former assistant general counsel and author of the book *Softwars,* downplayed the sinister aspect of this trading in an interview. "They're not doing it to be unfair or conspire," he said. "In the Cold War, there was a certain amount of making available information about what was going on on either side. They had the red phones. There was a certain amount of pressure being released by providing information through back channels. That's what this is like. I'll cross-license, you'll cross-license, and we'll get enough freedom of operation."

He also downplayed the disadvantage to smaller inventors. "In theory and in philosophy, I don't think there is anything that favors the larger," he said, but added, "It's just that life favors the larger entity."

But Aharonian, the patent agent, has a different view. He feels the big companies care little about patents because the value of even a great patent is about $20 million, which adds little to their balance sheet. Patents worth more than that are rare. The little companies that can blossom with a $20 million patent don't have the ability to influence Washington. Aharonian said, "No one wants to spend a year or two arguing whether the patent is valid. If we want to encourage the small people and the start-ups, we'll have to clean up the patent system. Those people aren't being served."

Sander of Sightsound.com agrees with this pronouncement. "During the turn of the last century, when technology was really exploding, people were putting forth the same arguments that the Patent and Trademark Office had lost the ability to keep pace with that much innovation," he said in an interview. "It's essential for companies to protect their intellectual property in times of great change." Otherwise, he added, "It all ends up in Redmond, Washington," in the hands of the biggest companies like Microsoft.

17. Financial Business Method Patents: Nothing New under the Sun

P. Michael Nugent

In 1984 Jay Walker, founder of priceline.com, started Visual Technology Corporation. Visual Technology invented and manufactured plasma light sculptures that sold for $800 to $1,200 apiece. Visual Technology entered into a lucrative contract with Sharper Image to distribute the light sculptures through the famous Sharper Image catalog we all know and love. In the late 1980s, Radio Shack began to produce knockoffs of the light sculptures and sold them at half the price. Sharper Image ceased marketing Visual Technology's products and there ensued contractual disputes between the parties as to who was to pay for incurred catalog expenses and inventory.

Had Jay Walker obtained a patent for the plasma light sculptures—which he could certainly have done—Visual Technology would not have had a competitor in Radio Shack and the messy dispute would have been avoided. Jay Walker didn't make the same mistake with priceline.com.

In 1998, Walker Digital was issued the so-called priceline.com patent (5,794,207). Far from being a mere "business method" patent, far from being a patent on "reverse auctions," the priceline.com patent is a method and apparatus patent for a cryptographically assisted commercial network system designed to facilitate buyer-driven conditional purchase offers over the Internet and other media. There is a raft of other patents underlying the priceline.com business, including so-called "adaptive marketing" patents, which cover methods and systems for inducing and offering on a real-time basis third-party cross-subsidies at point of purchase.

Citibank started early obtaining patents, in 1979 getting a seminal patent (4,134,537) on a "transaction terminal" that covered ATMs, smart phones, and handheld transaction devices of all kinds. In 1995, anticipating the coming surge in software-, system-, and business method-based patents, John Reed said in his "Chairman's Intellectual Property Letter":

> Patents . . . are available for step-by-step procedures that solve problems, if the procedures are novel, appropriately described and are part of a computer product or system. Some of our innovative, electronic solutions and services for customers are patented. . . . Similarly, our innovative software that drives today's electronic banking . . . can receive the benefits of patent protection in certain cases.

Over the following years, Citibank obtained patents for such inventions as methods and systems for remote delivery of retail banking services, methods and systems for creating and managing synthetic currency, and methods and systems for open electronic commerce using trusted agents where the transfer of electronic merchandise or electronic money is provisional until the transaction is finalized.

Although the banking community, and other industries, debated whether the courts would uphold software, system, and business method patents, Citibank and a few others within and outside the financial industry worked to obtain financial system and method patents in the belief that patent law clearly blessed patents for such inventions. They were vindicated a few years later.

On July 23, 1998, the U.S. Court of Appeals for the Federal Circuit in *State Street Bank & Trust Co. v. Signature Financial Group, Inc.* held that methods of doing business were to be treated like any other "process" invention that, under U.S. patent law, is patentable subject matter.[1] The court upheld a patent issued to the Signature Financial Group that covered a novel method or system for pooling assets of a number of mutual funds to achieve economies of scale typically enjoyed by larger funds. Specifically, in a decision the Supreme Court later refused to consider on appeal, the lower court stated:

> Today we hold that a transformation of data, representing discrete dollar amounts, by a machine through a series of mathematical calculations into a final share price, constitutes a practical application of a mathematical algorithm, formula or calculation, because it produces "a useful, concrete and tangible result," a final share price momentarily fixed for recording and reporting purposes and even accepted and relied upon by regulatory authorities and in subsequent trades.

After the decision, the number of applications for business method or process patents shot through the roof, only to be matched by the number of cries and complaints that the patent system had been undermined, innovation would be deterred, and general havoc would ensue.

The outcry and complaints are not warranted. Business method patents are not new. Financial method or process patents are not new. When it comes to such patents, there is nothing new under the sun.

The U.S. patent regime anticipates and is riddled with method inventions. Class 734 of the U.S. patent classification scheme, the pigeonhole system patent examiners have to use to examine and reward the novelty and usefulness of claimed inventions, covers patents on methods of teaching. Methods of playing games fall under Class 273. Methods of improving crop yields spring up under Class 47. Indeed, one researcher found over 445 financial method patents awarded under Class 705/35, 705/36, 705/37, 705/38 and 705/4 between the years 1971 and early 2000.[2] The award of process and business method patents is the natural culmination of patent decisions by the courts in the 1970s and 1980s that allowed an extraordinary range of software and computer system and process patents, highlighted by key decisions in 1994 (*In Re Alappat*) and 1995 (*In Re Beauregard*) by the U.S. Court of Appeals for the Federal Circuit.

Financial method patents have been granted since the beginning of the patent system, according to the U.S. Patent and Trademark Office (PTO).[3] The first patent statute, enacted by Congress under its Constitutional grant of authority[4] to protect the discoveries of inventors, was signed into law on April 5, 1790. A few months later, the first U.S. patent was issued, a chemical *method* patent for making potash and pearl ash. The first financial patent was issued March 19, 1799, for an invention for detecting counterfeit notes. The first financial patent for which the Patent and Trademark Office still has file wrapper detail was issued April 28, 1815, and covered a printing method entitled "A Mode of Preventing Counterfeiting." According to the PTO, 41 financial patents were issued in the first 50 years of the U.S. Patent Office, in the arts of bank notes (2), bills of credit (1), bills of exchange (1), check blanks (4), detecting and preventing counterfeiting (2), coin counting (1), interest calculation tables (5) and lotteries (17). The first financial method patent specifically cited as a business method patent by the PTO was issued in 1889 to the later founders of IBM. In fact, three method and apparatus patents for automating the tabulating and compiling of statistical information for businesses and enterprises—essentially comprising the punch card method of computing—were issued to the Tabulating Machine Company.

With the widespread adaptation of computer software and systems to the workplace and the home throughout the late 1980s and 1990s, the commercialization of the Internet, and the introduction of the browser in the early 1990s, it was only natural that the inventions seeking patent protection during this time period were software and computer system-based and business method-based. It is only natural to find that modern inventions consist of new electronic methods, systems, and processes for doing business over multiple media and appliances. As the PTO put it, "We are at the beginning of a change in the approach to how inventors choose to describe their inventions." The new electronic methods, systems, and processes are the statutory "manufactures" of today in a world more intangible, virtual, and electronic than it has ever been. What is a "1-click" procurement system but a modern machine? What is a hyperlinking invention but a modern process? What is a system for authentication and transfer of secure electronic notes if not a 21st century manufacture?

It should not be surprising that the upsurge of patent applications for business method, system, and process inventions occurred when it did, leading up to and following the State Street *Bank* decision. The upsurge is not merely a matter of inventors getting relief and clarity at long last thanks to an esoteric court decision. Rather, the upsurge in these patent applications followed a pattern. Whenever a business revolution occurs—be it an information revolution or an industrial revolution—patent applications surge as businessmen and -women, as inventors, seek to erect barriers to entry where few exist. During the late 1980s and 1990s American business and society underwent an unparalleled information, computing, and communications revolution. It is only natural that patent applications emerged that were suitable to a new age aborning with novel electronic methods, systems, and processes. It is only appropriate that a living, breathing system of patent law adapted to the new inventions.

During the industrial revolution in the 1870s and 1880s, new patents soared 56 percent a year, engineered by advances in the railroad, telegraph, telephone, and electric industries. Then, like today, inventors were asked, "How can you patent the process for moving electrons down a wire?" Between 1902 and 1916 patents doubled as the auto and aircraft industries geared up.[5]

It should be noted that the so-called "surge" in business method patent applications is a moderate one and the number of issued business method patents is not remarkable, which should be some relief to those alarmed by the business method patent "craze." Of a total number of 375,000 patent applications of all kinds expected by the PTO in fiscal year 2001, 10,000 are likely to be classified as business method patents ("BMPs") in Class 705.[6] BMP applications are less than 3.7 percent of applications filed and represent less than 1percent of all patents issued. Whereas 330 BMP applications were filed in FY95 and 126 BMPs issued, 7,800 BMP applications were filed in FY2000 and 899 issued. In FY2001, the PTO projects 9,360 BMP applications and gives no numbers on projected grants.

The BMP numbers are not alarming, nor are the trends. In FY2000, 57 percent of BMP applications were granted. In FY2001, the PTO projects that 47 percent of BMP applications led to grants, and an even smaller 37 percent grant rate took hold in the fourth quarter of 2001.

What explains the trends indicating that allowance of BMPs is decreasing? A number of countervailing factors have taken hold as the alarmists and the outcry over BMPs have had effect. In March of 2000, the PTO launched its "BMP Initiative," which consisted of an increase in examiner technical training, an increase in prior art research resources, second-level examiner review for BMP applications in Class 705, efforts to reach out to industry for prior art, and more BMP reexaminations generally. The courts and Congress have sent a signal, too. The infamous preliminary injunction against B&N.com's 1-click ordering system, won by Amazon in the height of the 1999 holiday buying season, was vacated when the court found that evidence of prior art rebutted the likelihood that Amazon would prevail on the merits. The court was referring to the early 1990s CompuServe Trend System that enabled stock charts to be ordered with a single mouse-click.[7] Congress passed the American Inventors Protection Act,[8] a misnomer of sorts, which allows a defense (but not a license) against another's invention claims if the party relying on the defense has commercially engaged in a business practice continuously for at least a year before the claimant's patent application arguably covering the practice was filed (the Act applies to applications filed after November 29, 1999). Finally, we may be seeing the depressing effects on BMP applications of the so-called "offer-for-sale" doctrine, which prohibits PTO patenting of an invention if it has been disclosed or offered for sale more than one year before the filing of a patent application. Little is required for an invention to be the subject of an offer for sale: it can be a single offer, the mention of a price for a future offering at an industry trade show or venture capital forum, or the shopping around of ideas and methods at a restaurant, at a conference, or on the phone. This doctrine, in particular, has had and will tend to have disproportionate impact on the "dot-com" business method inventions that triggered so many alarms.

Abraham Lincoln, an inventor of a device for buoying vessels over shoals, has been quoted as saying the "[p]atent system added the fuel of interest to the fire of genius." And, indeed, there are many good reasons for modern inventors to look to patents for protection. Patents protect the underlying concept of an invention, the method and the process and the system. Other forms of intellectual property protection accomplish less. Trademarks protect the association of a mark in commerce with goods or services, not the goods or the services themselves. Trade secret law protects commercially valuable trade processes, systems, and methods, but they do not prevent—as patents do—"independent" or original discovery and commercialization of your invention or secret. Copyrights protect the creative expression in a tangible medium of your idea, but they do not prevent independent or original expression of your idea.

Patents give you the right to exclude others from making, using, or selling your invention, giving you a barrier against others' entry into your field and helping you to avoid getting crushed by outsized competition. Patents are the tools of competitors from patent cultures—like Microsoft, AOL Time Warner, IBM, General Electric, Hewlett-Packard—and it is these competitors moving into the electronic space. Patents accord you prudent protection for the expenses and resources poured into research and development. Patents are real assets, giving you valuation in spin-offs, sales, divestitures, M&As; currency in strategic partnerships, cross-licensing arrangements and deals; and a measure of value for Wall Street and venture capitalists. Patents can enable beneficial return for your risk and investment by allowing you to establish a market position and to derive licensing revenue. Patents are the only legal tool in the intellectual property realm that protects you against innocent, independent origination of an invention that duplicates yours, and that means a lot when you have an innovative business method or process that is easy to reengineer or copy. Finally, patents are an important supplement in your intellectual property war chest, giving you a leg up on the competition and protection from vendors and employees who might be inclined to steal your secrets.

Jay Walker learned all this about patents—a little late for his Visual Technology Corporation endeavor but not too late for his Walker Digital and Priceline initiatives.

Notes

1. 35 U.S.C. 101, which describes patentable subject matter, provides: "Whoever invents or discovers any new and useful process, machine, manufacture, or composition of matter, or any new and useful improvement thereof, may obtain a patent therefore, subject to the conditions and requirements of this title."

2. "Where Does State Street Lead? A First Look at Finance Patents, 1971–2000," National Bureau of Economic Research, Unpublished Working Paper 7918, September 2000.

3. See generally "A USPTO White Paper, Automated Financial or Management Data Processing Methods (Business Methods)," July 19, 2000, www.uspto.gov/web/menu/busmethp/index.html, for data and sources discussed in this paragraph.

4. U.S. Const., Art. I, §8.

5. See Kevin G. Rivette and David Kline, *Rembrandts in the Attic: Unlocking the Hidden Value of Patents* (Boston: Harvard Business School Press, 2000), pp. 14–15.

6. Class 705 covers computer-implemented processes and methods related to e-commerce, the Internet, and data processing; other business method applications are assigned according to their implementing technology or mode. Class 705, "Data Processing: financial, business practice, management, or cost/price determination," is defined as "machines and methods for performing data processing or calculation operations in the (1) practice, administration or management of an enterprise; (2) processing of financial data; or (3) determination of the charge for goods and services."

7. Amazon and B&N.com announced they had settled the lawsuit on March 6, 2002. See news.com.com/2100-1017-854105.html?tag = cd_mh.

8. Pub. L. 106-113, 113 Stat. 1501 (1999).

18. The Patentability of Internet Business Methods: A Systematic Approach to Evaluating Obviousness

Ron Laurie and Robert Beyers

In July 1998, the U.S. Court of Appeals for the Federal Circuit in *State Street Bank & Trust Co. v. Signature Financial Group, Inc.* (hereafter, *State Street Bank*)[1] explicitly ended the ban on business method patents. The *State Street Bank* decision expanded the scope of the "useful arts" that may be patented under the U.S. Constitution to include any process (also referred to as method) that produces a "useful, concrete, and as elsewhere tangible result." Since that decision, entrepreneurs and e-commerce companies have flooded the U.S. Patent and Trademark Office with patent applications covering a wide range of Internet-based business methods.

It is difficult to find anyone involved in commercial applications of the Internet these days who doesn't have a strongly held view on the subject of business method patents. At one extreme are those who predict that allowing patents on such processes will surely stifle innovation on the Internet;[2] at the other are those who bear personal witness to the fact that a successful e-commerce company would never have attracted the investment capital that gave it life were it not for the existence, or at least the possibility, of a strong proprietary position based in large part on the exclusionary rights provided by patent protection.

When one listens carefully to the impassioned arguments against patenting "business methods" it becomes apparent that the arguments, and the basic intellectual property policy positions that consciously or unconsciously underlie them, can be classified into three categories: (a) patents are bad; (b) business method patents are bad; and (c) bad business method patents are bad.

The first position is most often heard in the halls of academia and raises fundamental social and economic issues that go far beyond the scope of the present inquiry. The second position is frequently advanced by established companies that constitute a large target for individuals and start-up (sometimes referred to as upstart) companies obtaining these patents. The third position is the most widely held, and for obvious reasons, the easiest to defend. It reflects the fact that the U.S. and other patent offices are ill-equipped to properly examine these types of applications. One reason is that examiners typically have training in computer science and engineering, not business, economics, and finance. Another is that the best "prior art" is not in the form of previously issued patents (the database historically used by patent examiners) but rather in the form of products and services that are largely unknown to the examiner.

In the heat of the debate over business method patents, the boundary between the second and third philosophical positions described above tends to blur, but it is important to address them separately. The "business method patents are bad" position relates to the question of patentable *subject matter*—that is, whether such patents *as a class* ought to be allowed. The "bad business method patents are bad" position relates to the question of whether a *particular* business method is not patentable because the method is either old—that is, not "novel"—or because it is "obvious to a person having ordinary skill in the art." According to the Federal Circuit (or at least the three-judge panel that decided the *State Street Bank* case), the subject matter question is no longer on the table. Thus, the debate should be focused on the questions of novelty and nonobviousness.

Because it is relatively straightforward to determine novelty,[3] the key legal inquiry becomes, How should obviousness be evaluated for business method patents? To help answer this question, we first suggest a claims taxonomy for use in evaluating obviousness. Next, we examine the problem-solving process itself—that is, the creation of "technology," and its relation to the traditional legal framework for evaluating obviousness—the *Graham* framework (named for an important 1966 Supreme Court decision). Finally, we suggest how the *Graham* framework should be applied specifically to business method patents.

The substantive analysis presented here is an important component of any comprehensive system for granting or litigating Internet-related patent rights. Other articles have examined the procedural components of such a system, such as better prior art databases, improved training of patent examiners, and the use of European-style patent opposition proceedings.[4] The analysis of the substantive legal principles presented here complements those previously suggested measures. Indeed, the procedural improvements will be for naught if the substantive analysis is flawed. In addition, the cries of alarm regarding business method patents should subside if patent offices and courts undertake a proper analysis of obviousness.

Section 101 Statutory Subject Matter and Utility—The Old Issue

The traditional way to articulate the main requirements for patentability is to say that a patentable invention must be new, useful, and nonobvious.[5] These three requirements are covered by Sections 102, 101, and 103 of the patent statute, respectively.

Under 35 U.S.C. Section 101, "Whoever invents or discovers any new and useful process, machine, manufacture, or composition of matter, or any new and useful improvement thereof, may obtain a patent therefor, subject to the conditions and requirements of this title."

The Section 101 "useful" requirement derives from Article I, Section 8, Clause 8 of the Constitution, which gives Congress the power "to promote the Progress of Science and useful Arts."[6] A number of decisions by the Federal Circuit (and its predecessor, the Court of Customs and Patent Appeals) have equated "useful arts" with "technological arts," but the scope of the subject matter that falls under the umbrella of these two terms for the purposes of Section 101 patentability has been changing over time.[7]

Case law developed a number of specific exceptions to the subject matter categories that are not patentable under Section 101.[8] The historical exceptions were laws of nature, scientific principles, and natural phenomena on the one hand and abstract ideas on the other.[9] The *State Street Bank* decision specifically addressed two exceptions of more recent origin—the"mathematical algorithm" exception and the "business method" exception.

With respect to the "mathematical algorithm" exception, the Supreme Court has held that mathematical algorithms that are merely abstract ideas with no practical application are not patentable.[10] However, in the *State Street Bank* case, the Federal Circuit held that the transformation of data by a machine (e.g., a computer) through a series of mathematical calculations is a practical application of a mathematical algorithm (and thus patentable) because it produces a "useful, concrete, and tangible result."[11] The *State Street Bank* opinion emphasized that this result applies even when the data being transformed represent nonphysical (abstract) quantities, such as the balance in a financial account.

With respect to the "business method" exception, the court explicitly put this "ill-conceived exception to rest," noting that business methods should be subject to the same legal requirements for patentability as applied to any other process or method.[12]

Placed in context, the *State Street Bank* decision may be viewed as just one more step in a line of cases that have expanded the scope of "technology" that constitutes patentable subject matter. Indeed, the Federal Circuit's decision in *AT&T Corp. v. Excel Communications, Inc.*,[13] which followed *State Street Bank*—and held that a process that applies a mathematical principle to produce a useful, concrete, and tangible result without preempting other uses of the mathematical principle lies well within the scope of Section 101—has arguably extended patentable "technology" to include algorithms that are not limited to implementation on a *machine* (e.g., a computer). (In contrast, the *State Street Bank* holding concerned transformations of data by algorithms implemented on a machine.[14])

As discussed below, the net effect of this line of cases will be a broader, more general view of what constitutes patentable technology. Given the trend away from a manufacturing-based economy toward an information-based economy, a broader scope of patentable subject matter that promotes progress in new areas of the "useful arts" is warranted. Indeed, the Federal Circuit has explicitly stated that it is trying to make its understanding of the scope of Section 101 responsive to the needs of the modern world while also remaining true to basic legal principles.[15]

There is currently no universally accepted definition of what constitutes "technology" for either legal purposes or general understanding. Some definitions are more narrowly focused. For example, the Manual of Patent Examining Procedure states, "The definition of 'technology' is the 'application of science and engineering to the developments of machines and procedures in order to enhance or improve human conditions, or at least to improve human efficiency in some respect.'"[16] Limiting the scope of technology to the practical application of scientific and engineering principles reflects our industrial past—a manufacturing-based economy that was primarily focused on making better "widgets."

However, as our economy becomes more information-based, a broader definition of technology may be more appropriate. For example, combining the *Webster's New World Dictionary* definitions for "technology" and "technical"[17] suggests the following definition for technology: a method or process for handling a specific technical problem—that is, a method for solving a specific problem in the practical, industrial, or mechanical arts or the applied sciences. This broader definition encompasses traditional industrial inventions (making better widgets). It also maintains the Supreme Court's prohibitions on patents for laws of nature, natural phenomena, and abstract ideas by requiring that a specific problem be solved. At the same time, it also broadens the scope of "technology" to cover the practical arts. Note that the industrial arts, mechanical arts, and applied sciences are just particular examples of the practical arts. Thus, *at the highest level of generality, technology is just a solution to a specific practical problem.*

Recent case law supports this expansive definition of technology. In particular, the court in *State Street Bank* stated that the question of whether a patent claim encompasses statutory subject matter should not focus on which of the four Section 101 categories of subject matter a claim is directed to (i.e., a process, machine, article of manufacture, or composition of matter), but rather on the *practical utility* of the subject matter— in other words, whether the claimed subject matter produces a "useful, concrete, and tangible result."[18]

Thus, in light of recent case law, the three traditional requirements for patentability can be restated as follows: a patentable invention must be a new and nonobvious solution to a specific practical problem.

Internet business methods will almost certainly provide solutions to specific practical problems. Moreover, it is fairly simple to determine if the claimed subject matter in a business method patent is identical to an existing business method and thus not "new." Therefore, the real issue for the patentability of claims in business method patents will be whether the claimed subject matter is obvious.

Obviousness—The Real Issue

The statutory basis for the nonobviousness requirement is 35 U.S.C. Section 103(a), which states:

> A patent may not be obtained though the invention is not identically disclosed or described as set forth in section 102 of this title [i.e., the invention is novel], if the differences between the subject matter sought to be patented and the prior art are such that the *subject matter as a whole would have been obvious at the time the invention was made to a person having ordinary skill in the art to which said subject matter pertains.* Patentability shall not be negatived by the manner in which the invention was made.

The traditional legal framework for determining if an invention is obvious (and thus not patentable under 35 U.S.C. Section 103) was originally articulated by the Supreme Court in *Graham v. John Deere Co.*[19] In 1998, the Federal Circuit provided an extended explanation and discussion of this analytical framework in *In re Rouffet*. The court explained the showing needed for an examiner to reject an application on grounds of obviousness. At that point, the court explained:

> An applicant may specifically challenge an obviousness rejection by showing that the Board reached an incorrect conclusion of obviousness or that the Board based its obviousness determination on incorrect factual predicates. The *factual predicates* underlying an obviousness determination include:
>
> 1. the scope and content of the prior art,
> 2. the differences between the prior art and the claimed invention, and
> 3. the level of ordinary skill in the art.
>
> The secondary considerations are also essential components of the obviousness determination. This objective evidence of nonobviousness includes:
>
> 1. copying,
> 2. long felt but unsolved need,
> 3. failure of others,
> 4. commercial success,
> 5. unexpected results created by the claimed invention,
> 6. unexpected properties of the claimed invention,
> 7. licenses showing industry respect for the invention, and
> 8. skepticism of skilled artisans before the invention.

When a rejection depends on a combination of prior art references, there must be some teaching, suggestion, or motivation to combine the references.

Therefore, when determining the patentability of a claimed invention which combines two known elements, the question is whether there is something in the prior art as a whole to suggest the desirability, and thus the obviousness, of making the combination.

Obviousness is determined from the vantage point of a hypothetical person having ordinary skill in the art to which the patent pertains. This legal construct is akin to the "reasonable person" used as a reference in negligence determinations. The legal construct also presumes that all prior art references in the field of the invention are available to this hypothetical skilled artisan.

Virtually all inventions are combinations of old elements. Therefore an examiner may often find every element of a claimed invention in the prior art. If identification of each claimed element in the prior art were sufficient to negate patentability, very few patents would ever issue. Furthermore, rejecting patents solely by finding prior art corollaries for the claimed elements would permit an examiner to use the claimed invention itself as a blueprint for piecing together elements in the prior art to defeat the patentability of the claimed invention. Such an approach would be an illogical and inappropriate process by which to determine patentability.

To prevent the use of hindsight based on the invention to defeat patentability, the examiner must show reasons that the skilled artisan, confronted with the same problems as the inventor and with no knowledge of the claimed invention, would select the elements from the cited prior art references for combination in the manner claimed.

This court has identified three possible sources for a *motivation to combine* references:

1. the nature of the problem to be solved,
2. the teachings of the prior art, and
3. the knowledge of persons of ordinary skill in the art.

To show a proper prima facie case of obviousness, the examiner must explain the specific understanding or principle within the knowledge of a skilled artisan that would motivate one with no knowledge of the applicant's invention to combine the references.

While the skill level is a component of the inquiry for a suggestion to combine, a lofty level of skill alone does not suffice to supply a motivation to combine. Otherwise a high level of ordinary skill in an art field would almost always preclude patentable inventions. As this court has often noted, invention itself is the process of combining prior art in a nonobvious manner. Therefore, even when the level of skill in the art is high, the Board must identify specifically the principle, known to one of ordinary skill, that suggests the claimed combination. In other words, the Board must explain the reasons one of ordinary skill in the art would have been motivated to select the references and to combine them to render the claimed invention obvious.[20]

The analytical framework described in *In re Rouffet* (i.e., three factual predicates + secondary considerations + motivation to combine) can be applied to any invention, including a new method of doing business. However, before describing its application specifically to business method patents, it is useful to develop a claims taxonomy for such patents and to consider the problem-solving process itself (i.e., the creation of "technology," and its relation to the *Graham* framework.

A Claims Taxonomy for Internet Business Method Patents

In general, any business method claim can be written as follows:[21]

A method for doing business, comprising step A, step B, and step C. Symbolically, this claim to a combination of steps can be written as $[A + B + C]$. Each of the steps ("elements") in the claim can either be a new step (e.g., A_{new}) or an old step (e.g., A_{old}). "New" here refers to a step invented by the patent applicant, rather than a step previously invented by someone other than the patent applicant. In other words, a step previously developed by another person is "old," not "new," even if it was recently made.

Even if all of the *individual* steps are old, the claim may still be patentable if the *combination* of steps is a new and nonobvious solution to a specific practical problem— for example, $[A_{old} + B_{old} + C_{old}]_{new}$. Thus, at the highest level of generality, business method claims may be divided into three categories:

1. $[A_{old} + B_{old} + C_{old}]_{old}$ – old steps combined in an old combination,

2. $[A_{old} + B_{old} + C_{old}]_{new}$ – old steps combined in a new combination, and

3. $[A_{new} + B_{old} + C_{old}]_{new}$ – at least one new step (which automatically makes the combination of steps new).

Type I Patent—Old Steps Combined in an Old Combination

The first type of business method claim is not patentable because it is not new. It fails to pass muster under Section 102 of the patent statute. This category is simple to understand, so it does not require an extensive explanation. Two points about this category, however, are worth noting.

First, claims in this category are unpatentable if a single prior art reference can be found that teaches each and every step in the business method claim. For most technologies, prior patents are one of the best sources for such references. For business methods, however, there is not an extensive collection of patents because of the previous, now discredited, business method exception to patentability.[22] Consequently, other sources, such as prior business methods in public use and nonpatent printed publications (e.g., news articles) describing business methods will need to be found and examined.

Second, an unusual type of method claim that appears at first glance to belong in this category lends credence to the broader definition of technology proposed in the preceding section. In particular, it is well established that a person can receive a method claim for a new use for a known product. For example, suppose that a person found that a chemical commonly used as a weed killer could also be used to cure cancer. He could not patent the chemical itself but could patent the method of using the chemical to cure cancer. At first glance, such a method claim might appear to be of the form $[A_{old} + B_{old} + C_{old}]_{"old"}$. Here, quotation marks are put around the "old" combination because the combination is in fact new (i.e., Type II). Such an invention creates no new "technology" if technology is defined in a very narrow sense because the operative "widget" in this technology is a known chemical. However, this invention does create new "technology" if technology is viewed in a broader sense, i.e., using a weed killer to cure cancer is a new, nonobvious solution to a specific practical problem. Moreover, awarding a method patent here promotes progress in the useful arts by encouraging people to find new uses for "old" solutions in nonanalogous fields.

Type II Patent—Old Steps Combined in a New Combination

The majority of business method patents will belong to this category. Indeed, most patents in general belong to this category. Moreover, there are compelling reasons why new combinations of old steps (or elements) should be patentable:

> [T]he defendant argues that the supposed invention is no more than a substitution of materials familiar to the art in the same uses; an aggregation of which each part performs what it did before. We may concede as much arguendo, for the same may be said of every invention. All machines are made up of the same elements. . . . All compositions are made of the same substances. . . . But the elements are capable of an infinity of permutations, and the selection of that group which proves serviceable to a given need may require a high degree of originality. It is the act of selection which is the "invention" and it must be beyond the capacity of the common-place imagination.[23]
>
> Because virtually *every* invention is an assembly of old elements, . . . the statement cannot be universally applied without risk of destroying the patent system. Unable to create from nothing, man must use old elements, which must perform their normal functions. . . .[24]
>
> The dictionary, a mere book of words, contains the great novels of the future which will appear only when those words are combined to create a great work by those skilled in the art.[25]

For methods of doing business on the Internet, the generic business method claim can be written as follows: a computer-implemented method for doing business,[26] comprising step A, step B, and step C.

In some cases, the steps done in the computer system may merely correspond to business method steps previously performed in the physical world. In other cases, one or more of the steps performed in the computer system will have no close analogs in the physical world. In either case, by definition, the combination will be "new" if it is the first time those steps have been carried out in a computer system.

Determining if a method of doing business on the Internet is new (thereby satisfying Section 102) should not be difficult. As noted above, a significant difficulty here is that there is not an extensive database of business method patents to search, so other sources of prior art must be examined.

The more complex question for these types of patents will be whether the combination of steps as a whole is obvious. If a well-known business process in the physical world is merely replicated in ("ported to") cyberspace, the likely answer will be that the combination is obvious and the method is not patentable under Section 103. However, if an Internet business process involves steps without close analogs in the physical world, the answer will not be as obvious (pun intended).

Type III Patent—At Least One New Step

The strongest arguments for patentability can be made for business method claims that fall into this category. Such claims satisfy the Section 102 novelty requirement for two reasons: they contain one or more new steps and the presence of these new steps automatically makes the combination of steps new as well. If it is questionable whether any of the steps are in fact new, the applicant still has the fallback argument that the combination is new.

Some Type III claims may also be less controversial because they correspond to narrower, more traditional notions of technology. For instance, if an inventor develops collateral technology (e.g., a new hardware widget or software application) that "enables" a new business method, then the inventor will have an easier time arguing that business method claims based on the inventor's own collateral technology are not obvious. (The effect of the development of collateral technology on the determination of obviousness is discussed in more detail below.)

The invention claimed in the Priceline patent[27] is arguably a classic example of a Type III invention—or, more specifically, a Type III.A invention (see Table 1 below). For example, claim 1 covers:

> A method for using a computer to facilitate a transaction between a buyer and at least one of a plurality of sellers, comprising:
>
> (a) inputting into the computer a conditional purchase offer which includes an offer price;
> (b) inputting into the computer a payment identifier specifying a credit card account, the payment identifier being associated with the conditional purchase offer;

    (c) outputting the conditional purchase offer to the plurality
        of sellers after receiving the payment identifier;
    (d) inputting into the computer an acceptance from a seller,
        the acceptance being responsive to the conditional pur-
        chase offer; and
    (e) providing a payment to the seller by using the pay-
        ment identifier.[28]

This claim describes a process of "buyer-driven commerce" wherein a single potential buyer can essentially make an irrevocable (via the credit card) offer to hundreds, thousands or even millions of potential sellers anywhere in the world, and the first seller to accept the offer (e.g., by clicking on an "I accept" button) creates a legally enforceable contract. It is submitted that this new business process simply could not have been done before the Internet because the real-time (or nearly so) communication mechanism that is essential to the invention did not exist. Thus, the business steps in the Priceline claim are "$business_{new}$" However, the Priceline inventors did not invent the collateral computing technology that makes these new business steps possible (i.e., the computing technology that is part of the claim is $computer_{old}$).

Overall, the Priceline claim can be described as $[business_{new} + computer_{old}]_{new}$, which we classify as Type III.A. As discussed below, such claims fall into a grey area for obviousness, between arguably obvious $[business_{old} + computer_{old}]_{new}$ claims that merely transpose (or "port") well-known business methods to the Internet with existing computer technologies and $[business_{old\ or\ new} + computer_{new}]_{new}$ claims that cannot be found obvious based on advances in collateral computing technology because the inventor developed the computing technology that enabled the new business method.

Creating New Technology—The Problem-Solving Spectrum

Having defined technology as the solution of specific practical problems, it is useful to consider how technology is created—the problem-solving process itself. This consideration will assist in understanding and applying the *Graham* framework for determining obviousness.

Problems and solutions are often thought of as distinct entities with a sharp dividing line between the two. For this simple view, the problem-solving process involves just two steps: identifying a problem and then finding a solution. On closer inspection, however, the separation between problems and solutions is not sharp. Instead of a crisp boundary, there is often a broad band with many shades of gray.

This blurring of the distinction between problems and solutions arises because problems can be stated at varying levels of generality. Typically, a problem is first identified and stated at a high level of generality. For example, for methods of doing business on the Internet, a very general problem is, How does one create a profitable business on the Internet? This question shows that stating a problem at a high level of generality provides little or no insight into its solution. A solution to a very general problem is usually not obvious.

After identifying a problem at a high level of generality, the problem-solving process then typically involves creating a feedback loop between the synthesis of possible solutions and the analysis of the problems associated with each solution. With each iteration of the feedback loop, the problem gets redefined and restated at successively more specific levels of generality. Eventually, at some level of specificity, the problem can be stated in such a way that its solution is obvious—that is, the problem can be stated in terms of its solution.

The problem-solving process may proceed through many shades of gray as it moves from general recognition of a problem to a specific solution. For the purposes of this obviousness analysis, however, the problem-solving "spectrum" can be divided into four main areas: no recognition of a problem, general recognition of a problem, specific recognition of a problem—which includes "discovering a problem's source"[29] —and solution of the problem.

The problem-solving spectrum provides useful guidance when one considers the factual predicates in the *Graham* framework. In particular, it should be apparent that asking about the scope and content of the prior art and the differences between the prior art and the claimed invention correspond to asking, Where was the prior art on the problem solving spectrum when the invention was made? The prior art could have been at any of the four different points on the simplified spectrum when the invention was made. Consider the implications of each of these for determining obviousness.

No Recognition of a Problem

"[T]here is no requirement that persons of ordinary skill have been aware of the problem, or have been seeking solutions. The inventor is not required to have been the winner of a race to a common goal. Certainly, an invention may create a new want and still be nonobvious and therefore patentable."[30]

This category corresponds to the case in which an inventor sees and solves a problem that no one else has previously recognized. The inventor's contribution spans the entire problem-solving spectrum. Moreover, the lack of awareness of the problem by those of ordinary skill in the art provides strong evidence of nonobviousness:

> If, as appellants claim, there is no evidence of record that a person of ordinary skill in the art at the time of appellants' invention would have expected the problem . . . to exist at all, it is not proper to conclude that the invention which solves this [problem], would have been obvious to that hypothetical person of ordinary skill in the art.[31]

In the past, some legal commentators with a narrow view of what constitutes technology have also taken a narrow view regarding the patentability of solutions to unrecognized problems:

> [W]hen an innovation results merely from the perception of a problem, rather than the working out of a non-obvious solution, no patent should issue[32]
>
> Often a given solution is a "good idea" from a business point of view because it meets human needs not theretofore recognized. However, the solution from a technological point of view may have been obvious after the problem was recognized, and patents issue only for new and nonobvious solutions to technological problems (i.e., developments in the "useful arts"), not for good business ideas.[33]

This narrow view seems unduly restrictive, especially given the broadened scope of patentable "technology" after *State Street Bank*. Moreover, this perspective leads to the anomalous result that a person whose inventive contribution spans the entire problem-solving spectrum can be denied a patent whereas another person whose contribution spans a smaller range of the spectrum (e.g., an inventor who solves a previously recognized but unsolved problem) can receive a patent.

Finally, note that this starting point in the problem-solving spectrum is not a clear point. Problem recognition itself depends on the level of generality with which the problem is stated. Stated broadly enough, virtually any problem becomes a "recognized" problem. For example, the question raised above—How does one create a profitable business on the Internet?—is a "recognized" problem. Thus, at this high level, problems related to methods of doing business on the Internet are generally recognized. (This discussion simply shows that the boundaries between different regions of the simplified problem-solving spectrum are blurred. This blurring should not be a surprise because the problem-solving spectrum itself reflects the fact that the interface between problems and solutions is blurred.)

General Recognition of a Problem

If there is a general recognition of a problem in the prior art, the inventor's contribution lies in identifying the specific source of the problem and then providing a solution. The invention as a whole is not obvious (and thus patentable) if *either* (1) identifying the problem's source *or* (2) providing a solution would not have been obvious to one of ordinary skill in the art at the time the invention was made.

Two key cases, *Eibel Process*[34] and *In re Sponnable*,[35] discuss nonobviousness in situations in which an inventor provides an "obvious" solution after identifying the nonobvious source of a generally recognized problem. According to the Supreme Court in *Eibel Process*, "[I]t was the discovery of the source not before known and the application of the remedy for which Eibel was entitled to be rewarded in his patent."[36] Or, as the Court of Appeals stated in *In re Sponnable*, "[A] patentable invention may lie in the discovery of a source of a problem even though the remedy may be obvious once the source of the problem is identified. This is *part* of the 'subject matter as a whole' which should always be considered in determining the obviousness of an invention under 35 U.S.C. Section 103."[37]

In addition, a "simple" solution itself may still be nonobvious: "An inventor will not be denied a patent simply because his invention embodies a solution which seems simple and obvious with the benefit of hindsight."[38] As another court put it, "The invention here in dispute is simple and there is an inclination to find such simple things to be obvious. However, if the invention were so obvious why hadn't anyone come up with it . . .?"[39]

Specific Recognition of a Problem

If there is specific recognition of a problem in the prior art— for example, the source of the problem is known—the inventor's contribution lies in providing a solution to the known problem. The comments made in the preceding section about "simple" solutions apply here as well. Indeed, as noted in *American Safety Table Co. v. Schreiber*, "the very simplicity of a new idea is the truest and most reliable indication of novelty and invention, when others have devoted extensive efforts and exhausted their resourcefulness in a futile search for a solution of the same vexing problem."[40]

Nevertheless, if the prior art has reached this stage in the problem-solving process, then it is more likely that an inventor's solution will be obvious: "[I]f an apparently obvious invention is made very shortly after the [prior] art identification of a need, the short period of time between identification of the need and the making of the invention bolsters the conclusion of obviousness."[41]

Thus, it is important to correctly determine that the prior art had indeed reached this stage in the process, rather than merely having a general recognition of the problem: "The district court's formulation of the problem confronting the inventors presumes the solution to the problem ... Defining the problem in terms of its solution reveals improper hindsight in the selection of the prior art relevant to obviousness."[42]

Solution of the Problem

If the prior art recognized the problem and arrived at the same solution as the inventor claims, the inventor has a Type I—[A_{old} + B_{old} + C_{old}]$_{old}$—claim that is not patentable because it is not new. Note, however, that the inventor may still have a patentable invention if the inventor's solution is sufficiently different from the prior art solutions. Moreover, the inventor's solution does not have to be better than the prior art solutions, it just has to be new and nonobvious.[43] (Of course, a patent claim to an inferior solution will not have much value.)

Applying the *Graham* Framework to Internet Business Method Claims

The preceding discussions of a claim taxonomy and the problem solving-process can be applied to any type of invention. Keeping these general principles in mind, we now examine specific issues in the *Graham* framework (as described in *In re Rouffet* above) that will likely decide whether an Internet business method claim is obvious.[44]

For each issue, the arguments for and against obviousness will be offered in a point-counterpoint style.

Step One: Factual Predicates

Scope and Content of the Prior Art. The scope and content of the prior art includes references from those areas a person with ordinary skill in the art would look to in solving a particular problem.[45] For methods of doing business on the Internet, the prior art will include both business and computer "technologies."

There is a strong argument for the obviousness of claims that merely port well-known business methods to the Internet. The scope and content of prior business and computer technologies would make such Type II combination claims—that is, [$business_{old}$ + $computer_{old}]_{new}$? obvious.

One counterargument against obviousness is that moving known business methods from the physical world to the virtual world creates new problems that must be solved. For example, Microsoft recently received a patent for an electronic purchasing system.[46] The invention automatically matches methods of payment registered by a purchaser with methods of payment accepted by a merchant: it is the online equivalent of the familiar question typically asked in a face-to-face purchase: Cash, check, or charge? This invention seems to be an obvious transfer of known business methods onto the Internet, yet, as the patent notes, new problems arise in online transactions that are different from those encountered in face-to-face transactions:

> With the increasing demand to electronically purchase and pay for goods and/or services, there are a number of issues that arise. For instance, the purchaser must choose a method of paying for the goods and/or services that is acceptable to the merchant. But this task is not so simple, because the purchaser most likely will not have access to payment methods that are accepted by the merchant. Unlike a point-of-purchase transaction where the accepted payment methods are often posted, the purchaser in the electronic transaction is often blind to the requirements of the merchant.
>
> Another issue concerns how to protect the purchaser's wallet from the merchant. Given a choice, the merchant would most likely choose one particular payment method (such as using the merchant's own charge card) that the purchaser might not wish to use. Moreover, for obvious

reasons, it is in the purchaser's interest not to reveal his/her bank account or credit card information to the merchant. An electronic purchasing system should block the merchant from access to the purchaser's payment options and to this confidential account information.

Another concern is protection from fraudulent transactions, both on the part of the merchant and the purchaser. For instance, how can the purchaser be sure that the merchant is authentic and truly has the represented goods or services to sell? How can the purchaser know that he/she will not be billed for more than the amount that was agreed upon? From the merchant side, how can the merchant be assured that the purchaser really exists and that payment will be forthcoming? These issues are less troublesome in a point-of-purchase context because the purchaser and merchant can see one another, the goods are often readily apparent, and payment is typically tendered on the spot. However, in an electronic purchasing system where the purchaser might live in one state or country and the seller might live in another, these issues become rather important. A suitable purchasing system should address these issues to reduce or prevent the occurrence of fraudulent transactions.

Another issue that arises in the electronic environment is whether the purchaser has sufficient funds to pay for the goods or services. Still another issue concerns how to authenticate the purchaser and merchant, as there is no opportunity for either of them to visually authenticate one another like in the point-of-purchase context.

Many of the issues raised above are born out of the difficulty and complexity of converting from a "paper-trail" purchase transaction system where these concerns are addressed in large part through the use of paper checks, receipts, physical credit cards, debit cards, and penned signature verification?to a "paperless" computerized purchase transaction system.[47]

However, this counterargument against obviousness can be rebutted by noting that there is extensive prior art concerning online authentication, digital signatures, and so on that would still render the invention obvious. The invention might not be obvious if *only* business prior art were consulted, but it is arguably obvious when *both* business and computer technology prior art are considered.

As alluded to above, business method claims typically combine business steps (i.e., "business$_{old}$" or "business$_{new}$") with computer

Table 18.1
Claims Taxonomy for Computerized Business Methods

Claim Type	Comment
I. [business$_{old}$ + computer$_{old}$]$_{old}$	Lacks novelty, thus invalid under Section 102.
II. [business$_{old}$ + computer$_{old}$]$_{new}$	Strong argument for obviousness where existing business steps are merely combined with collateral technology "enabler" created by a third party (computer$_{old}$) (e.g., see discussion of Amazon "one-click" patent).
III.A. [business$_{new}$ + computer$_{old}$]$_{new}$	Very fact specific, grey area for obviousness; collateral technology "enabler" created by a third party (computer$_{old}$) argues for obviousness, but new business step argues against obviousness (e.g., see discussion of Priceline patent).
III.B. [business$_{old}$ + computer$_{new}$]$_{new}$	Strong, traditional argument for patentability; patent applicant invents key technology "enabler" (computer$_{new}$).
III.C. [business$_{new}$ + computer$_{new}$]$_{new}$	Strong, traditional argument for patentability; patent applicant invents key technology "enabler" (computer$_{new}$).

steps (i.e., "computer$_{old}$" or "computer$_{new}$").[48] Thus, as shown in Table 18.1, the claims taxonomy for computerized business methods can be further subdivided.

Advances in collateral technology made by persons other than the present inventor, especially advances in computing technology, will be a major factor arguing for obviousness in business method patents. For example, microprocessors will continue to get faster and more powerful, memories and storage devices will pack more information into less space, and communications bandwidth will continue to increase for at least the next decade. These advances will in turn enable new methods of doing business that were previously impractical. As recently noted by Lawrence Lessig, "[w]hen the world was given TCP/IP[49] and the collection of protocols it induced, a billion ideas became obvious to anyone who took the time to think. These were not ideas that were discovered because some lone inventor spent years toiling away in his basement, but because TCP/IP was a language with which practically anything could be done."[50]

Broadly speaking, the Internet itself can be thought of as a computer step in a business method patent (e.g., Step A = communicating over the Internet). If an inventor uses a new, improved method of communicating over the Internet to create a new business method, but the new communications method was developed by someone else then that is a Type II or Type III.A claim (i.e., computer$_{old}$); if the new communications method was developed by the present inventor, that is a Type III.B or Type III.C claim.

A Type II business method claim will be obvious if "the new combination is but a natural use for the improved element:"[51] "[O]nce another supplied the key element, there was no long-felt need or, indeed, a problem to be solved by [the inventor]."[52]

The impact of collateral technology on the analysis of obviousness is well illustrated by the Federal Circuit's February 14, 2001, decision in *Amazon.com, Inc. v. BarnesandNoble.com, Inc.*[53] The patent in suit, generally known as the "one-click" patent,[54] describes and claims a product ordering method for use in online shopping. It solves the problem of having to fill out an order form with purchaser identification, billing and shipping addresses, and credit card information each time a customer visits a merchant's Web site and purchases one or more items. By analogy to a supermarket or department store, this order form is usually referred to as the "checkout" page, and the process whereby items are accumulated prior to checkout is referred to as the "shopping cart ordering model," that is, each time a customer adds an item to the list of items to be purchased, it is metaphorically placed in the customer's virtual shopping cart.

In contrast to the shopping cart model, in the patented one-click method the customer enters the required personal, shipping, and credit information only once, during a registration process, and the information is thereafter stored in a database on the merchant's computer for reuse during subsequent shopping sessions. A customer identifier, called a "cookie," is stored on the customer's computer and links to the customer's full information record in the database on the merchant's computer. Each time a registered customer visits the shopping site and makes a purchase, the merchant's computer examines the cookie and automatically fills out the order form. Thus, when a customer sees an item that he or she wishes to purchase, a single "click" on an on-screen representation of the item, such as a "place order" button, submits the order without requiring the customer to go through a "checkout" process. The one-click method thereby makes online purchases less cumbersome.

The claims in the one-click patent are illustrated by Claim 1, which reads as follows:

> A method of placing an order for an item comprising: under control of a client system, displaying information identifying the item; and in response to only a single action being performed, sending a request to order the item along with an identifier of a purchaser of the item to a server system; under control of a single-action ordering component of the server system, receiving the request; retrieving additional information previously stored for the purchaser identified by the identifier in the received request; and generating an order to purchase the requested item for the purchaser identified by the identifier in the received request using the retrieved additional information; and fulfilling the generated order to complete purchase of the item whereby the item is ordered without using a shopping cart ordering model.

However, one-click-checkout business methods were known in the prior art (i.e., one-click checkout is business$_{old}$) as were cookies (i.e., cookies are computer$_{old}$). Thus, the claims in the Amazon patent are arguably obvious Type II claims— [one-click$_{old}$ + cookie$_{old}$]$_{new}$— or even anticipated Type I claims—[one-click$_{old}$ + cookie$_{old}$]$_{old}$. Indeed, the Federal Circuit remanded the case to the District Court because BarnesandNoble.com had "mounted a substantial challenge to the validity of the patent."

However, a Type II claim is not necessarily obvious. In rebuttal to Lessig's arguments quoted above, the following points can be made.

First, although the creation of TCP/IP may have made a billion ideas immediately obvious, it has been many years since TCP/IP was given to the world. Thus, the new Internet business ideas being generated *today* (i.e., many years later) to take advantage of TCP/IP are arguably nonobvious ideas. In other words, if today's new ideas are obvious, why weren't they thought of years ago when TCP/IP was first created?

Second, Lessig's reference to the lone inventor spending years toiling away in his or her basement is an emotional appeal to the lay public that is without merit. Section 103(a) makes it explicitly clear that the manner in which an invention is made is irrelevant: "Patentability shall not be negatived by the manner in which the invention was made. " In other words, "sweat of the brow" is not a prerequisite to patent protection.

Third, a strong rebuttal to Lessig's argument that "TCP/IP [is] a language with which practically anything [can] be done" can be found in the historical arguments made in support of combination claims. (See the discussion in "Type II—$[A_{old} + B_{old} + C_{old}]_{new}$—old steps combined in a new combination" above.) In particular, Lessig's argument is analogous to saying that all of the great novels to be written in the future are obvious given the words contained in a dictionary.

The arguments against obviousness for a business method claim will be much stronger if an inventor creates the new communications method (computer$_{new}$ in Table 1) that enables the new business method. The inventor will thus be making a Type III.B or Type III.C claim for the business method. This situation corresponds to the more traditional case in which an inventor creates a new widget and can then get claims to both the widget itself and to methods that use the new widget. It is more difficult to show that Type III claims are obvious because both the new element created by the inventor and the combination of elements incorporating the new element must be shown to be obvious.

There are a number of practical problems dealing with the scope and content of the prior art for business method patents. Patent examiners must understand both business and computer technologies—they need cross-disciplinary insight. The Patent and Trademark Office is already struggling to find enough examiners who understand computer technology alone, so finding examiners who understand business as well (and know the business prior art) will be even more difficult. In addition, the lack of business method patents means that more nonpatent prior art will need to be found.

President Clinton's 1997 Framework for Global Electronic Commerce recognized these problems and called for the PTO to:

(1) significantly enhance its collaboration with the private sector to assemble a larger, more complete collection of prior art (both patent and non-patent publications) and provide its patent examiners better access to prior art in [Global Information Infrastructure]-related technologies;

(2) train its patent examiners in [Global Information Infrastructure]-related technologies to raise and maintain their level of technical expertise; and

(3) support legislative proposals for early publication of pending patent applications, particularly in areas involving fast-moving technology.

Another part of the solution to these problems may be to involve an inventor's competitors in the patenting process because they will have a better knowledge than the PTO of commercial products in the prior art and they will have more incentive to find invalidating prior art.[55] In addition, researchers and academics will frequently have access to the best prior art in the form of publications other than patents.

Some combination of these solutions will make much more sense than the prior expedient of simply banning business method patents. The following hypothetical problem makes the inadequacy of the previous approach clear. Suppose that the PTO had a shortage of examiners with expertise in mechanical engineering. It would be silly to suggest that the way to fix this problem is to ban patents on new widgets! Instead, the PTO should hire more people who understand widgets, teach its current examiners about widgets, and also try to leverage private-sector and academic knowledge about widgets.

Similarly, the PTO needs to develop expertise in new areas of technology as these areas emerge. If the PTO can also adjust the examination system to tap into private-sector expertise without undermining the patenting process, then so much the better.

Differences between the Prior Art and the Claimed Invention. The prior discussion about the problem-solving spectrum covers many of the key points regarding this factual predicate in the *Graham* framework. Indeed, comparing where the prior art was in the problem-solving

259

process with the inventor's solution is essentially equivalent to examining the differences between the prior art and the claimed invention.

The prior discussion of "simple" solutions should also be borne in mind here because many new methods of doing business on the Internet seem simple. For example, the CyberGold patent on "attention brokerage" (U.S. Patent No. 5,794,210), which compensates Internet users for viewing targeted advertising on the Internet, seems simple, yet no one had thought of it before. Although the lay public may be inclined to believe that simple inventions are obvious, this is usually true only with the benefit of hindsight. The courts have emphasized repeatedly that "simplicity is not inimical to patentability:"[56] "This change, which has been extraordinarily popular, certainly seems simple. Any graduate of a high school art class could design the essentials with a piece of paper and pencil in ten minutes. But no one did."[57]

Another argument against obviousness is the "comparative utility" of new methods of doing business on the Internet: "The theory behind the use of comparative utility is one of inference based on motivation. If an invention is advantageous but obvious, it is likely that persons in the art would have been led by normal economic incentives to develop it sooner."[58]

In other words, "the prior art's failure to reveal the claimed invention despite its advantageous qualities tends to confirm that it was unexpected and nonobvious."[59]

However, the inference of nonobviousness based on comparative utility can be rebutted. For new Internet business methods, the most likely source of the rebuttal will be recent developments in collateral computing technologies. In other words, the prior art did not reveal the new, advantageous business method sooner because the new method depends on recently developed computing technologies, generally referred to as "enablers."

The Level of Ordinary Skill in the Art. For this factual predicate, an important argument for obviousness is likely to come from near simultaneous invention of similar Internet business methods. To paraphrase the discussion of "near simultaneous invention" in *Phillips Petroleum Co. v. U.S. Steel Corp*:

> Common sense dictates that if an alleged infringer is able to show that [Internet business methods] similar to those claimed in the patent-in-suit were developed independently

and simultaneously, those "inventions" would be probative of the level of knowledge in the art at the time of the patent-in-suit's invention. Of course, unlike a reference under [Section102] anticipation, "simultaneous invention" is not preclusive or conclusive; it is but one of the factors considered by the Court en route to the legal conclusion on the obviousness issue.[60]

In today's environment, those skilled in the art of Internet business methods include literally millions of people trying to figure out how to create unique (and profitable) Internet businesses. Thus, it is not surprising to see Internet businesses with very similar business methods springing up almost overnight. Contemporaneous and independent invention of the same business method would tend to indicate that nothing beyond ordinary skill in the art was required. However, the "near simultaneous invention" argument for obviousness can be rebutted in several ways.

Although two or more Internet businesses may have sprung up almost simultaneously with similar business methods, their business methods may not have been developed independently. Information about Internet business methods is disseminated widely and rapidly via the Internet itself. Moreover, the low barriers to entry on the Internet encourage copycat business models.

In addition, change occurs so quickly on the Internet that a couple of months on the calendar is sometimes referred to as an "Internet year." What is almost simultaneous in "real time" may seem much longer when measured in "Internet time."

Lastly, "[b]ecause Title 35 [i.e., the patent statute] provides for interference proceedings, it implicitly recognizes that contemporaneous independent invention may not alone show obviousness. . . . Accordingly, this court weighs evidence of contemporaneous invention 'in light of all the circumstances,' . . . , especially in light of evidence of long-felt need."[61]

Step Two: Secondary Considerations

In re Rouffet lists eight different types of secondary considerations, which are objective measures of nonobviousness that must be considered in the *Graham* framework: copying, long felt but unsolved need, failure of others, commercial success, unexpected results created by the claimed invention, unexpected properties of the claimed invention, licenses showing industry respect for the invention, and skepticism of skilled artisans before the invention. Of these, the following considerations are likely to have the most relevance to Internet business methods.

Copying. Copying relates to the ideas of "comparative utility" and "near simultaneous invention" discussed above. Not surprisingly, new methods of doing business will be copied if they are better than prior methods. The prior art's failure to implement the new business method despite its advantages tends to confirm that the new business method was unexpected and nonobvious.[62] Moreover, copying by those who were aware of a new business method is a possible rebuttal to contemporaneous "independent" invention.

Long-Felt but Unsolved Need. "Establishing a long-felt need requires a showing that others skilled in the art in fact perceived a need and that this perception persisted over a long period of time without resolution by the prior art."[63]

Long-felt need will depend on the level of generality with which the prior art described the problem—that is, where the prior art was on the problem-solving spectrum. The higher the level of generality used to state the problem in the prior art (e.g., How does one create a profitable business on the Internet?), the more likely there is to be a finding of long-felt need. Conversely, if the problem was defined very specifically in the prior art (e.g., if the problem could practically be defined in terms of its solution), then there is less likely to be a finding of long-felt need. Indeed, the solution of a problem shortly after its identification in the prior art (i.e., "short-felt need") bolsters the conclusion of obviousness.[64]

Consequently, those arguing for obviousness will try to show that a short period of time elapsed between the identification of a narrowly defined problem in the prior art and its solution by the inventor. Moreover, for Type II and Type III.A Internet business method claims, they may also argue that changes in collateral infrastructure technology reduce the significance of prior needs and failures.[65] (See the discussion in "Scope and content of the prior art" above.)

On the other hand, those arguing against obviousness will try to show that there was a long-felt need to solve a problem that had only been identified at a very general level in the prior art. Alternatively, they may try to show that there was no recognition of the problem, so that there was no motivation to combine prior art references to create the present invention. (See the discussions in "No recognition of a problem" above and "Nature of the problem to be solved" below.)

Failure of Others. "Logically, there are three possible causes for the failure of others to solve a problem. Either they were unfamiliar with the prior art, they lacked ordinary skill in the pertinent art, or the solution was in fact not obvious."[66]

This secondary consideration is closely related to the consideration of long-felt need, which was just discussed. As noted there, for Type II and Type III.A business method claims, the evidentiary significance of the failure of others will be reduced by changes in collateral computing technology. The significance of actual failures will also be diminished if those who failed did not consider all of the prior art in the pertinent business and computing fields: "Thus the fact that those with ordinary—and indeed, extraordinary—skills failed for a time in finding the solution may be attributable to the simple fact that they failed to take advantage of the massive body of knowledge already in the public domain. And the more massive that body of knowledge becomes, the more common this explanation of failure becomes."[67]

The vast, largely untapped reservoir of business methods knowledge that lies outside the patent database will probably diminish the importance of the failure of others. In addition, the lack of cross-disciplinary insight by those who failed will also diminish the significance of their failures. For example, an inventor claiming a method that improves the security of commercial Web sites cannot point to the failure of some sites to use adequate security in view of the massive body of existing knowledge concerning Internet security.

Commercial Success. The traditional rationale for using commercial success as an indicator of nonobviousness certainly applies to new Internet business methods: "It is the foreseeability of commercial success at that point in time before the problem is solved which is relevant to the obviousness determination. If individuals believe there is a 'fortune waiting in the wings' for the person who solves the problem, we infer that with such an incentive, many artisans were attempting to find the solution."[68]

Indeed, the "fortune waiting in the wings" is arguably the foreseeable goal of all new Internet business methods, which has motivated many people to try to develop such methods.

Early discussions of commercial success often described it in terms of the success of a patented *device*, thereby reflecting the narrower view of technology that was prevalent at that time: "Commercial success demonstrates that there was a market for the patented device and implies that persons skilled in the art had an economic incentive to make it as soon as they could; the failure to produce a device satisfying a known demand indicates that the inventor's solution was not obvious."[69]

These comments, however, can be modified to reflect the new, broader view of technology simply by changing the word "device" to "business methodology."

Those trying to diminish the evidentiary weight given to commercial success will attempt to show that there is no nexus between the claimed business method and its commercial success. For example, they will argue that the success of a particular business (using the claimed business method) is due to extensive advertising rather than the intrinsic value of the new business method.

In addition, like long-felt need, the evidentiary weight given to commercial success will be diminished if there were recent developments in collateral technologies by those other than the present inventor that enabled the new business method. In other words, commercial success will carry less weight for Type II and Type III.A business method claims than for Type III.B and Type III.C claims.

Licenses Showing Industry Respect for the Invention. The evidentiary weight given to this secondary consideration will probably be marginal for business method patents. Those arguing against obviousness will claim that licensees would not pay royalties if they thought the patent was invalid. Conversely, those arguing for obviousness will claim that the licensees merely wanted to avoid costly litigation in a new, uncertain area of patent law.

It seems likely, however, that more patents with Type III claims will be licensed than patents with Type II claims because there is a greater chance that the more traditional Type III claims will be found nonobvious.

Teaching, Suggestion, or Motivation to Combine. "Before obviousness may be established, the examiner must show that there is either a suggestion in the art to produce the claimed invention or a compelling motivation based on sound scientific principles. . . . Logic compels that the suggestion or motivation be accompanied by a general knowledge of the existence of art recognized techniques for carrying out the proposed invention. . . . It is wrong to use the patent in suit as a guide through the maze of prior art references, combining the right references in the right way so as to achieve the result of the claims in suit. Monday morning quarterbacking is quite improper when resolving the question of nonobviousness in a court of law."[70]

As noted in *In re Rouffet*, the Federal Circuit has identified three possible sources for a motivation to combine references:

1. The nature of the problem to be solved,
2. The teachings of the prior art, and
3. The knowledge of persons of ordinary skill in the art.

Nature of the Problem to Be Solved. The nature of the problem to be solved depends on where the prior art was in the problem-solving process. In particular, note that there can be no motivation to combine if there was no recognition of the problem: "Lack of identification of the problem facing the inventor has long been a basis for finding that the references could not have suggested a solution to the problem nor, without more, be properly combinable one with the other."[71] "[T]o say that the missing step comes from the nature of the problem to be solved begs the question because the Board has failed to show that this problem had been previously identified anywhere in the prior art."[72]

Conversely, knowledge of a problem provides motivation for its solution: "The significance of evidence that a problem was known in the prior art is, of course, that knowledge of a problem provides a reason or motivation for workers in the art to apply their skill to its solution."[73]

Teachings of the Prior Art. The prior art can make either an explicit or implicit suggestion to combine prior references with each other or with knowledge generally known to those of skill in the art. An explicit suggestion is easy to understand and need not be considered further.

For Internet business method patents, two types of implicit suggestions may be especially important in showing obviousness—trends and broad concepts in the realm of the obvious: "A 'trend' might very well constitute a suggestion or teaching to one of ordinary skill in the art to make 'minor' changes from the prior art in accordance with that trend to produce the claimed invention."[74]

As previously discussed, there are clear trends in collateral computing (infrastructure) technologies (faster processors, greater bandwidth, etc.). These advances will produce corresponding trends in business methods. For example, new business methods based on fast anywhere-to-anywhere information distribution are emerging, with a clear trend toward the communication of more sophisticated information (first text, then data, then voice + data, etc.). The movement of conventional business methods onto the Internet is another clear trend that provides a motivation to combine the elements in Type II [business$_{old}$ + computer$_{old}$]$_{new}$ claims, thereby making such claims obvious and unpatentable.

Broad concepts in the realm of the obvious correspond to information so ubiquitous as to warrant judicial notice.[75] This type of implicit suggestion provides another motivation to combine the elements in Type II [business$_{old}$ + computer$_{old}$]$_{new}$ claims.

Knowledge of Persons of Ordinary Skill in the Art. In re Rouffet established that a high level of skill in the art alone is not sufficient to provide a motivation to combine references:

> While the skill level is a component of the inquiry for a suggestion to combine, a lofty level of skill alone does not suffice to supply a motivation to combine. Otherwise a high level of ordinary skill in an art field would almost always preclude patentable inventions. . . . the Board must identify specifically the principle, known to one of ordinary skill, that suggests the claimed combination.[76]

For many Type II business method claims, the crux of the obviousness analysis will often be whether there is an implicit suggestion to combine prior references with the common knowledge of those of skill in the art. Yet this component of the *Graham* framework is not well settled in general, let alone for business methods in particular:

> Basic areas of continued uncertainty had also arisen, however, particularly the seemingly unsolvable question of the nature of the teaching, motivation, suggestion or reference necessary to lead one of ordinary skill in the art to make the combination; the continued uncertainty as to the proper source and level of explicitness of that teaching, motivation, suggestion or reference; the uncertain effect of difference in the problem solved in the reference compared to the claimed invention; . . . and the growth in basing [combined reference

obviousness] rejections on the revitalized *In re Bozek* concept of common knowledge and common sense of persons skilled in the art, which did not rely upon any specific suggestion in a particular reference or references.[77]

In the future, these uncertainties may be reduced by analyzing them more systematically in the context of the problem solving spectrum.

Conclusion

Cries of alarm and calls for drastic changes are typically heard when the law attempts to address new areas of technology. Often, however, the most appropriate response can be found in a return to basic legal principles. This is arguably what happened with respect to Section 101 statutory subject matter. With the Section 101 issue now largely resolved for business method patents (at least those implemented using technology in the traditional sense, such as the Internet), our attention should turn to the real issue, namely Section 103 obviousness.

We have outlined some simple analytical models (i.e., the claims taxonomy and the problem-solving spectrum) to bear in mind when analyzing obviousness. Using these tools, we have also tried to give a balanced view of how the basic legal principles regarding Section 103 obviousness should be applied specifically to Internet business method patents.

The analysis of the law presented here complements previously suggested procedural improvements. Arguably most (if not all) of the cries of alarm regarding business method patents should subside if the PTO and the courts perform a proper substantive analysis of obviousness.

Notes

1. *State Street Bank & Trust Co. v. Signature Financial Group, Inc.*, 149 F.3d 1368, 47 USPQ2d 1596 (Fed. Cir. 1998), *cert. denied*, 119 S.Ct. 851 (1999).

2. See, for example, Scott Thurm, "A Flood of Web Patents Stirs Dispute over Tactics," *Wall Street Journal*, October 9, 1998, p. B1 ("The fear: Companies with new-fangled Web patents will demand license fees from other Web merchants for aspects of everyday business."); Lawrence Lessig, "The Problem with Patents," *The Industry Standard*, May 3, 1999, p. 20 ("There is growing skepticism among academics about whether such state-imposed monopolies help a rapidly evolving market such as the Internet."); Dan Gillmor, "Absurdity Can Be Patented—U.S. Office Proves It," *San Jose Mercury News*, August 17, 1999, p. 1C; Kurt Kleiner, "Patently Silly," *New Scientist*,

October 16, 1999, p. 22 ("Fierce battles over intellectual property rights . . . are now the main threat to the Net.").

3. Analyzing novelty merely requires determining whether the claim is "anticipated" by the "prior art," that is, the claimed subject matter is identical to a previously used or described business method.

4. See, for example, William J. Clinton and Albert Gore, Jr., *A Framework for Global Electronic Commerce* (1997), www.ecommerce.gov/framewrk.htm; Robert Merges, "As Many as Six Impossible Patents before Breakfast: Property Rights for Business Concepts and Patent System Reform," *Berkeley Technology Law Journal* (1999): 577.

5. There are additional requirements for patentability under §112 relating to the patent "disclosure," such as the *enablement, best mode,* and *written description* requirements, but these need not be considered here.

6. This clause is the basis for both the patent and copyright laws. The phrase "useful arts" is the basis for patent law, and the word "science" is the basis for copyright law.

7. *In re Musgrave*, 431 F.2d 882 (CCPA 1970); *In re Alappat*, 33 F.3d 1526 (Fed. Cir. 1994). Both of these cases were decided by Judge Rich, the author of the *State Street Bank* decision.

8. Statutory subject matter and utility are usually considered two different inquiries under §101: (1) Does the invention belong to at least one statutory subject category (process, machine, manufacture, or composition of matter) and (2) is the invention useful? As discussed herein, however, the *State Street Bank* decision makes clear that the statutory subject matter inquiry has essentially been subsumed by the utility inquiry.

9. *Diamond v. Diehr*, 450 U.S. 175, 185, 101 S.Ct. 1048, 67 L.Ed.2d 155 (1981).

10. *State Street Bank*, 149 F.3d 1368, 1373 (citing *Diehr*, 450 U.S. 175, 101 S.Ct. 1048, passim; *Parker v. Flook*, 437 U.S. 584, 98 S.Ct. 2522, 57 L.Ed.2d 451 (1978); *Gottschalk v. Benson*, 409 U.S. 63, 93 S.Ct. 253, 34 L.Ed.2d 273 (1972)).

11. Ibid.

12. Ibid. p. 1375.

13. *AT&T Corp. v. Excel Communications, Inc.*, 172 F.3d 1352, 50 USPQ2d 1447 (Fed. Cir. 1999).

14. *State Street Bank*, 149 F.3d at 1373.

15. *AT&T Corp.*, 172 F.3d at 1356.

16. *Manual of Patent Examining Procedure*, 7th ed. (Washington: Government Printing Office, 1998), pp. 2100–2106, quoting *Computer Dictionary*, 2d ed. (Redmond, Nash.: Microsoft Press, 1994).

17. *Webster's New World Dictionary*, 2d ed. (Springfield, Mass: Merriam-Webster, Inc., 1974), p.1460 (Technology is defined as "a method, process, etc. for handling a specific technical problem" and technical is defined as "having to do with the practical, industrial, or mechanical arts or the applied sciences.").

18. See footnote 8 above.

19. *Graham v. John Deere Co.*, 383 U.S. 1 (1966).

20. *In re Rouffet*, 149 F.3d 1350, 47 USPQ2d 1453 (Fed. Cir. 1998) (citations omitted, numbers added, and some minor changes in wording made for clarity).

21. Note that a business method claim need not be written as a method claim per se. Any method claim can also be written as a system (apparatus) claim. For example, the generic business method claim given here can be rewritten as "a system for doing

business, comprising: means for doing step A, means for doing step B, and means for doing step C."

22. Through clever claims drafting, a limited number of patents covering business methods were issued before the business method exception was put to rest.

23. Donald S. Chisum, *Chisum on Patents* § 5.04[5], at 5-421 (Rel. 51, 1994), quoting Judge Learned Hand in *B.G. Corp. v. Walter Kidde & Co.*, 79 F.2d 20, 21-22, 26 USPQ 288 (2d Cir. 1935).

24. Ibid., p. 5-422, quoting *Nickola v. Peterson*, 580 F.2d 898, 912 n. 22, 198 USPQ 385, 403 n. 22 (6th Cir. 1978), *cert. denied*, 440 U.S. 961 (1979).

25. Ibid., p. 5-423, quoting *Shields v. Halliburton Co.*, 493 F. Supp. 1376, 1390, 207 USPQ 304, 317 (W.D. La. 1980), *aff'd*, 667 F.2d 1232, 216 USPQ 1066 (5th Cir. 1982).

26. "Doing business" can be replaced by the particular business being done—for example, "conducting an auction" or "creating a market between buyers and sellers."

27. U.S. Patent 5,794,207.

28. Ibid.

29. Ibid. § 5.04[7][c], at 5-503 (Rel. 51, 1994).

30. Ibid. § 5.04[1][c], at 5-271 (Rel. 51, 1994), quoting *Leif v. Louis Milan & Sons, Inc.*, 726 F.2d 734, 740, 220 USPQ 845, 849 (Fed. Cir. 1984).

31. Ibid. § 5.04[7][c][iii], at 5-510 (Rel. 51, 1994), quoting *In re Nome* 509 F.2d 566, 572, 184 USPQ 607 (CCPA 1975).

32. Ibid. § 5.04[5], at 5-421 (Rel. 51, 1994), quoting Kith, *Graham v. John Deere Co.: New Standards for Patents*, 1966 Sup. Court Rev. 293, 3401-41 (1966).

33. Ibid. § 5.04[1][c], at 5-271 (Rel. 51, 1994).

34. *Eibel Process Co. v. Minnesota & Ontario Paper Co.*, 261 U.S. 45, (1923).

35. *In re Sponnable*, 405 F.2d at 578, 160 USPQ 237 (CCPA 1969).

36. Chisum, *Chisum on Patents* § 5.04[7][c][I], at 5-504 (Rel. 51, 1994), quoting *Eibel Process Co. v. Minnesota & Ontario Paper Co.*, 261 U.S. 45, 67-68 (1923).

37. Ibid. § 5.04[7][c][ii], at 5-506 (Rel. 51, 1994) quoting *In re Sponnable* 405 F.2d at 578, 585-86, 160 USPQ 237, 243-244 (CCPA 1969) (emphasis in original).

38. Ibid. § 5.04[7][a], at 5-500 (Rel. 51, 1994) quoting *Globe Linings, Inc. v. City of Corvallis*, 555 F.2d 727, 730, 194 USPQ 415, 418 (9th Cir.), *cert. denied*, 434 U.S. 985 (1977).

39. Ibid. quoting *State Industries, Inc. v. Mor-Flo Industries, Inc.*, 639 F. Supp. 937, 945, 231 USPQ 242, 247 (E.D. Tenn. 1986), *aff'd*, 818 F.2d 875 (Fed. Cir. 1987), *cert. denied*, 484 U.S. 845 (1987).

40. Ibid. § 5.04[7], at 5-499 (Rel. 51, 1994), quoting *American Safety Table Co. v Schreiber*, 269 F.2d 255, 263, 122 USPQ 29, 36 (2d Cir.), *cert. denied*, 361 U.S. 915 (1959).

41. Ibid. § 5.04[5], at 5-420 (Rel. 51, 1994), quoting *Lifting Technologies Inc. v. Armstrong Steel Manufacturing Inc.*, 19 USPQ2d 1935, 1941 (D. Minn. 1991).

42. Ibid. § 5.04[1][e], at 46 (Rel. 70-V.2, 1999), quoting *Monarch Knitting Machinery Corp. v. Sulzer Morat GmbH*, 139 F.3d 877, 45 USPQ2d 1977 (Fed. Cir. 1998).

43. Ibid. § 5.03[5], at 5-241 (Rel. 51, 1994), quoting *Ryco, Inc. v. Ag-Bag Corp.*, 857 F.2d 1418, 1424, 8 USPQ2d 1323, 1328 (Fed. Cir. 1988) ("Nothing in the patent statute requires that an invention be superior to the prior art to be patentable.").

44. See Ibid., Chapter 5, for an extended discussion of the various issues that can arise in determining obviousness for any sort of invention. The analysis here highlights those issues that are likely to be particularly relevant to business method patents.

45. Ibid. § 5.03[1], at 6 (Rel. 70-V.2, 1999).

46. U.S. Patent 5,878,341.

47. U.S. Patent 5,878,141, column 2, line 53 to column 3, line 37.

48. As noted above, "new" here refers to a step invented by the patent applicant rather than a step previously invented by someone other than the patent applicant. In other words, a step previously developed by another person is "old," not "new," even if it was recently made.

49. TCP/IP stands for "Transmission Control Protocol/Internet Protocol," a suite of software protocols for communicating over the Internet.

50. Lawrence Lessig, "The Problem with Patents," *The Industry Standard*, May 3, 1999, p. 20.

51. Chisum, *Chisum on Patents* § 5.04[5], at 5-420 (Rel. 51, 1994).

52. Ibid. § 5.05[1][b], at 5-574 (Rel. 51, 1994) (quoting *Newell Companies, Inc. v. Kenney Manufacturing Co.*, 864 F.2d 757, 768, 9 USPQ2d 1417, 1426 (Fed. Cir. 1988)).

53. *Amazon.com v. BarnesandNoble.com et al.*, 239 F.3d 1343 (Fed. Cir. 2001).

54. U.S. Patent 5,960,411.

55. Robert Merges, "As Many as Six Impossible Patents before Breakfast: Property Rights for Business Concepts and Patent System Reform," *Berkeley Technology Law Journal* 14 (1999): 577.

56. Chisum, *Chisum on Patents* § 5.04[7][a], at 113 (Rel. 70-V.2, 1999), quoting *In re Oetiker*, 977 F.2d 1443, 24 USPQ2d 1443 (Fed. Cir. 1992).

57. Ibid. § 5.04[7][a], at 113 (Rel. 70-V.2, 1999), quoting *Gentry Gallery Inc. v. Berkline Corp.*, 939 F. Supp. 98, 102, 41 USPQ2d 1345, 1349 (D. Mass. 1996) *aff'd in part, rev'd in part*, 134 F.3d 1473, 45 USPQ 1498 (Fed. Cir. 1998).

58. Ibid. § 5.03[5], at 5-240 (Rel. 51, 1994).

59. Ibid., quoting Chisum, *Intellectual Property: Copyright, Patent and Trademark* 7-103, 104 (1980).

60. Ibid. § 5.05[7], at 5-639 (Rel. 51, 1994), quoting *Phillips Petroleum Co. v. U.S. Steel Corp.*, 673 F. Supp. 1278, 1319, 6 USPQ2d 1065, 1097 (D. Del. 1987), *aff'd*, 865 F.2d 1247, 9 USPQ2d 1461 (Fed. Cir. 1989) (citing Treatise).

61. Ibid. § 5.05[7], at 136 (Rel. 70-V.2, 1999), quoting *Monarch Knitting Machinery Corp. v. Sulzer Morat GmbH*, 139 F.3d 877, 884, 45 USPQ2d 1977, 1983 (Fed. Cir. 1998).

62. Ibid. § 5.03[5], at 5-240 (Rel. 51, 1994), quoting Chisum, *Intellectual Property: Copyright, Patent and Trademark* 7-103, 104 (1980).

63. Ibid. § 5.05[1][a], at 123 (Rel. 70-V.2, 1999), quoting *Markman v. Lehman*, 987 F. Supp. 25, 43, 45 USPQ2d 1385, 1399 (D. D.C. 1997), *aff'd*, 178 F.3d 1306 (Fed.Cir. 1998).

64. Ibid. § 5.04[5], at 5-420 (Rel. 51, 1994), quoting *Lifting Technologies Inc. v. Armstrong Steel Manufacturing Inc.*, 19 USPQ2d 1935, 1941 (D. Minn. 1991).

65. Ibid. § 5.05[1][b], at 5-574 (Rel. 51, 1994).

66. Ibid. § 5.05[1][b], at 5-577 (Rel. 51, 1994), quoting *Tennant Co. v. Hako Minuteman, Inc.*, 22 USPQ2d 1161 (N.D. Ill. 1991) (citing Treatise).

67. Ibid. § 5.05[1][b], at 5-575 (Rel. 51, 1994), quoting *Dickey-John Corp. v. International Tapetronics Corp.*, 710 F.2d 329, 346, 219 USPQ 402, 416 (7th Cir. 1983).

68. Ibid. § 5.05[2][a], at 5-580 (Rel. 51, 1994) (quoting *Dickey-John Corp. v. International Tapetronics Corp.*, 710 F.2d 329, 346, 219 USPQ 402, 417 (7th Cir. 1983)).

69. Ibid. § 5.05[2], at 5-590 (Rel. 51, 1994), quoting *Chicago Rawhide Mfg. Co. v. Crane Packing Co.*, 523 F.2d 452, 187 USPQ 540 (7th Cir. 1975), *cert. denied*, 423 U.S. 1091 (1976).

70. Kenneth R. Adamo, "The Power of Suggestion (Teaching, Reason or Motivation) and Combined-Reference Obviousness," *Journal of the Patent and Trademark Office Society* 76(1994): 177, 188, 191; quoting *Ex parte Kranz*, 19 USPQ2d 1216, 1217-18 (Bd. Pat. App. & Int. 1990) and *Orthopedic Equipment Co. v. U.S.*, 702 F.2d 1005, 1012, 217 USPQ 193, 199 (Fed. Cir. 1983).

71. Ibid., p.194, citing *In re Shaffer*, 229 F.2d 476, 479-80, 108 USPQ 326, 329 (CCPA 1956).

72. Chisum, *Chisum on Patents* § 5.04[1][e], at 44 (Rel. 70-V.2, 1999), quoting *In re Zurko*, 111 F.3d 887, 890, 42 USPQ2d 1476, 1479 (Fed. Cir. 1997), *reh'g in banc granted*, 116 F.3d 874 (Fed. Cir. 1997), *rev'd* 142 F.3d 1447, 46 USPQ2d 1691 (Fed. Cir. 1998), *cert. granted sub nom. Dickinson v. Zurko*, 119 S. Ct. 401 (1998).

73. Ibid. § 5.04[7][c][iii], at 5-510 (Rel. 51, 1994), quoting *In re Nomiya* 509 F.2d 566, 572, 184 USPQ 607 (CCPA 1975).

74. Ibid. § 5.04[1][e], at 42 (Rel. 70-V.2, 1999), quoting *Monarch Knitting Machinery Corp. v. Sulzer Morat GmbH*, 139 F.3d 877, 45 USPQ2d 1977 (Fed. Cir. 1998).

75. Donald S. Chisum, *Patent Law Digest* (1998): 173–74, citing *In re Raynes*, 7 F.2d 1037, 28 USPQ2d 1630 (Fed. Cir.1993).

76. *In re Rouffet*, 149 F.3d at 1359, 47 USPQ2d at 1459.

77. Adamo, pp. 177, 209; citing *In re Bozek*, 416 F.2d 1385, 163 USPQ 545 (CCPA 1969).

Contributors

John Perry Barlow

John Perry Barlow is a retired Wyoming cattle rancher, a former lyricist for the Grateful Dead, and cofounder of the Electronic Frontier Foundation. Since May 1998, he has been a fellow at Harvard Law School's Berkman Center for Internet and Society, following a term as a fellow with the Institute of Politics at Harvard's John F. Kennedy School of Government. He has written for numerous publications, including *Communications of the ACM*, the *New York Times, Time*, and *Wired* magazine. His "Declaration of the Independence of Cyberspace" is posted on thousands of websites.

Tom W. Bell

Tom W. Bell is a professor of law at Chapman University and an adjunct scholar at the Cato Institute. Formerly director of telecommunications and technology studies at Cato, he is an expert on such topics as telecommunications deregulation, Internet law, intellectual property, and public policy for the high-tech sector. He has written for numerous publications, including the *University of Chicago Law Review, Wired, Los Angeles Daily Journal, Reason, Michigan Law Review, Bridge News Services*, and others.

Robert Beyers

Robert Beyers is an associate at Skadden, Arps, Slate, Meagher and Flom in Palo Alto, California, where he advises clients in the semiconductor, computer, telecommunications, and financial services industries on intellectual property strategy.

Rick Boucher

Rep. Rick Boucher (D-Va.) is a member of the House Energy and Commerce Committee, serving on two subcommittees—Telecommunications and the Internet; and Energy and Air Quality, of which he is the ranking member. He also sits on the House Judiciary Committee, serving on the Courts, the Internet and Intellectual Property Subcommittee. He originated the House Internet Caucus in 1996 and currently serves as one of two House cochairmen of the more than 170 member group. Congressman Boucher, a native of Abingdon, Virginia, where he currently resides, earned his law degree from the University of Virginia Law School. He has practiced law on Wall Street and in Virginia. Prior to his election to Congress, he served for seven years as a member of the Virginia State Senate.

Drew Clark

Drew Clark, senior writer at *National Journal's Technology Daily*, is an award-winning reporter who has covered business, politics, society and law for a variety of newspapers, magazines and websites. He covers courts, law, and crime, including the Microsoft antitrust lawsuit; issues of online privacy; and copyright and computer security. His past work has included assignments with the *San Francisco Chronicle*, the *Weekly Mail* (now *Mail and Guardian*) of Johannesburg, the *Washington Business Journal*, and, most recently, *American Banker*. At the Columbia University Graduate School of Journalism, Clark assisted in the launch of the *New York Times* on the Web.

James V. DeLong

Jim DeLong is a senior fellow at the Competitive Enterprise Institute's Project on Technology and Innovation. Before joining CEI, DeLong was vice president and general counsel of the National Legal Center for the Public Interest, a nonprofit legal education foundation in Washington, D.C. His prior professional positions have included research director of the Administrative Conference of the United States, assistant director for special projects in the Bureau of Consumer Protection of the Federal Trade Commission, director of programs for the Drug Abuse Council (a private foundation), and staff analyst in the Office of Program Evaluation of the U.S. Bureau of the Budget. DeLong's writings have appeared in the *Wall Street Journal, Los Angeles Times, Washington Times, Intellectual Capital, TechCentralStation, New York Times, National Law Journal, New Republic*, and others. He is a contributing editor for *Reason*.

Mitch Glazier

Mitch Glazier is senior vice president of government relations and legislative counsel for the Recording Industry Association of America. Previously he served as the chief counsel to the Subcommittee on Courts and Intellectual Property, Committee on the Judiciary, U.S. House of Representatives. Prior to that he served as law clerk to the Hon. Wayne R. Andersen in the U.S. District Court for the Northern District of Illinois and practiced with the Chicago law firm Neal, Gerber and Eisenberg.

Mike Godwin

Mike Godwin is senior policy fellow for the Center for Democracy and Technology, where he researches and writes about Internet issues, ranging from the First Amendment and criminal law to computer crime and copyright policy. Godwin has published articles for print and electronic publications on topics such as electronic searches and seizures, the First Amendment and electronic publications, and the application of international law to computer communications. In 1991–92, Godwin chaired a committee of the Massachusetts Computer Crime Commission, where he supervised the drafting of recommendations to Gov. William F. Weld for the development of computer-crime statutes. Godwin has written about social and legal issues on the electronic frontier have appeared in the *Whole Earth Review, Quill, Index on Censorship, Internet World, Wired,* and *Playboy.* He is an "IP Land" columnist for *The American Lawyer,* and a contributing editor for *Reason.*

Robin D. Gross

Robin D. Gross is an intellectual property attorney with the Electronic Frontier Foundation. She specializes in intellectual property policy and digital music legal issues and serves as Director of EFF's Campaign for Audiovisual Free Expression (CAFE), which she helped launch in June 1999 to explore the interaction of intellectual property and freedom of expression in a digital world. Gross frequently speaks and publishes on cyberspace legal issues such as digital copyright, and the MP3 and DeCSS legal wars, and she has testified before the U.S. Copyright Office on the dangers to freedom of expression presented by the anti-circumvention provisions of the Digital Millennium Copyright Act.

Frank G. Hausmann

Frank G. Hausmann is the chairman and CEO of CenterSpan Communications Corporation. Before joining the company in 1998, Hausmann was vice president of finance and CFO of Atlas Telecom, a developer of enhanced facsimile and voice-mail solutions. From 1995 to 1997, he served as vice president, corporate development, and general counsel of Diamond Multimedia Systems, a designer and marketer of computer peripherals such as modems and graphics and sound cards. Prior to Diamond, Hausmann was executive vice president and CFO of Supra Corporation, a designer and marketer of modems that was acquired by Diamond Multimedia Systems in 1995.

Orin S. Kerr

Orin Kerr is a former Justice Department attorney now at George Washington University. After graduating from law school in 1997, Professor Kerr was a law clerk to Judge Leonard I. Garth of the U.S. Court of Appeals for the Third Circuit. He then served as a trial attorney in the Computer Crime and Intellectual Property Section of the Criminal Division at the U.S. Department of Justice for three years. At Justice, Professor Kerr developed special expertise in computer search and seizure and electronic privacy law. He also served as a special assistant U.S. attorney for the Eastern District of Virginia.

Ron Laurie

Ron Laurie is a founding partner of Skadden, Arps, Slate, Meagher and Flom's office in Palo Alto, California, where he cochairs the firm's information technology practice. He has worked in Silicon Valley for more than 40 years, first as a computer programmer and systems engineer and later as a patent attorney. His practice focuses on IP strategy in the context of complex business transactions.

Stan Liebowitz

Stan Liebowitz is a professor of economics at the University of Texas at Dallas and a fellow at the Independent Institute, where he specializes in the economics of knowledge goods and intellectual property issues. He is the author of *Internet Cents and Non$sense*, to be released in 2002, and co-author of *Winners, Losers, and Microsoft* and *The Economics of Qwerty*. He has written for such publications as the *George Mason Law Review, Wall Street Journal, Upside, Harvard Journal of Law and Technology,* and *Encyclopedia of Law and Economics,* among others.

Jessica Litman

Jessica Litman is a professor of law at Wayne State University, where she teaches courses in copyright law, Internet law, and trademarks and unfair competition. Before joining the Wayne faculty in 1990, she was an associate professor at the University of Michigan Law School. Professor Litman is the author of many articles on copyright; her work has been cited by the Supreme Court and reprinted in House hearings. She is the author of *Digital Copyright: Protecting Intellectual Property on the Internet* and a co-author of the second edition of *Trademark and Unfair Competition Law: Cases and Materials* (1996). Professor Litman has testified before Congress and before the White House Information Infrastructure Task Force's Working Group on Intellectual Property.

Declan McCullagh

Declan McCullagh is the Washington bureau chief for *Wired News.* An award-winning journalist, he has been a reporter for *Time Digital Daily,* the *Netly News,* and *Time* magazine, as well as a correspondent for *HotWired.* His writings on technology and politics have also appeared in *George* magazine, the *New Republic,* the *Wall Street Journal, Playboy, Communications of the ACM,* and the *Harvard Journal of Law and Public Policy.* He has appeared on NPR's *All Things Considered,* ABC *Good Morning America,* NBC News, Court TV, and CNN, among other programs. In 1994 he founded Politech, a well-known mailing list that looks broadly at politics and technology.

Michael P. Nugent

Michael Nugent is a lawyer with Heller Ehrman White and McAuliffe where he heads the Financial Technology Group. He has practiced technology and intellectual property law since 1978 and was formerly Citigroup General Counsel for Technology and Intellectual Property for over a decade and was concurrently General Counsel and Head of Business Affairs for e-Citi, Citigroup's unit for Internet operations and investments. He also served as Executive Vice President and General Counsel for Walker Digital, LLC (the incubator that invented, patented and launched new business models representing breakthrough Internet and e-commerce applications such as Priceline.com).

Tom G. Palmer

Tom G. Palmer is senior fellow at the Cato Institute and director of Cato University. Before joining Cato he was an H. B. Earhart Fellow at Hertford College, Oxford University, and a vice president of the Institute for Humane Studies at George Mason University. He regularly lectures in America and Europe on public choice, individualism and civil society, and the moral and legal foundations of individual rights. He has published reviews and articles on politics and morality in scholarly journals such as the *Harvard Journal of Law and Public Policy, Ethics, Critical Review,* and *Constitutional Political Economy,* as well as in publications such as *Slate,* the *Wall Street Journal,* the *New York Times,* and the *Washington Post.*

David G. Post

David Post is an associate professor of law at Temple University Law School, where he teaches intellectual property law and the law of cyberspace, and a senior fellow at the Tech Center at George Mason University School of Law. He is also the cofounder and codirector of the Cyberspace Law Institute, ICANNWatch, and Disputes.org. He has published articles on the law of cyberspace in the *Stanford Law Review,* the *Journal of Online Law,* the *University of Chicago Legal Forum,* the *Computer Law Reporter,* and the *Wayne Law Review,* as well as several articles on complexity theory and the legal system in the *Journal of Legal Studies,* the *Georgetown Law Journal,* and the *Vanderbilt Law Review.* He has appeared as a commentator on the law of the Internet on such programs as the *News-Hour, Morning Edition,* the PBS "Life on the Internet" series, NPR's *All Things Considered,* and Court TV's *Supreme Court Preview.*

Emery Simon

Emery Simon is counselor to the board of directors of the Business Software Alliance. He advises the BSA on a broad range of policy issues including copyright law, electronic commerce, trade, and encryption. Until January of 1996, Simon was the executive director of the Alliance to Promote Software Innovation. Previously, he served as the deputy assistant USTR for intellectual property at the Office of the United States Trade Representative. In that capacity he was the U.S. negotiator on intellectual property for the North American Free Trade Agreement, and the TRIPs Agreement. Simon has also worked for the Congressional Budget Office, the Senate Budget Committee, the Inter-American Development Bank, the Council on Environmental Quality, and Kaye, Scholer, Fierman, Hays, and Handler.

Peter Wayner
Peter Wayner is a Baltimore-based writer whose work appears frequently in *Salon* magazine and the *New York Times*. His latest book, *Disappearing Cryptography* (2nd edition) explains how to hide information in pictures, music, and text. He is the author of nine other books on software technology, including *Translucent Databases, Digital Cash: Commerce on the Net, Free for All: How LINUX and the Free Software Movement Undercut the High-Tech Titans, Digital Copyright Protection,, Java and JavaScript Programming, Java Beans for Real Programmers, Compression Algorithms for Real Programmers,* and *Agents Unleashed: A Public Domain Look at Agent Technology.*

Index

About the Editors

Wayne Crews

Wayne Crews is the director of technology studies at the Cato Institute where he studies Internet and technology regulation, antitrust, and other regulatory reforms. Earlier, Crews was director of competition and regulation policy at the Competitive Enterprise Institute, and a legislative aide to Sen. Phil Gramm (R-Tex.), responsible for regulatory and welfare reform issues. He has been an economist and policy analyst at the Citizens for a Sound Economy Foundation, and has worked as an economist at the Food and Drug Administration and a research assistant at the Center for the Study of Public Choice at George Mason University. Crews has published in the *Wall Street Journal, Forbes,* the *Washington Times,* the *Journal of Commerce, American Enterprise, Policy Sciences,* the *Electricity Journal,* and others. He has appeared on various television and radio programs including CNN, Fox News, Tech TV, TechnoPolitics, PBS, and others.

Adam Thierer

Adam Thierer is the director of telecommunications studies at the Cato Institute where he conducts research on how government regulations are hampering the evolution of communications networks, including telephony, broadcasting, cable, satellite, and the Internet. He also examines the broader economic and constitutional aspects of telecommunications policy. His writing has been published in the *Washington Post, Newsweek, Wall Street Journal, Investors Business Daily, Journal of Commerce, Forbes,* and *The Economist.* He has made media appearances on NPR, PBS, Fox News Channel, CNN, MSNBC, BBC, Radio Free Europe, and Voice of America. Prior to joining Cato, Thierer spent nine years at the Heritage Foundation, where he served as the Alex C. Walker Fellow in Economic Policy. In that capacity, he covered telecommunications and Internet policy and also wrote extensively on antitrust, electricity and energy policy, the airline industry, and federalism. Before moving to Washington, Thierer worked at the Adam Smith Institute in London, England, where he examined reform of the British legal system.

Cato Institute

Founded in 1977, the Cato Institute is a public policy research foundation dedicated to broadening the parameters of policy debate to allow consideration of more options that are consistent with the traditional American principles of limited government, individual liberty, and peace. To that end, the Institute strives to achieve greater involvement of the intelligent, concerned lay public in questions of policy and the proper role of government.

The Institute is named for *Cato's Letters*, libertarian pamphlets that were widely read in the American Colonies in the early 18th century and played a major role in laying the philosophical foundation for the American Revolution.

Despite the achievement of the nation's Founders, today virtually no aspect of life is free from government encroachment. A pervasive intolerance for individual rights is shown by government's arbitrary intrusions into private economic transactions and its disregard for civil liberties.

To counter that trend, the Cato Institute undertakes an extensive publications program that addresses the complete spectrum of policy issues. Books, monographs, and shorter studies are commissioned to examine the federal budget, Social Security, regulation, military spending, international trade, and myriad other issues. Major policy conferences are held throughout the year, from which papers are published thrice yearly in the *Cato Journal*. The Institute also publishes the quarterly magazine *Regulation*.

In order to maintain its independence, the Cato Institute accepts no government funding. Contributions are received from foundations, corporations, and individuals, and other revenue is generated from the sale of publications. The Institute is a nonprofit, tax-exempt, educational foundation under Section 501(c)3 of the Internal Revenue Code.

CATO INSTITUTE
1000 Massachusetts Ave., N.W.
Washington, D.C. 20001